Ann,
'all my love
Tony
December 6th
2015.

# THE
# GRAVEDIGGER'S
# APPRENTICE

By

Tony Buckingham

*To Cath for putting up with me for over 50 years.*

# CONTENTS

# ACKNOWLEDGMENTS

I would like to thank Ross for pre-editing it.

# CHAPTER 1

## *The Grave Digger's Apprentice*

*"We will all go together when we go*
*All infused with an incandescent glow."*
*— Tom Lehrer*

"No more, 'ee won't come back," growled Harry in a broad Hertfordshire accent.

Once again, I was being given the wisdom and thoughts of old Harry the grave digger. We were, at the time, filling in a grave after the mourners had left. I suppose it was pretty obvious that the occupier of the coffin was unlikely to make a reappearance. It was nice of Harry to tell me in case it had not occurred to me. Harry looked me in the eye and pointed down at the coffin in a strange emphatic way.

"'Ee were a good man, 'ee were a good man," continued Harry in that strange semi-moronic tone of his. He then started to bend his elbow in a very weird way.

"Rose and Crown," he growled, "Rose and Crown."

1

He kept making the strange gesture and at last I realised he was indicating that the dead man had been the publican from the Rose and Crown. The gesture was him pulling a pint.

Harry was a strange character. He seemed to be left over from some Dickensian novel. Everything about him seemed to have come from a jumble sale. His face was like old parchment, brown and gnarled. He'd been in the open air all his life and where the sun hadn't browned his face, the dirt had. He wore those funny mittens where the fingers stick out, trousers tied up at the turn-ups with string, probably to prevent mice or rats running up them, a dirty old tie as his belt, a filthy shirt, a beige woolly sweater, and a leather jerkin with a red handkerchief tied at the neck.

At the time, I'd been a grave digger for about an hour and wasn't at all sure whether in fact I'd been promoted from third class council labourer to grave digger. Certainly the job was different!

Harry was at that certain age, God knows what it was, probably a hundred. He certainly looked a hundred and he was very much larger than life which was more than could be said about his customers. After we'd shovelled the earth and stones and rocks back in to the hole and made it look reasonably tidy, we went off for our morning break.

"Cuppa tea?" called Harry as he handed me the dirtiest mug I'd ever seen. As neither Harry nor George, his assistant, seemed to agree with washing the crockery, or themselves for that matter, I was facing a difficult dilemma. There were a number of options: I could knock it over – could be good but I would almost inevitably be given a further one and it

2

would look odd to keep throwing my tea all over the floor; "Sod off," I could cry, "I'm not ready to die yet by drinking that filthy mug of dog's turd," would undoubtedly work but could be interpreted as being slightly rude; perhaps I could say it was too hot for tea – this would be true in this particular case but would not work on a cold day. So I decided in this instance the truth was best.

"I'm afraid I can't drink tea or coffee or any other hot drink due to my illness. It wouldn't really be fair to you if I did use the mugs because you'd possibly catch it." As I said, the truth is always the best. They certainly didn't want to catch 'it' whatever 'it' was and so no further offers were forthcoming.

The cemetery was a strange place to work. These two old men had been digging graves there for decades and were very much set in their ways. George, a rather plump, red-faced labourer, who invariably wore the traditional dark blue boiler suit and spoke very slowly. He obviously felt very superior to Harry who my father would have described as a diddykeye. I was never quite sure what a diddykeye was but I assume it was like a gypsy but not as good.

I had come across Harry once before. His family lived in a series of old caravans in the middle of the old Roman road at the back of Stevenage. They'd worked quite a clever trick: they hadn't cultivated right up to any road, they'd opened up in the middle stretch. It was quite impressive the way they had hidden themselves away from prying eyes. George, on the other hand, lived in a Council house quite close to the cemetery which made him much higher in the pecking order. Mind you, George found Harry quite annoying. He was something of an expert in racing. Every break he would study the Hotspur tips, the Punter's Club from the *Mirror* and any other publication which would help him decide which nag was going to win that particular day. After weighing up all the options he would make his choice and place his bet. Normally Harry would ask him to place one for him. I wasn't quite sure of Harry's technique. I had a feeling it was more of a pin and I wasn't a hundred per cent sure if he could actually read. The ironic thing was that Harry regularly won and George, despite all the effort he put in, lost.

"I don't know how he does it," confided George to me while we were digging a grave on the far side of the cemetery. "I always reckon he's got some friend that gives him a tip. He doesn't know anything about horses himself."

"He could just be lucky," I said cheerfully.

"Could be, I suppose," said George miserably, "but not all the time. I'll tell you what he is good at though, spotting new business."

"What do you mean?" I asked.

"Well, he writes down the names of those he thought wouldn't last the winter on the bottom of his wheelbarrow. He's pretty accurate as well."

"You mean if you start seeing him looking at you and shaking his head, you should get worried?"

"Yes, I would! He's not often wrong."

George was not a very cheerful sort of character, and the fact that we seemed to have so much work to do didn't seem to help.

"Not get it all done!" grunted Harry. "Too much! Gotter have help."

Looking back to those weeks in a cemetery, I often wondered why business was so good. Why were so many people dying that summer? Was there a serial killer at large? Was it the return of the Black Death? Was it simply that people died rather than going to Clacton for their summer holidays? But certainly, as there were so many people who were inconsiderate about their dying, we had to have extra help. This turned up in the form of Bob. Now, I've seen some big men in my time, but this man was enormous. He had hands twice the size of the average man and must have stood the best part of six foot seven. Mind you, I don't think he'd have qualified for the Brain of Britain or done very well in Mastermind but he certainly looked very useful for digging graves.

Bob, however, proved to be a great problem for the original old pair. I'd already worked out their little racket; working for the Council had made me look at things in a different way. When I first started I was given a job weeding the roadside flower-beds. I set about it with great enthusiasm and very soon had gathered a small crowd of workmen. I wondered why the men started to gather round my particular flower-bed. Could it be my technique interested them? Had I the green touch when it came to removing stinging nettles? Or could it be the fact that I was a local cricket star and they wanted to say how much they enjoyed my six for twenty-one on Sunday?

"What the bleeding 'ell do you think you're doing?" shouted a rather large object dressed in check shirt and blue jeans. Before I had a chance to reply he continued: "I asked you a bloody question. What the 'ecking 'ell is up?"

I did perhaps contemplate for a moment a reply, "Weeding, and my, my, our manners have been forgotten haven't they? What's wrong with 'please'?" However, I didn't like the look of him, although he was no doubt loved by his poor wife, so I played it cool.

"Er, what do you mean?" I politely asked.

"The f***ing Council don't f***ing pay you to f***ing work!" he screamed.

"That's right!" said his shorter right-hand man. "They pay us to turn up! We don't f***ing earn f***ing enough for these f***ing bastards to f***ing work so bleeding well slow down!"

I understood at last. My co-workers, and in particular the man with the Shakespearean touch with words, was alarmed. It was a little bit like Ian Carmichael in 'I'm all right Jack', the famous Bolton Brothers film, when his efforts on a forklift truck brought about a major strike. His problem was like mine, he was just too quick. Well, I certainly didn't wish to embarrass my newfound friends so I hastily apologised and had a fag break which went down well with the rest of the band.

"Sorry, I'm new and didn't realise the way to do things. I'll get it right eventually."

However, it did seem rather odd as I was earning over fifty per cent more than I got in the last vacation when I was in an office doing responsible work but, rules is rules! After a second fag and a little walk round chatting to the blokes, I returned to my slow,

slow, slow weeding. At this point the heavens opened up. Rain stopped weeding.

"What do we do now?" I asked the obvious boss, the large ugly one with the fluent use of Anglo-Saxon.

"We'll have to go up the f***ing barn to f***ing shift f***ing soil. The f***ing bastards will send a f***ing lorry."

With that he gobbed out a rather unpleasant green lump and belched rather loudly. A particularly unpleasant odour followed and I noticed he belched rather often, almost as often as he farted. In all fairness though, he rarely belched and farted and gobbed at the same time! On the scale of vile people he would be about an eight. With training he could become world class. I had to admit that I forgot to mention the smell. Now, that was a certain something. I used to watch a spy thriller called 'Callan' in which there was a character called Lonely who stunk, and jokes were always being made about soap. Believe me, Lonely smelt like roses compared with this oaf!

The lorry duly turned up and we climbed aboard. The Noel Coward of the Council workforce continued with an interesting story about his early morning adventures. In order to save paper, the reader is asked to imagine the Anglo-Saxon expletive beginning with an 'f', which you'll already have learnt was his favourite word, to be added after every other word. For example, "I f***ing got f***ing up this f***ing morning and my f***ing wife got the f***ing breakfast." This fascinating story told in between farts, belches and gobs included nearly a hundred 'f***ing's. Had I been stupid like a friend of mine, Tip

Tipping, I would have tried to educate him. Tip in similar circumstances in Brighton did:

"Here," he said to a hard-looking Irish man, "I don't mind you swearing, it doesn't bother me, but it would be nice if we could get a little bit of variety. Now, what I want you to do is to repeat after me. 'Bastard.'"

The Irish man's reply was more physical than intellectual. He smashed Tip in the face. At the time, in addition to breaking a tooth and causing severe discomfort, it also convinced Tip that perhaps labouring was not for him.

Forewarned is forearmed so I didn't attempt to use my teaching skills, simply counted the expletives and waited for the end of the journey to the barn and whatever new slow job I had to do. Sifting soil was the treat awaiting us and as soon as the foreman left all the men sat down and lit up fags. Some of them either produced a *Mirror*, comics, or played cards.

"Aren't you going to sift any soil?" I asked, as it turned out, rather stupidly.

"No bloody point is there?" answered the short right-hand man. "We've sifted that soil at least ten times. They just can't bear the thought of us going home on a wet day!"

I had to say, it wasn't particularly good man-management to sift the same soil hundreds of times but then, what did I know about Council practices?

However, back at the graveyard the same attitude continued. Harry and George were experts in nursing graves. They never finished a grave on a Thursday or Friday which always meant that Monday or Tuesday burials needed overtime over the weekend: time and a half on Saturdays, double time on Sundays. Need I say more? Neither of them had a family so it was no skin off their noses to read the *News of the World* at the cemetery rather at their Council flat or in a caravan. Bob, however, was a threat to the establishment and the sensible order of things. Bob, as I've said, was rather large. He was given the first grave to dig and set about it as if he wanted to get it done in the first ten minutes. I've never seen earth come out of a grave so quickly. It was like some cartoon film! He didn't appear ever to stop. It was like a steam piston machine, on and on and on. The hole got bigger and deeper. Harry and George were shocked. They huddled together, nattering and moaning, as they watched in horror. I could imagine what was going on through their minds: no more double time, no more time and a half, perhaps no more job! This man looked as if he could dig six graves a day. Bob started humming a little tune, at least I think it was a tune, caught my eye and looked up at me.

"I like a little digging," he said, an enormous grin lighting up his face. A little digging was not how I described this human grave machine. "I think I'll dig the garden tonight," he added as he got stuck in once again. Harry and George's moaning got worse. I had to say I felt very sorry for them so I tried to explain to Bob why he was upsetting them and their concern about their overtime.

"Here, Bob, can I have a word for a minute?"

"All right," he said, springing out of the hole. We went and sat by the grass up by the hedge.

"Bob, you're very good at grave digging."

"Oh, thank you."

"The problem is you're very quick."

"I am, aren't I?"

"Harry and George are a bit worried."

"What are they worried about?" said Bob.

"Well, they think you're going to come and take their job."

"No, I'm only here for two weeks. I'm not even from this area. I'm from 'atfield."

"Ah," I said, "that'll please them." I left Bob demolishing the earth once again and went across to talk to George and Harry. "You don't have to worry about Bob," I told them, "he's only here for two weeks."

Their faces lit up. "Reckon you could ask him to slow down?" said George. "We don't want to be shown up." Harry nodded in agreement.

"I've got a better idea," I said. "Why don't you get him to get most of the work done, and you, as the experts, finish them off?"

This suggestion went down very well with them both. It meant they could take it very, very easy and still appear to be working very hard, thus becoming part of normal Council working practices. Bob duly finished his two weeks and he was replaced by a Cypriot called Nico. It was while he was with us that the shocking incident of the five shilling bounty occurred.

It appeared that for every grave dug the grave digger was granted a bounty of the enormous sum of five shillings, in today's money 25p. It might not sound much, but five shillings would buy forty cigarettes or a few pints of bitter so it was appreciated, particularly by old Harry. Nico was a Greek Cypriot, and I guess he was very short of money. The bounty to him was important so he was very keen on receiving his due entitlement. Normally it was paid before the actual funeral. He was very annoyed when nothing had been forthcoming and the actual mourners were marching behind the coffin. Nico became very sullen and muttered angrily to himself: "Is not fair, just 'cos I'm a Cypriot. I should 'ave it. I need the money, cheating the poor is not fair. I'm going to do something about it! You can't do that to me, I'm entitled. I should be allowed. It's my five shillings!"

Nico prattled on, Harry ignored him. He continued to sip his disgusting brown liquid during his break. No-one was allowed to dig a grave while a funeral was actually taking place. I sat thinking of great triumphs ahead at the weekend: nine for twenty and a hat-trick to boot (the probability was nought for plenty, but then we can all dream). I must admit, I never saw Nico leave. Whether I could have stopped him was another matter. After all, I knew he carried a knife and I wouldn't describe myself as a natural hero.

"Where's a-my five shillings?" shouted Nico at the very large undertaker who tried to remain solemn and dignified in his morning suit leading the procession. "You're not a-going to cheat-a me, just because I'm a Cypriot," he continued, his voice getting higher and higher.

As Nico was rather short and the funeral director

was exceptionally tall, Nico had to jump up to make the impression he thought necessary. None of this helped to create the correct atmosphere of a funeral. I hadn't noticed Nico leave, nor did I see Harry follow, but suddenly the boy was grabbed very firmly and removed behind the office. Digging graves obviously made you enormously strong and Nico didn't argue. The procession continued on in a more sombre note and Nico, realising he might have perhaps done something wrong, sat sullenly for the rest of the time. Nico was right to have been upset. When the funeral was over and the facts were sorted out, it appeared that a bounty had been paid – to Harry.

The next week, we were in the middle of a bit of a rush job. Time was ticking away and the funeral party was due any minute. It was a re-opener, in other words a double plot which had already one permanent resident.

"Harry, shouldn't we stop digging?" I asked worriedly.

"Uh-uh! Not deep enough!" muttered Harry as he kept digging.

"Harry! Look what you're digging up! Shouldn't we stop now?"

Harry leant on his shovel and surveyed the grave.

"Bones!" he cried. "Too many bones! No good! No good! Too many bones!"

"That's what I've been trying to tell you. We are digging up the previous occupant and it's highly likely that some of the present mourners will know the person," I explained.

"Too many bones! No good! No good! Not deep enough! What's to do?"

We were running out of time. The graveside was covered with all sorts of human bones. It was really horrific, but somehow, being in a graveyard it, seemed normal.

"Cover with grass!" grunted Harry. "Cover with grass!"

It won't grow that quickly," I said, thinking that he'd flipped his lid at last.

"I'll get the grass, you stay!"

With that, Harry went across to a small shed next to the extreme end of the cemetery. I watched with interest. Harry returned, his arms filled with artificial grass that looked like a large carpet. He quickly laid it all over the mounds of earth and bits and pieces of the rightful occupier.

"Not see." He pointed to the grass. "Not see!"

We were only just in time, because the funeral party had arrived. I watched from the shed in a sort of horrified wonder as the mourners actually stood on the previous occupant. It was all pretty gruesome.

"I 'ate re-openers," muttered George, "they're never deep enough."

After the funeral party had left, we moved over to refill the cavity. I wanted to do it as quickly as I could in case somebody came back to pay their last respects. As I shovelled the first load in to cover the coffin, a rock went right through the lid. I stood back, appalled.

"Not good wood!" called Harry. "Not good wood!"

"No good!" he continued muttering throughout the refilling. "Cheap coffins! No good! No respect! Cheap coffins! No good!"

It happened to me more than once and on one ghastly occasion, I actually thought that I could see a face looking up at me from the grave. It wasn't pleasant work dealing so closely with death.

George appeared from his morning visit to the betting shop bringing with him Harry's winnings and, as usual, a series of excuses.

"My horse must of had one leg too short," he explained. "I couldn't have known about it. I should really have got my money back!" he continued. "Problem is, they don't want to know so what's the point?" He sat miserably while Harry counted his ill-gotten gains.

"'Alf crown short! There's 'alf crown missing," he muttered accusingly. "Where's my 'alf crown?" he demanded of poor George.

"I put it on my 'orse," he miserably explained. "It was a dead cert. Well, I thought it was a dead cert. Honestly, I thought I was doing you a favour!"

"Well you didn't," moaned Harry, and continued to count his money. "Pay day tomorrow," he added as if that changed everything and promptly forgot the two and six. Turning to me, he started whispering confidentially. "Big grave for him. Would be a lot of work, wouldn't want to dig that one!"

At first I thought he was maliciously referring to George, thinking he should do the decent thing and die as he'd lost him his two and sixpence. Then I realised he was looking through the window at the undertaker. He certainly was a very large man, had to be six foot five and big with it. Twenty-six stone, I should imagine! I could see Harry's point, it would be a very large grave. I suppose I should have taken more notice of his mutterings, he had a horrible habit of looking at people and then shaking his head.

"Not long, not long," he'd cry with amazing accuracy. True to form, the undertaker was buried while I was still in the cemetery. Even worse for me, I remember saying to a friend of mine that the whole burial scene was so bizarre I dreaded the next funeral I attended as I was sure I'd get the giggles. I remembered those words at my father's funeral, the very next one I ever attended. Needless to say, I didn't get the giggles.

The Foreman, the superintendent, was a small crinkly-haired Geordie. Surprisingly he was actually called Geordie. At first he seemed a complete bastard but, working with some of the weirdos, I suppose it was important to keep them in their place. He relaxed with me pretty quickly and enjoyed serious discussions; politics, economics, sport, current events. He loved to chat, it was obvious that he was a very intelligent man who didn't have the educational advantages of today.

"They don't know they're born today, youngsters," he continued in his usual tirade against lazy bastards, "but when I was a boy, you knew when you were well off. I had one good suit and that was for weddings, funerals and important dates, and one good pair of shoes. That's all we could afford in those days. You had to take care of them, they were meant to last for years." He took another sip of his tea and looked up in the sky and sighed. "They think I'm a real sod but if they had my first boss, they'd know about real bastards." And his eyes went glazed and obviously went back to the events of his youth.

"I went a party one night in nearby Heaton and I missed the last bus home. We started work in those days at 7.30am so I had to go straight to work. The foreman, he was a red-faced boozer with a nasty sense of humour." He paused, lit up another cigarette and then leaned back, enjoying the sunshine. He actually grinned when he saw my suit. "Get up on the heap," he shouted, "and start shovelling. I want all that moved today!" Of course he knew it would ruin my suit but I couldn't refuse as jobs were hard to come by. I stood up to my knees in this filthy slime, hating the bastard, but what could I do? I've never forgiven him for it. "What do you think this lot would do if I tried that on them?" he enquired.

"Have a strike?" I suggested.

"Too right," he replied, "it's hard enough getting them to actually start in the morning, let alone work!"

I chuckled, thinking of the 'they don't pay us to work' remark. "You're probably right," I said and drifted back to work.

It was very good that I had a good relationship with him because I needed time off for my cricket, particularly with Cricket Week coming up. I must admit, I wasn't as yet the star of the team. It wasn't that I didn't perform, it was just I wasn't given a chance. I desperately needed a good week to push me in to the first team and towards the minor Counties place I desperately wanted. I had a dream of County cricket and needed to keep moving towards my goal. Trouble was, I was surrounded by jealous players, grudge holders and simply fools. Of course, you understand I was not biased in any way! But one thing I did learn that summer was cheap fun at somebody's expense can often backfire later in life.

A major problem at this time was an exceptionally fat ginger-haired man who'd been one of my main teachers and who didn't actually like me. I had hated him from the time he wouldn't even let me practise with the team when I was eleven and, for some reason he actually seemed to enjoy stopping me play. I'd managed to overcome his stranglehold on my future by joining a local club. I went over with a friend, Mandy, who, despite the name, was a boy. He was the school opening bowler and really a decent bloke.

"And what do you do boy?" asked the second eleven Captain at Knebworth. "Bat or bowl?"

Lying through my teeth, I replied I opened the bowling for the school. Mandy kept quiet and so, as I was bigger than him, I opened the bowling for the second eleven. Believe it or not, I actually got three wickets on my debut! I thought I was Freddy Trueman and Brian Statham rolled into one. However, I was quickly brought back to reality in the second game when some Greek god with a very heavy old bat proceeded to hit me over the moon or, in this case some very tall trees, with embarrassing regularity. He was a very impressive figure and taught me a very painful lesson. Ironically, I was to play on the same side as him a few weeks later where I learned even more about the complexities of village cricket.

It was a very, very hot day. In fact, it had been a very hot week. In a heatwave that had dried out the countryside and actually parched it brown, the wicket, if you could call it that, was like concrete with nasty cracks all over it. Not quite like Lords! The opposition had a blacksmith who bowled faster than Typhoon Tyson. The major difference was that Tyson probably knew where he was bowling and this chap did not.

The opposition had batted first and scored a hundred and forty-six. Despite this ferocious onslaught, we were actually doing reasonably well. The Captain, who went by the very appropriate name of Split, was struck on the head and pole-axed. His cap probably saved his life. Everyone rushed here and there. He was taken by car to the nearest hospital. When all the panic had died down the next sacrifice – whoops! I mean batsman – was required to enter the furnace.

"Smith!" called the Vice Captain, the local chemist. "Has anyone seen Smith?" he continued.

"I think he went to the hospital with Split," called one of the players.

"Oh well," continued the chemist. "Jacko, where's Jacko? Jacko?"

"I think he went too," came the reply.

"Oh dear! Who's next? Dave? Dave? Don't tell me, he's gone to the hospital as well!"

"Yep, in the car," came the reply.

"Buckingham," continued the chemist.

*Oh God!* I thought. *Why didn't I go in the car?*

"Buckingham, you're next in. Get your pads on!"

A suit of armour would be more appropriate. I honestly can say I wasn't scared. That would have been all right, I was terrified. I've never been so frightened in my life. I pushed my box in, grabbed a bat and walked very, very slowly into the middle.

"Guard?" asked a white-haired undertaker.

"T-t-t-two legs," I stuttered. I thought it was more adult and sophisticated than calling centre-guard. Where I put my bat down, the earth was simply red with blood. It was horrible and not just on the surface. Split must have really been split in two! I took my stand and looked in horror as a twenty stone madman killer started to run up the wicket to hurl his missile at me. I lunged hopefully forward, shutting my eyes. The ball touched my ear as it screeched by at ten million miles an hour. It actually touched my ear! In fact it burnt it. I was out next ball backing away to China. I was never more pleased to be out in my life!

The next batsman was the Greek god who'd taken the delight in hitting me over the tall trees. It appeared he also liked blacksmiths and had no fear, like some hero in a comic strip. He proceeded to win the game single-handed, despatching the ball to all parts of Hertfordshire and probably into all the neighbouring counties. Poor old Split, he lived but never played cricket again. I suppose today he would have sued.

From that very humble beginning I'd become a star at Knebworth. You know the sort of thing: Buckingham routs Gravely, then St Dunstans Blind School have no answer to Buckingham, another seven wickets with Knebworth's Buckingham against a kindergarten. Guaranteed head-swelling stuff but, alas, Knebworth's wicket was not very flat whereas the pitch at Stevenage was, in comparison, a billiard table. A new ball game indeed!

For the first match in Cricket Week, I'd obtained permission from Geordie and had turned up despite the fact that I was only twelfth man. I mentioned my problems earlier in this narrative turning the easy win that leads to losing. It may sound Irish but it has a sound basis. Now, I'd made two very large mistakes while I was still at school. The first concerned the ginger-haired runt who I mentioned before. To say that I hated his guts would be an understatement. The feeling was mutual, revenge was short-lived but, at the time, so sweet! The secret of life is being in the right place at the right time.

But to come back to the point that cheap fun at somebody's expense can often backfire later in life. Fate put me in a dream position one evening shortly before the first eleven versus the staff. Ginger wanted some practice. Well he would, wouldn't he? To quote that well-known personality, whom we naughtily called Randy Nice-Davies (actually it was Mandy Rice-Davies, Randy Nice just summed her up so well), I just happened to be there in whites and, obviously, wanted to help my old 'friend'. There was quite a crowd at the nets. He had arranged for some small boys to help him get some confidence. They were delighted that the first eleven opening bowler would also help. Ginger looked rather unhappy at this turn of events.

"Don't worry," I encouraged him, "I won't bowl flat out *at first*."

By his look, he knew I was not going to be

worrying about earning brownie points that evening. My first effort struck him rather satisfactorily in the ribs.

"Sorry," I cried, "a bit short!"

The second removed his off-stump and strung it up in the netting. It took him a few minutes to untangle it. I got a round of applause. The next two balls hit Ginger first on the thigh (very painful), the second on the shoulder.

"Sorry!" I called, not very convincingly. I finally uprooted the off-stump, again to much applause.

I didn't want to give him any credit, but to give him his due, he called out to the appreciative crowd,

"Well bowled! You see boys why he's the school's best bowler. Thanks for your help, Buckingham. I think I'm all right now!"

Probably a good move on his part.

The next day, in front of the whole school, he had to repeat the exercise. I did actually consider hurting him again but decided against it. The sight of his stumps splattered first ball was a great source of pleasure and amusement.

Every triumph has its price. After some success at Knebworth, my captain suggested that I should try for the Stevenage cricket team, because it was a very good standard. I was told that I could not go straight into the first eleven, despite my growing reputation, I'd have to prove myself by starting in the third eleven and work my way up. To my disgust Ginger was now the captain of Stevenage third eleven.

"I can't possibly bowl you on this wicket,

Buckingham," he would say regularly, "you're far too quick, it wouldn't be fair."

The question was, how did I get into the second eleven without taking wickets in the third eleven, and how could I take wickets without bowling? Ginger, again, had the last laugh.

The second mistake involved the Captain of the Stevenage first eleven, who was also my school coach. He was a Colossus, a giant in the cricketing world. However, as one wag described him in the Stevenage pavilion: "A man amongst boys, but a boy amongst men!" He had a rather special tradition, he scored at least one century against the first eleven every summer, usually two. When he got up to a hundred, he ostentatiously gave the bowler his wicket. It was sickening but what could you do?

Well, my mistake was ginormous, elephantine, mind-blowing. I just had one of my major school triumphs in destroying yet another school-boy team. Needless to say, my cap wouldn't fit. I also had trouble getting into the car as the door seemed much lower. My head wouldn't quite fit in! The fan club in the car were telling me all the things I wanted to hear: "God, you bowled well today, Tony! That yorker number three was incredible!" You know the sort of thing.

Suddenly Boy remarked, "It's all very well getting out schoolboys, but you don't *move* the ball. You're just straight up and down. You'll never amount to anything unless you learn to move it."

It was a bit deflating at the time, but very honest. I *was* ordinary and despite probably being a bit pissed off, I took it reasonably well. The library was the best starting point. I looked at the books on bowling. Today, Geoff Boycott and other great cricketers give you free coaching in graphic detail on the television. I would really have liked that! But, in my day it was strictly do-it-yourself. I studied, practised and managed to swing the ball for the very first time. Luckily I had plenty of time available because it was the A-levels and we'd been given time off to study for the exams. I spent all my time studying how to bowl in-swingers. Eventually I was pleased with my newfound skill.

The first time I could show off was against Stevenage and who should be opening the batting but Boy himself. I have to say the ball that bowled him was a peach. It swung late and of course *he knew* I didn't move the ball. In all honesty I think roaring at him and jumping up and down was not a tactful thing to do. It went down very well with the seven hundred plus boys watching, but not with Boy.

"Well bowled," he muttered as he slowly walked back to the pavilion, looking even smaller than usual.

A few weeks later he was to retrace those same steps when I repeated the trick. This time I remembered not to roar. Boy was still not amused. He always scored a hundred and he was not to be thwarted in his endeavour.

For the first time the school first eleven played the staff. As readers may remember, I'd already settled a score with Ginger. But I didn't bowl to Boy. He just didn't bat, he thought nobody had noticed. He was, of course, very, mistaken. Boys can be very cruel. The general comment was that he was scared of facing me.

After I'd finished my bowling spell he came in to bat. He'd scored about ten when he hit the ball to me on the boundary. I had no great reputation as a fielder. In fact, quite the contrary. Fast bowlers bowled, we were not expected to be great athletes like they are today. I stopped the ball and, apparently, fell over with it.

"Yes, one more," shouted Boy. He had not noticed that I had thrown the ball in before I fell. If I threw the ball in a hundred times I suppose I might get a few perfect throws right above the stumps. I've always been a great believer in sod's law and that day it worked very well. The ball sailed, fast and true, straight into the wicket keeper's gloves perfectly above the stumps. The wicket keeper screamed, "Howzat!" as he smashed the wicket to the ground. Boy didn't even have to wait for the umpire, he knew he was out. He glared at me as he passed, walking back to the pavilion, muttering something about a moral victory. I don't think Boy ever forgave me for humiliating him. When you're young, you just don't understand.

So anyway, there I was hanging round on that first day of Cricket Week, twelfth man with no chance of having a game because all the players had turned up. However, the opposition had turned up with one short so I was loaned to them for the day.

In the morning session Stevenage did incredibly well, reaching a hundred and ten for one. The bowling was all right but hardly inspired. They did have one good spinner who'd keep the runs down but the rest were very ordinary. I ran round the pitch. I did my best but it was very boring.

"Young Buckingham can bowl a bit," drawled Justice Pigshit. I'm never quite sure how the name came about but that's what everyone called him. Not to his face however, he was, after all, the Chairman of the Governors of the school, the President of the Cricket Club, and the local JP. A friend of mine once came up before him for a minor traffic offence on a motor scooter.

"I know you, young Powell?" said JPS.

"Yes sir," came the polite reply.

"Well, you have the right to be tried by someone else," stated JPS firmly.

"Oh no, sir, I'll stick with you," came the smart reply. He always regretted those words as he got the maximum sentence. But, I digress.

JPS was very convincing and I was given the right to open the bowling after lunch. During the break the sun had disappeared and the atmosphere had become very humid, hot and sticky; ideal swing bowling conditions. We all have good days and this was one of mine. On that day I was magic! I could do no wrong, nobody could score any runs. I gradually worked my way through the team. The new Captain immediately brought back the spinner and we proceeded to grind Stevenage into the dirt. Being young and inexperienced, I thought this would make me a star and I would play for the first team.

Wrong! Boy was not amused. It virtually ended my cricket for that season. It was getting towards the end of that season and I was off to Brighton to learn to be a teacher, and meanwhile I was earning as much money as I could, so I could enjoy myself there.

"You just watch Harry go!" laughed Geordie as I was talking to him up at the cemetery. Harry was deep in a grave when suddenly he pulled himself out like an Olympic athlete and ran towards the shed.

"What on earth's going on? I can't believe it! I've never seen Harry move like that!"

"Pay wagon's comin'," laughed Geordie. "He can hear it a mile away!" Sure enough the wagon arrived and Harry was first in the line.

"He's always first, you'll see!" Geordie was certainly right. All the time I was at the cemetery, Harry was always first for his money.

"He'll die up here," continued Geordie. "I thought he had one day last December."

"What happened?" I asked.

"Well, I came up here. It as a misty day, cold and wet. Harry was standing by a grave on the far side. Then, all of a sudden, he fell in. I knew it would happen one day. He's gone and died and fallen in one of those holes. I suppose it wouldn't be right to just fill it in though it would be the cheapest option. I walked across to the grave. Just as I got there a hand came out. 'Fallen in the grave,' he said. 'Gis a hand.' I helped him out. He dusted himself down and walked off back to the office. It gave me a right turn, I can tell you."

"I don't think I'd want to be working up here in December," I said to Geordie. "It's gruesome enough when the sun's shining, but with the dark and the mist it would be a bit like a Hammer Horror film. Anyway, I'd better get on. I'm off to cricket this evening!"

"I don't know what you see in cricket," complained Geordie. "I actually went down to watch you the other day. I watched for nearly an hour and saw three runs. It's a bore!"

"Not for me it wasn't!" I chuckled. "I was king for an afternoon."

King I might have been, but I still had some very dirty jobs. Lavatory cleaning for one. I don't recommend it. Now, park keeping was much better. But picking up the used johnnies was, again, not very pleasant. Sometimes they were still being used when I came across them as I patrolled the park in the early evening. Nobody told me the correct procedure when stumbling over a rutting couple. Should I accost them by saying, "Excuse me, this park is not for copulating unless you've brought the correct licence. I don't mind what you're doing but please take home the empties!" In reality I, embarrassed, wandered by pretending I hadn't noticed, which was probably the best way to deal with the situation.

I never progressed past third class labourer during my Council interlude but I did get an excellent tan and developed some superb muscles. I also put about half the work force off sick with one of my improvised work games.

We were sent down to clear a field of stones. I suggested throwing them into the waste area. It was easy for me, as throwing cricket balls was part of my training but the others reported sick the next day; they couldn't use their throwing arms. How was I to know? Besides, I had enough to worry about with my evening job of selling locally grown King Edward potatoes.

# CHAPTER 2

## *The Potato Lark*

*"No income tax, no VAT"*
— *Del Boy's song*

It had all started when I was offered a job by my sister's ex-fiancé. I'd been an egg picker part-time for some time but, to be honest, the smell of the chickens and the disgusting conditions they lived in put me off. It seemed to me horrifying that the cages were sloped so the eggs, once laid, would run down into a basket and the chickens had to live on a permanent slope. The reason for this was apparently, if the eggs were left in the cages, the chickens pecked them and made them unsellable. They also pecked your hands as you gathered their eggs and chickens have vicious little beaks.

Anyway, the new job was described as 'working with potatoes'. I imagined a very dirty occupation and so turned up in what was, for me, very scruffy clothes. My co-workers were very similarly dressed. If anything, it appeared that I had overdressed for the occasion.

Imagine my surprise when it turned out the actual job was door-to-door selling. The local farmer had become angry with the money paid to him by the local wholesaler and decided to sell direct. I was selling a labour-saving dream; seven pounds of locally grown potatoes delivered to your door for the same price, or cheaper, than older and probably inferior foreign potatoes from the shop. The concept was very good.

I knew nothing about potatoes but I was young, charming, and spoke reasonably well. I tried hard and, despite, my scruffy appearance, persuaded twenty-four households to switch to our new season King Edwards. I was somewhat surprised that this was about twice as many as the rest of the experienced team managed between them. The money paid was quite good. In fact, generous for our age and it seemed ridiculous that I should apparently do so well as a novice.

The next night I dressed up for the part and found selling much, much easier. When I got to thirty new orders I thought I'd see how the others were doing. At that point, they didn't know how well I'd done the night before.

"Er, could I come round with you for a while?" I asked Ern, one of the group.

"'Elp yourself mate," he replied in broad Cockney. "It's not an easy job so don't worry, it took me a while to get the hang of it."

We approached his next possible customer. He rang the bell and kicked the nearby shrubs with impatience. The door finally opened and he began his sales patter.

"Er, er, er, would you er, like, er… well, what I mean is, er, would you er, would you like some spuds?" The door had already shut in his face – about the norm for Ern.

"I told you it was 'ard," he muttered, and took his high-pressure selling technique to the next house.

I thanked him for his help and moved on.

Compared with some Ern was a class act to follow. The worst was an unpleasant-looking yob called Trev, whose sales pitch was somewhat unusual. First he would beat the door with his fist regardless of whether there was a bell or knocker. He had a very large fist. When the door opened he would shout abusively: "Want any spuds, mate?"

His technique was, I'm afraid, not very successful. The only good thing that could be said that if he got a customer it was a good one who was desperate for potatoes. Young as I was, it was obvious that all the sales force should go as soon as possible. I also worked out how to remove them and make me rich, or at least well-off, at the same time.

Now, our boss was that particular type of bloke who drove old Jaguars and wore sheepskin jackets, smoked pipes and generally thought well of themselves. Peter was the playboy of Stevenage. For all I knew he could have been the playboy of the whole of Hertfordshire. He was the sort of cad that complete books are written about. To give an example of his social skills, he announced his engagement on his wedding day. So what? He was in a hurry.

Not so, the wedding was meant to be to his live-in partner, a divorcee who was waiting for the decree absolute to come through. It had been arranged that they would get married on the day of freedom for her. She was a beautiful woman, slightly older than Peter, but she certainly got approving eyes from all the men when he turned up with her. I, for one was completely besotted. She was gorgeous and very, very pleasant to talk to. It must have come as a terrible shock that not only did he not marry her, but he actually did get engaged to someone else on that very day. Apparently, there were hundreds of thousands of reasons why he should marry the new girl, and money always talked to Peter, usually to say goodbye!

As a Romeo he certainly earned nine out of ten, but as a business man, somewhat less. How on earth he picked his sales team, I'll never know, except for the fact that he probably wouldn't want to do the job himself and was so grateful for anyone doing it. My fiendishly clever idea was that there should be an incentive for getting orders.

"Peter, have you got a few minutes? I've got an idea for your business that I think will make you money." That was the way to make him listen; sex and money were his favourite interests. Although he preferred them together, he was prepared to deal with either separately.

"We'll, what's the deal?" he snapped.

"I don't think you're getting value for money with your sales efforts and I'd like to reorganise it for you." He'd have had to have noticed that I was the star salesman, in fact I was the only salesman.

He turned on his most charming manner, the one which had women undressing before he'd even asked:

"Go on young Tony. Explain!"

"Well, at the moment you're paying eight shillings an hour for three hours a night. You're not getting three hours' work, nor are you getting many orders."

"Well, how would you change it then?" he asked.

"Easy," I continued, "pay per order and reduce the hourly rate. Why not make it four shillings per hour and then pay the salespeople two shillings an order. You'll need a set number of orders before the bonus starts, how about ten?" I finished my scheme and waited for his answer. It was obvious to Peter that it would save a lot of money, only he was somewhat concerned.

"Do you think you could actually improve sales?" he asked doubtfully. "I'm not sure they would work for that."

"I'm sure you're right," I said, "but as they're doing more harm than good, what's the point in keeping them? If I worked an hour longer I could replace all their orders and, better still, I could find you one more salesman. You would probably double the orders if we really worked hard."

"Yes, you could be right," he admitted, "we'll give it a wang."

I knew I was right.

Nobody was really working for four hours a night. I certainly wasn't and I knew I could do a lot better. The next few nights were fun. I averaged over forty per night; very nice increase in my wages. As for the others, they gradually stopped coming as they could never get ten orders. By the second week, I'd reached fifty a night and I was earning about five pounds a night which was a very good weekly wage for a youngster working full-time.

"You mentioned you'd got a friend?" asked Peter as we careered over a humped bridge at eighty miles an hour. That was one of the big disadvantages of the job: Peter's driving. "Do you reckon he'd join us?"

With the sort of money I was earning, who wouldn't join us? In retrospect this is where I went wrong. I should have known better than to introduce Tip Tipping into the lark. The game was never the same again.

Tip was a complex character and always felt he believed he was superior to the very ordinary couple that had taken him in. He lived on a Council estate and although he was obviously very intelligent, he used most of his energy to create mischief. Being around Tip was always amusing, sometimes dangerous but never quiet! When he was younger, to annoy his neighbours, he rigged out a mega speaker system with the speakers pointing out of his bedroom into the street. About five o'clock one morning he broadcast a bit of Johnny and the Hurricanes' latest hit 'Reveille Rock'. Thus his whole neighbourhood was wakened by the sound of "Come on you guys, rise and shine," followed by the Hurricanes' rendering of the army rise and shine call. It was not a popular move, but harmless.

"Well, what's the game then?" demanded Tip. "And, more importantly, what's in it for me?" His mercenary streak was showing.

"Well, it's easy money," I explained, "but the

important thing is not to milk it. If we keep to, say, fifty orders per night we knock in thirty to forty pounds a week, and he pays cash in the hand."

Tip considered for a few minutes and agreed, as I knew he would. The first night was fine. We both got fifty orders but on the second night Tip started his games.

"I thought we'd agreed fifty," I moaned, "you got sixty-two."

"Oh, sorry, I must have missed a page, I miscounted."

Peter was very pleased with Tip. He was now his star man. This annoyed me. The next night I got seventy. Tip got sixty-five.

"Things are on the up," said Peter as he took our sheets.

The next night Tip got eighty-five, I got seventy-five. *Bastard*, I thought. We passed a hundred shortly after that. It got hairy; a hundred and twenty, a hundred and thirty, a hundred and fifty. We were coining it. We were also cheating. Tip was worse than me but we both used dubious tactics.

For example:

"Knock knock!" Small girl answers door.

"Is your mother in?"

"No, she's out. Is there a message?"

"Yes, tell them we'll call again on Thursday. Thanks!" Seven pounds of potatoes Thursday for number sixteen.

"Ring ring!" Man answers the door.

"Is your wife in?"

"No. Sorry, anything I can do?"

"It's about the potatoes. Can you tell her that seven pounds will come on Thursday. By the way, is seven pounds enough?"

"Well, she never mentioned it but we usually have fourteen pounds." he adds cautiously.

"Ah, she probably didn't want you to carry them. It's a much better service and it doesn't cost any more. So, never mind, we'll make it then the fourteen pounds on Thursday. Thanks very much!"

The amazing thing was a large number of all these orders stuck. In fact, most of them. After all, potatoes are heavy and these were cheap. There were no large supermarkets in those days. I suspected that Tip also made up orders, but couldn't prove it. Mind you, we were both feeling very rich. After all, we were earning fifteen pounds per night, tax free. To put this in perspective, my first teaching job brought me thirty-seven pounds a month. The fact that we were having to go further and further from Stevenage made it all the more exciting.

By now, my boss had well over ten vans delivering potatoes over a very large area. We hadn't realised people change their minds, not just the ones that Tip had tricked. All the rounds needed re-canvassing but this meant a much more difficult job. Virgin streets seemed much more interesting to the sales force.

"We've got to re-canvass some of the areas," said Peter one evening. "Sales are getting unprofitable."

"Yeah, I can understand that," I said, "the trouble

is it's obviously going to be much more expensive. Why not make the bonus four shillings per order for re-canvassing?"

However, this idea didn't go down very well. We turned up to be paid one Friday evening. He took out a wad of money from his back pocket, looked at it and, to our amazement, told us he was a bit short that night as he was going up west. Tip was not amused but this was nothing compared with two weeks later when he had worked back through all the orders for the last four weeks, and totalled the bad ones.

"Well, it only seems fair that you don't get paid for the no-show orders," said Peter determinedly. We both looked in horror.

"Well Tipping, you had seven hundred and two bad ones which means I only owe you six pounds this week. Tony, you were better so you got fifty-four pounds." With that, he paid us. Tip was not happy.

"No-one's getting fat here anymore," he shouted. "Even the dog's getting thin. I'm quitting!" He walked off. The remark about the dog was slightly unfortunate. It had a serious illness and was dead within a week.

I carried on for as long as the game lasted. I realised it was very good money and I needed it as living in Brighton as a student was very expensive.

At the same time as the great potato game, and running concurrently, was the party season. For some reason, the whole of the south-east became obsessed with big parties. It all started in a small way as far as I was concerned, but it was certainly very exciting. The ground rules were: go to the Coffee Cabin, a trendy coffee bar in Stevenage New Town, buy one cup of coffee and make it last forever while you wait for the instructions to find the right party. It was all rather cheeky because no-one was actually invited but that didn't seem to bother anyone. Perhaps the best example of what could happen was when we gate-crashed a party at Tewin.

It was a very good party; plenty of attractive girls, lots of food and drink. We only had one problem really, an obnoxious drunk who nobody could stand. At last, by common consent the guests threw him out. I only found out later that it was his house! Another time, hundreds of people turned up to a six-year-old's birthday party. Obviously, somebody had got their wires crossed!

The biggest and most extraordinary of these parties was held at a white house on the river near St Neots. It was advertised as the biggest and best party in our area. Tip and I persuaded an occasional friend of ours to run us up there after the potato work. He had access to his father's Jaguar, a very old petrol-guzzler. It was the only car I'd ever travelled in where you actually saw the petrol gauge move steadily down. We agreed to pay the petrol and we started off late to catch the action.

"How many times do we have to stop for petrol on the way?" I asked, watching in horror as our money disappeared down the throttle of the car.

"Oh, he'll get us there," said Tip, "and probably back as well if we're lucky."

As we drove closer to St Neots we seemed to be driving into mass crowds of people.

"What on earth's going on?" I asked incredulously. Police cars, black Marias and all sort of other entertainment lined the road. We cruised round in amazement. Eventually, we stopped and asked a group of youngsters what was happening.

"It's all a bloody hoax!" shouted one of them. "There is no party at the White House."

"Whoever had the idea invited people from hundreds of miles away," continued his friend. "We've met people from Norwich, Peterborough, Oxford, Cambridge, Chelmsford, St Albans, and all parts of London. There are thousands of them all over the place. If that wasn't enough they've tipped off the police. It's a shambles. You're not going back to Norwich are you, by any chance?" he added hopefully.

"Sorry, no, we're off down the A1," I said. "Come on Tip, let's get going!"

With that, we turned round and returned home. Ironically, when I first went to college I roomed in a hotel with a farmer's son from Little Paxton, just outside St Neots. He was actually helping the police that night and confirmed how serious it was for the area and just how many arrests there'd been. It's amazing how small the world is!

***

"She's the most beautiful girl I've ever seen." I confided this to Dave one evening at the Mecca ballroom.

Dave was a near neighbour of mine, whose main claim to fame was his infamous brother. In every small town the police have favourites for various types of crimes. For example, if there'd been a beating they would bring in Terry the Nutter, a vicious teddy-boy who enjoyed maiming people. On the other hand, if it was a theft their preference was Dave's brother. We regularly heard the police bells ringing as they rushed to arrest him yet again. I felt very sorry for Dave, not only did he have an infamous thief for a brother, but his mother was also rather odd. I'd been going to his house for quite a long time before I realised the gardener/handyman was in fact his father.

Dave, however, was all right. We regularly went to the Mecca to enjoy the top groups: Freddy and Dreamers, Brian Pool and the Tremelos and occasionally American groups. It was also here we picked up the occasional bird. I was, admittedly, a bit fussy when it came to pick-ups. Some men are natural grazers, they seem to move from girl to girl adding up the score. I was more of your steady sort, I needed to actually like the girl. However, I was instantly in love with this angel I'd seen on the dance floor.

"You're mad," said Dave. "She's out of your league. She must be at least twenty-two."

I had to agree. She was much older than me but, what the hell, she was beautiful!

"Her friend's not bad, is she?" I said temptingly to Dave, knowing that if he didn't help me I'd have no hope at all.

"Yeah. But we got no chance."

"Yes, we have. Come on, follow me!"

I took the bull by the horns and asked the divine creature for a dance. Amazingly, she nodded her approval and Dave and I danced the next few dances including a fantastic slow number.

"Would you like a drink?" I suggested and, again, the vision nodded an approval. When we got into the bar it was quiet. I asked: "What is it to be?" It was here my world fell in. Her reply, innocuous in itself, finished my love affair. It wasn't what she said or the drink she asked for, a gin and tonic was fine, it was just I'd never heard such an awful voice in my life. Common didn't begin to describe it. I got the drinks and chatted about this and that for about thirty minutes after which I apologised: "I'm sorry but my poor old mother, she's widowed and very old and she needs looking after, so I'm going to have to go home and check on her. I'm very sorry."

Dave and I walked slowly back. As it happened, fate had a further twist for us that night. As we walked back along the old A1 two of the local girls were having problems with a cruising car and they ran back to us for help.

"Please can you help us? They're bothering us!"

The car stopped next and a yob called out: "Clear off, we saw them first!"

I rather pompously replied: "Why don't you go away? You're obviously annoying these girls."

With that the door opened and out stepped the first of three unpleasant-looking Teddy Boys.

"Quick, run!" I shouted to the girls. "And don't stop!"

Muttering thanks they ran off and I was left facing the leader of the band. Now, as I was getting on for six foot three I'd always found my height put people off so I just stared him straight in the face arrogantly. To my right, Dave was picked up and thrown into the hedge. In fact, he was thrown through the hedge. *Keep calm*, I thought. *Perhaps you can bluff it out.* I didn't really see the head coming, I just felt the pain as I crumpled to the floor. The next thing I knew was Dave standing over me.

"God, we've been lucky!" I said. "I thought they'd put the boot in!"

There had been some nasty attacks recently and normally the victims ended up with a long hospital stay. "At least it wasn't Terry the Nutter," I added.

"You ought to see yourself," said Dave, "it's no wonder they scampered. They must have been frightened out of their wits. They thought they must have nearly killed you."

"What do you mean? I'm not that bad," I said worriedly.

"Well, what do think all that blood is?" asked Dave. I then started to realise how much blood there was. It was all over my new coat, masses of it on the floor. It was horrible.

"They must have broken a blood vessel," I said. "It's probably saved me a lot of extra bother." Dave helped me back home and, amazingly, my mother took things very well – on that occasion!

The next week, she had something else to put up with.

"You know who we're playing next week, don't you?" said John with a big smile on his face.

"I don't know but it's obviously a good fixture," I replied, "otherwise you wouldn't be grinning like the proverbial Cheshire Cat!"

"It's Ablative Absolutes again, so we're in for a good night."

Ablative Absolutes were a very strange team. They wanted to call themselves Arseholes Anonymous but there was some reluctance by other clubs to allow them to play by such a name. It wasn't the fact that they were prudish, it was the fact that most teams have their fixtures printed and these fixtures were going to be put up in greengrocers, opticians, public houses, toy shops, and other assorted local venues. It was considered by some that the name Arseholes Anonymous would cause offence. They took the criticism to heart and changed the name to Ablative Absolutes.

In fact, they were a wandering band of ex-colonials, players form Australia, New Zealand, India, Pakistan, Canada, Hong Kong, and anywhere else that actually plays cricket. They played to a very high standard. In fact, they could easily turn up with an ex-test player but they also insisted on a good social game. They turned up with a jazz band, lots of pretty girls, and we always organised a big party for them after the game. The game itself was an all-day affair with lunch and was probably the most attractive game of the year.

"There's a rumour going around that you've given up smoking," said John. "Is it true?"

"Well, yes," I slowly answered, "I don't want to make a big deal of it because chances are, I won't have the willpower. But yes, I am trying to kick the weed."

"Why's that?" asked John. "I thought you enjoyed it."

"Well yes, I enjoy it, but I don't enjoy what it does to me. I seem to be coughing more and more and it's affecting my bowling."

"You've been getting enough wickets though."

"Yes, at the moment. But there was a nasty crack last week, I don't know if you heard it? I distinctly heard someone shout out, 'Don't take any notice of him, he's slowing down every over, he's not bowling at half the speed he was at the beginning.' I didn't find that very good for my confidence, particularly as I think it was true."

"Well you'll have to watch out," said John, "I've heard you put on weight if you stop smoking and that won't help your bowling either!"

The following Saturday the multi-national Ablative Absolute team turned up in a special coach along with jazz band, camp followers and special iced crates of beer. I'd been looking forward to the game, knowing that they were a good side, and I was probably going to get a lot of bowling. Over after over I bowled, ball after ball. Every so often I let off steam with a loud "Howzat!" usually more optimistically than genuinely. Occasionally I got lucky.

When the Ablatives had finally declared they set us two hundred and sixty-four to win, which was an unlikely total for us to get. We gamely struggled. Eventually, we battened down the hatches and the game ended in a draw with us on a hundred and ninety-six for eight. By a strange coincidence I scored as many runs as I got wickets: two. I thought the LBW decision that dismissed me was very harsh, but then, I normally did.

We had been drinking throughout the day and as we walked round the pub to continue our celebrations, one of the players who went by car had an accident in front of twenty witnesses. None of us thought it was his fault but then we were, to a certain extent, slightly biased. The chap in the other car asked us to confirm that he was in the right and was horrified to find that all twenty witnesses confirmed that he was wrong. He wasn't to know that we all were together, and knew the driver of the other car!

The party started promptly just after seven thirty, the jazz band was in full swing, as were the jugs of beer. I chatted round first the cricketers and then to some of the pretty girls who unfortunately were off limits as they were attached, but they were quite happy for a bit of harmless flirting. The drink flowed with only the occasional crisp or nut to soak it up. For some reason, around midnight when the jugs had run out, I switched to Dragon's Blood which was a strong ale brewed by Flowers. I had a few of them then decided I'd better go home.

"How are you getting home, Tony?" asked Ray, the Vice-Captain.

"Oh, I'll get the Green Line, there's one at one thirty, I should catch it easily," I replied jauntily.

"Oh, don't worry," he said, "I'll drive you home."

"You don't go my way, do you Ray?"

"No, but I'll take you home."

"Well that's very kind of you, but I'm happy to go on the Green Line."

"No!" he said loudly. "I will take you home!"

Well, I didn't see any point in arguing so he drove me back to Stevenage Old Town.

"Thanks for the lift, Ray. See you tomorrow! What time is it? Two thirty?"

"Yes," he said. "You'll be all right for tomorrow will you?"

"Oh, no problem. Looking forward to it, perhaps some easy wickets for a change!"

I got out of the car and walked up to the front door. My key seemed too large. I couldn't quite work it out really. I kept trying to put the key in the lock but it just wouldn't go in the hole. I was examining it rather carefully to find out what was wrong with it when my mother opened the door. She looked somewhat puzzled at me.

"Are you all right?" she said.

"Fine!" I said. "Very tired though, it's a bit late. Sorry you've had to come out of bed."

I went up the stairs, my mother watching me anxiously from the bottom.

*Can't think why everyone keeps asking me if I'm all right; very strange*, I thought. I got into my bedroom and took off my clothes. I went to the bathroom, cleaned myself up a bit, put on my pyjamas, came back to the bedroom and stopped. *What on earth have they done with my bed?* I thought. *It was never this high when I went out this morning! Well, never mind.* I started to climb up to try to get on to the bed which was about sixty foot tall. I kept falling off and somehow thought it was rather funny!

Giggling to myself, I eventually managed to climb

Everest, in this case my bed, and flung myself on it. Now, the strangest thing happened: the bed had become electric. As soon as I got on it, it spun round at a tremendous speed and threw me off. *That's not very nice*, I thought. So once again, I tried to climb Everest. Up, up, up I went, almost there – and fell off again. Eventually, after some time, I scaled the heights once again and flung myself on the bed. This time the bed was even more violent. The speed was more intense and I came off even quicker and I didn't feel very well.

I went to the bathroom and was violently sick. *Ugh!* I thought. *All in my nose, ughh, I hate being sick*. I rinsed my mouth, washed my face and crawled back in to the bedroom. By this time the bed was a hundred and twenty foot tall. *How on earth am I going to climb up there, is there a ladder anywhere?* Luckily, the edge of the bed had some bolt holes which allowed me to climb up, a bit like a ladder, not quite as steady. Up, and up, and up, and up I went, higher and higher till, at last, I fell on the bed. Again the bed picked me up and flung me round at tremendous speed and threw me off. "Ooh, ooh, wish it wouldn't do that," I said to myself. I rushed off to the bathroom once more to be violently sick.

Again, I cleaned myself up, washed my face and crawled slowly back to the bedroom. The bed now was three hundred foot tall and it had a Union Jack perched on the top. It took me longer to scale this enormous mountain. When I got there, I flung myself on the bed and someone, thank goodness, had switched the electricity off because the bed remained quiet. A great black mass from the ceiling descended on me like a big fog, suffocating me, squeezing the very life out of me.

I woke up, the sun was hitting me in the face through a chink in the curtain. The bed had returned to its usual size, thank goodness, as I didn't fancy jumping down. I got up, shaved, washed myself, got dressed and came down for breakfast. My mother still had that strange look on her face when she started the day's conversation.

"How do you feel?" she asked.

"Fine," I said, "in fact great! What's for breakfast?"

"Would you like toast or scrambled egg?"

"Oh, I think scrambled egg. I fancy a cooked breakfast." Mum's scrambled eggs were delicious: two thick slices of toast washed down with copious cups of tea, followed by toast and marmalade. I felt great!

"I've got another game this afternoon," I said.

"Are you sure you'll be all right?" asked Mum anxiously.

"Why shouldn't I be? It's not much of a game anyway, not like yesterday. I won't be late tonight. I think I could do with an early night anyway." I grabbed my kit and walked down to catch the bus at the bottom of the High Street. I arrived at the ground early and was ready, changed and fit for action when most of the other players arrived. Ray looked at me, puzzled.

"Are you going to be all right to play?" he asked.

"Of course! What's up with everyone? Do I look unfit?"

"No," he said, "to be honest, you don't. Well, all right!"

We lost the toss and Willian decided to bat. They were indeed a strange team. Nine of them were called Buck, it was almost like playing a family eleven. I was absolutely on fire, as they say. I don't know why but I seemed to be more aggressive than usual and proceeded to rip my way through the Bucks, getting seven Bucks for twenty-one. Perhaps it was the fact that they were unfinished: they needed an 'ingham' to make them better! We won the game very quickly and by six o'clock we were, once again, back in the bar.

"Do you know what you drunk yesterday?" asked Ray.

"No, not a clue, to be honest. That's the trouble with those jugs. I lost track."

"Well, I can't be sure," said Ray, "but I reckon you had about twelve pints to start with and then another ten bottles of Dragon's Blood."

"Well, that would mean that I drank sixteen and a half pints," I said. "I've never drunk that sort of amount."

"I know, that's why I took you home," said Ray. "I'm amazed you could walk! You certainly can take your liquor though!" he said and everyone agreed. "You're a lucky bugger though," said Ray, "at least it didn't hit you afterwards. If I'd drunk that sort of amount, I'd have been in a hell of a state. You must have a great constitution."

"Well, some of us have it, some of us don't," I said, "and I'm just, obviously, someone who can take my liquor." At the same time I was thinking to myself: *Never again, never do I want a night like last night! I'll certainly be more careful in future.* Getting drunk was not for me!

John had got some mates staying with him from his college and we'd all decided to go up west to have a good time. There were six of us and it was difficult to get in the car, especially as John (who was around 6'1") was the short man of the group. I was the next shortest at 6'3". The tallest being the Northumberland and Durham high jump champion who was about 6'9". John, majoring in PE, obviously went around with a very fit-looking crowd.

We drove round and round and round. London has that sort of effect on you.

"We want the next left turning," said John, "the trouble is, there's never any left turnings, only right turnings. So you turn right and then you want another right turning and there's only left turnings. Whatever you do, you never actually get where you want to go!"

It was all getting rather frustrating. We stopped the car to decide what to do next. We were engrossed in our argument when a rather unpleasant-looking Middle East type banged on the window. Jim, the high jump man, opened his window.

"Can I help you?" he said in broad Geordie. "What seems to be the trouble?"

"Move on," said our Middle Eastern friend, "or there'll be trouble!"

"Why should we move on?" said Jim. "We're doing no harm, we're just parked, thinking."

"You're not helping my business," came the stern

reply. "People don't like cars parked outside, it worries them."

What on earth was he talking about? And then the penny dropped. Looking up, we saw lots of girls leaning out of the windows, laughing. They didn't look the sort of girls that Mummy would like you to bring home for tea!

"You move on, and there will be no problem!" continued our rather short, darkish gentleman.

At this point, we decided to get out of the car. As we unfolded, the man's face was a picture. He must have been all of five foot two and suddenly to have six giants towering over him, all looking rather fit and healthy. In fact I should imagine he thought we were some form of gang or body guard patrol, his whole attitude changed as if by magic.

"No problem, you stay as long as you like! I don't-a mind, I don't-a mind!" The last words coming as he went back in the door and slammed it fast behind him.

"Funny fellow! Can't understand these places, what sort of man would pay for it?" said Jim. With that we all piled back in the car and drove off again.

Within minutes, we were again in trouble. Going down a narrow road, we were blocked by an open American sports car with two tough-ish looking men in it.

"Back up!" they shouted. "Back up!"

"I canna hear you!" cried Jim. "What's that you were saying? If you move back I can get my car through."

"Back up," came the reply, "quickly!"

"I canna hear you," Jim continued. "If you just go back a bit, I can get by. Why not go up the pavement?"

With that, the passenger got out of the car and walked towards us. He opened our door and Jim folded out. Again, the effect was dramatic. The man must have thought he was pretty big, probably around six foot. But six foot nine is bigger and Jim was broad and looked very strong indeed! The man ran back in the car and we heard him mumble to the driver: "Quick, back up the kerb, let them by, I don't like the look of them!"

We continued our evening, walking round enjoying space. It appeared that everyone wanted to walk on the other side of the pavement we were coming down! In retrospect we were probably very lucky we didn't come across anything unpleasant. But that night, nobody fancied the look of six giant athletes strolling round the town. Certainly, we all enjoyed a big night on the town!

"My parents are going away next week," said John. "I'm going to have a party!"

"Is that a good idea?" I enquired. "Not to say I wouldn't enjoy a party, but think what's happened to some of the other poor devils when they've had one."

"Oh, I'll organise it well," said John, "there'll be no gate-crashers. It'll be all carefully controlled, even numbers of men and women, no violence, no troubles. You'll help, won't you?"

"Of course I will," I said. "I think you're a bit optimistic. They all start off thinking they can control the gate-crashers. The trouble is, you end up being a prison warder rather than enjoying your party."

"Oh, you're just being wet," said John, "we can do it, don't worry!"

Well, to be honest, I wasn't worrying. It wasn't my house but I did know John's parents and I could see problems ahead should any damage occur. Still, we threw ourselves into the organisation, invited the right sort of people, only those who weren't going to puke all over the house or turn violent when they'd had a bit of booze. For example, we didn't invite Terry the Nutter although I'm sure he would have loved to have come.

"Put all that beer over there," said John. "Cover that table, put a sheet over it. We don't want that getting ruined. I think I'd better take this picture off the wall. I'll go and put it up in the bedroom."

Everything that could be protected, had been protected. We were feeling very confident by the time the party was due to start that evening.

"It's getting dark early, isn't it?" said John.

"Yes well, summer's nearly over. We'll soon be back at college."

"I suppose so. Funny, you would have thought people would have been here by now."

"Oh, they'll be along. Nobody likes to come early to a party."

At that point a double decker bus stopped outside the house. The entire bus, it appeared, got up and got off the bus.

"How many people are there on a double decker bus?" I asked John.

"Oh, I don't know. Seventy or eighty?"

"Well, how many people did you invite tonight?"

"Thirty-two. Why?"

"Well, I think we could have problems!"

The doorbell rang and John opened the door. He was smashed back behind the door in the crush as suddenly the party was full of people. There were certainly a lot more than thirty-two. I don't even think all the people that we'd invited were amongst the first wave. We must have had about forty gate-crashers straight away! Once they were in, it was very difficult getting rid of them. The main thing as far as I was concerned was to make sure I wasn't girl-less. Parties could be very miserable if you're the odd gooseberry left out. I made sure that my present girlfriend, Lou, was well tied to me before I did anything further. John, unfortunately, was not quite so lucky. The girl he'd thought was coming with him was immediately attracted to a gate-crasher and he ended up a gooseberry at his own party!

"I do feel sorry for him," I said to Lou while we'd crawled off into some distant corner, "but I did warn him!"

I don't remember much about the early part of the evening. Perhaps, we were involved in examining lips, tongues and teeth for hygiene reasons; and it was hot in the room. Despite my suggestions that it would be better to loosen clothing, Lou didn't seem inclined to agree, but seemed to prefer to be hot!

"You don't doubt my motives?" I asked.

"No," said Lou, "I don't doubt them at all. I know

perfectly well what your motives are, so forget it!"

Thus, disappointment once again! As I was coming to terms with the cruellest of cruel words, 'no', all hell broke out in the hall. I did feel some moral responsibility as I was part-organiser so I untwined myself from Lou and went out into the hall. Two of our guests, not that we actually knew them, had detached the poles from the bell push and were sword fighting in the hall. Above them hung a very expensive glass chandelier, John's parents' pride and joy! John rushed to the scene shouting: "Stop it! Give me that pipe!" He grabbed the pipe and the duellists let him have it immediately. John, unfortunately, was anticipating some aggression and used slightly more force than perhaps was necessary. The net result was that John smashed the chandelier himself with the long pipe.

*Oh God!* I thought. *That's all we need.* John's face was a picture. He just couldn't believe it. Of all things to happen, that he should have broken the chandelier.

"It's not too bad," I said optimistically to John. "I'm sure it can be repaired."

"Possibly," he said, "but not in time to save me. Oh why did you persuade me to have a party?"

I was somewhat hurt. It had been me that said it was a bad idea but then, memories are very short.

"Well, we can't do a lot about it tonight. Let's get the party over, clean up tomorrow and see what can be done."

Lou and a number of the girls stayed behind to help and we soon had the house pretty clean and shipshape. The exception, of course, was the chandelier. I then walked Lou back in the early hours of the morning. She asked seriously: "Will John be all right? What do you think's going to happen about the chandelier?"

"I don't know, they ain't going to be happy, that's for sure! But then, it was an accident. He was defending their property. Who knows, he might get away with it but I'd rather concentrate on other things." I put my arm round her and pulled her back to me to continue with my dental examination. Of all the girlfriends I'd had up to that point, Lou was undoubtedly the best kisser!

I got to know a whole group of girls who went to a convent. In the first place, I hadn't actually twigged all the girls went to the same school, which caused some slight embarrassment. The big problem was, I had a range of chat-up lines that I was rather proud of. I took inspiration from pop songs, from writing, and even from my own devious brain. I had one particular line that was, I thought, superb. It was very useful when someone had worked out that you had dated one of their friends.

"You've been out with Tessa, haven't you?" asked Wendy one evening.

"Tessa?" I said innocently. "Have I been out with Tessa?"

"Don't lie," said Wendy, "I know you've been out with Tessa. She's in my form."

*Oh dear*, I thought, *this is a bit awkward.* However, I had the answer in my patent chat-up line kit. "Yes, I did go out with Tessa. You're right. I'd almost forgotten."

"How could you forget going out with a girl?"

"Well it's you, you're so beautiful. You've sort of blotted out her memory. It's a bit like the moon and the sun. At night the moon glows bright and the sun can't be seen however, when the sun comes up at the dawn the moon is eclipsed and disappears. It's still there but just a pale version. Tessa is the moon and you're the sun. When you're there I can see nothing but your beauty."

"That's pretty good," she said, "almost word perfect."

"What do you mean 'word perfect'?"

"Well, I was talking to Diana the other day, she told me you said virtually the same as that and, on that occasion, she was the sun."

"Diana!" I exclaimed. "D-do you know Diana?"

"Oh yes," she said, "she's in my form. Didn't you know?"

No, I didn't know. As far as I was concerned, they all lived miles apart. What a mean trick to find they all went to a school together, miles away, and were in the same form. This was not good news! It was even worse news to find out that they compared notes. It seemed most unfair to me. I worked out these wonderful chat-up lines and then found they were being spread round by malicious girls.

"What else did Diana tell you?" I enquired rather nervously.

"Well, you'll find out, won't you? When you use the lines I'll tell you!"

This, I thought, was very unsporting. However, I suppose you've got to play the game. It was unfortunate that the rules had just all been changed. I was adaptable, I would learn the new rules. Perhaps the answer was to give up chat and get on with a bit of nuzzling, at least you're safe there! I pulled her to me, looked straight in her blue eyes. When I went to kiss her she broke away, exclaiming: "I don't hand my kisses round like toffees!"

Fine," I replied, "I prefer chocolates!" drawing her back and continuing to kiss her. She was a very pretty girl and kissed with great enthusiasm. The only problem was she did dress in the most extraordinary way which made one embarrassed to be seen with her in public. But then, that was no excuse for me to standing her up to go and play cricket instead, even if she did get her own back on me by beating me up on the boundary. But then, that's another story!

I had arranged to meet Wendy in the Town Square at 2 o'clock one Saturday. We were going to the Flea-pit for an afternoon matinee. I didn't know what was on, not that it mattered, we rarely saw the picture. After all it was warm, dark and fairly private.

"Thank goodness I found you, Tony," called Ray, my fellow fast-bowler from Knebworth.

"Hello, Ray. I thought you were playing against the Park this afternoon."

"Well I would be but for my back. It's completely gone. I told them I'd try to get you to play. It's a big game. Can you help us?"

"Of course I will!" I reassured him. "The only reason I'm not playing is that I thought I'd be working. Wait a minute, what about my kit?"

"Jump in the car, we'll fetch it on the way. You should get there in time for the start with a bit of luck!"

I had of course forgotten all about poor Wendy. It was a very hot day and I had just finished a long spell of bowling. I felt very tired. I had been put out to grass right on the boundary. I was happily dozing off when all of a sudden I heard Wendy's voice.

"Oh there you are, you bastard! I waited an hour for you!" she shrieked.

"Ah, well! I can – er – explain," I muttered.

"Oh no you can't!" she shouted and started hitting me over the head with her handbag. At that point I was conscious of a lot of uncouth laughter. I looked up and it appeared the game had stopped. Everyone was enjoying my embarrassment. Despite me moving round the boundary, Wendy continued to savagely attack me with her handbag and at the same time tell me all sorts of unpalatable home truths.

"Can I come in the slips?" I called hopefully.

"Not likely!" came the reply. "This is too good to miss!"

The rotten devils left me to be handbagged for a long time before they reluctantly recalled me to bowl.

Wendy never really forgave me for standing her up. It was, I admit, a rotten thing to do, but her display on the boundary was so good that it went down in Knebworth folk-history.

I suppose I was lucky that by the time I'd met Lou I'd realised that she was also in the same form and, therefore, didn't try my small repertoire of witty chat-lines. In fact, to be honest, I disposed of the lines and relied on honesty as the best policy – well, nearly always!

I also worked hard at the perfect date. I got free tickets to two cinemas in Letchworth through my father which meant I only had the cost of getting the girl to the cinema. I used to do that in style by buying first class day returns which, at that time, were very much cheaper after six o'clock at night. The advantage of the first class compartment was it was invariably empty. The journey from Letchworth to Knebworth took around fifteen minutes and was a very comfortable way of finishing off a perfect evening. As I got older and wealthier, I simply added a restaurant to the programme and also started to develop evenings in London with the theatre and meal at the Lyon's corner house and an even longer train journey home. Of course this was much more expensive and only for high days and holidays. Funny thing is though, once I started going out with Lou, I seemed to lose interest in all the other girls and thought she was perfect of course, until I met Cath at college. After all, when the sun comes out the moon disappears!

# CHAPTER 3

*Hearts full of Youth,*
*Hearts full of Truth*
*Three parts gin to*
*One part vermouth*
*— Tom Lehrer, 'College Days'*

## The Invasion of the Mods and Rockers

In the early sixties, a war was declared. Not a Cold War between Russia and NATO, but a more localised one between two groups of youngsters. In the dark corner, wearing leather and driving very large motorbikes, were the Rockers. These had been around for years, driving their bikes in groups like the outlaws in the Wild West. They liked playing with their machines and so tended not to be very clean and on top they sported long greasy hair.

In the light corner came the Mods. This group favoured smart suits and rode on small mopeds. They were a new phenomenon. They visited hair stylists, favoured clean shoes, and were generally neat in appearance. They also liked driving in groups, normally much larger than the Rockers but equally as vicious.

The majority of the Mods and Rockers were normal decent sorts of blokes but, as with all gangs, they became extreme. The papers were full of headlines: "Mods invade Southend!" or, "Hastings devastated by invasion of Mods and Rockers!" Mind you, it wasn't all bad news, there were few complaints from the manufacturers and distributors of mopeds and young men's clothes shops were laughing all the way to the bank!

Friday found me, as usual, hard at it at College. Could I go three no trumps or should I double? The other major decision was at what time I should visit the Dead Herring for my early morning cup of coffee. Personally I preferred Pejoes, a distinctly smarter coffee bar run by two nice boys, Peter and Joe. Their frothy coffee and cheese and tomato rolls were very classy and they kept the place immaculate, which was more than could be said for the Dead Herring. These difficult decisions were what College was really about. As I pondered on my bid, Cath arrived and announced: "The Mods and Rockers are coming to Brighton! I, for one, am going home for the weekend."

"Isn't that a bit drastic?" I replied curtly. "They probably won't bother us, we're not Mods or Rockers."

"Well, I don't care. I'm going, you do what you like."

After she left, I got to thinking; perhaps she was right after all. I had experienced the problem first hand but then, it was our own fault. When I say 'our', to be perfectly honest, I should have said Tip's fault. It was last summer. We'd been coffee-barring and talent spotting when about three million Mods appeared together with their miserable, pathetic little mopeds. All of them neat and tidy with pudding bowl hair-cuts. I sniggered and muttered to Tip: "Look at them. Aren't they pathetic!"

Tip obviously agreed as he shouted after them: "F***ing Mods!" Now, this was not a sensible course of action. They all started to move quickly in our direction.

"Run!" shouted Tip, apparently not noticing that we were both running rather quickly.

Doctor Roger Bannister may have broken the four minute barrier with his mile run but I reckon we could have done it in two minutes that particular afternoon. The expression 'fear lent us wings' sprung to mind. I honestly believe the three million Mods would have caught us, had we not run into the woods. They probably didn't want to disturb their hairstyles or dirty their mopeds, so they didn't follow.

"What on earth did you do that for, you stupid cretin?" I shouted at Tip once we got our breath back.

In typical Tip fashion he replied: "Well, it seemed a good idea at the time." Life was never anything but uncertain when around Tip Tipping! When I consider carefully that afternoon, I might slightly have exaggerated the number of Mods, but they wouldn't be interested in me now, would they?

I went out of College to get a beer at the Bombay Bar, a sort of poor man's Royal Pavilion. As I walked up the road, I saw a face I'd not seen for a while. Terry the Nutter in the flesh and twice as ugly! The last I'd seen of him, some idiot upset him by saying some offensive remarks. If I remember rightly it was "Hallo Terry." This, appears, was right out of order as he smashed the offending lad a few times to correct his error. After the educational process was finished, the lad benefited from a free holiday in the local hospital!

Terry the Nutter didn't need any excuses, he'd happily beat you up whatever your persuasion. It occurred to me that I was running out of clothes to wear. In other words those I could actually bear the smell of. A washing weekend would seem very much in order. It also helped me to get out of the area.

"I've been thinking about what you said," I confided to Cath. "I still think it's unnecessary, however, I'd rather see you safely onto the train and as you won't be here I'm going to visit Mum. She'd be delighted to have me home for the weekend."

"Well, I think it's the sensible thing to do. I'm almost packed, meet you in thirty minutes."

I rushed back to the home of the lewds and up to my steaming pit. Despite the fact I had two very large cases, I almost couldn't cram all the filthy clothes into them. *I hope Mum will be able to manage all those*, I thought.

I organised a taxi to the station for us and we managed to catch the Brighton Belle Pullman service. It was wonderful. For a shilling extra, you experienced the luxury of a single chair, individual lights, table cloths, and real linen serviettes.

Cath and I sat like Lord and Lady Muck in the Pullman car, drinking our coffee and eating the complimentary shortcake biscuits. As usual, we talked non-stop, saying nothing of importance but enjoying ourselves enormously. The hour on the train sped past so quickly that all too soon I was dragging my cases off to Paddington to see Cath on the train to Birmingham. As usual, I left the cases next to Isambard Kingdom Brunel and asked him to look after them for me. Cath and I had kissed as if we weren't going to see each other for a year or so, not simply for a weekend, and as her Birmingham train slowly pulled out I ran back to retrieve my luggage. As I grabbed the cases, a hand gripped my shoulder.

"Not quite so fast, sonny!"

I looked up and saw a large moon-faced policeman. His face was exceptionally white, probably because he lived in the dark at Paddington Station. His uniform seemed to be two sizes too small for him and I'm sure Sherlock Holmes could have told him his exact breakfast and lunch for the last two meals. He was certainly not one of London's most elegant policemen.

"Are those your cases?" he continued?

"Yes Officer," I replied politely.

"You're in a bit of a hurry, aren't you?"

"I'm going to King's Cross to catch a train, I've just left my girlfriend," I explained.

"Yes, and I'm sure that you could tell me exactly what's in each case?" he asked sarcastically. "Let's start with the cream one, shall we? What have you in there?" He glowered at me triumphantly, expecting, I'm sure, that I would know nothing at all about the contents.

"Dirty, smelly washing," I slowly replied.

"And in this one?" he continued, pointing to the green case.

"Just the same, just dirty, filthy washing."

It was obvious from his face he didn't believe a word I said.

"All right then, open this one and let's see for ourselves what's in it," he ordered me triumphantly.

"I don't think you'll want me to open up the case really. You just won't like it," I replied cheekily. "There'll be an awful smell."

"Just open the case please – now!" he shouted.

"OK, but I have warned you!" With that, I opened up the case. The stench was certainly not pleasant. Five weeks of dirty socks, filthy pants, etc. did not smell like Chanel No. 5, more like Canal No. 6.

"Christ Almighty!" he exclaimed. "That's disgusting. Shut it up at once."

As I shut the case I politely enquired: "Do you want me to open the other one?"

"No I do not! No doubt you're taking that lot home to your poor mother. You ought to be ashamed."

"Can I go now, Officer?" I politely asked.

"You're lucky I don't run you in for dumping dangerous chemicals on Paddington Station. Yes, go on but don't leave them there again!"

As I left, heading towards the Underground, I glanced back and saw him glaring after me. He didn't look a very happy policeman that day. I'm sure he thought he'd apprehended a dangerous bag-snatcher.

I met Cath the following Monday and, as we travelled down on the Brighton Bell, I told her all about my filthy experience on Paddington Station. As it was early, we ordered the English breakfast: eggs, bacon, sausage, fried potatoes, tomatoes, fried bread, in fact, the full monty. By the time we'd emptied two pots of tea and umpteen slices of toast and marmalade we were slowly approaching Brighton Station.

We had certainly done well to miss the invasion of the morons. Virtually every crime in the book had been carried out including murder and rape. Those who stayed behind had to hide indoors and wait for the crisis to end. My landlord had gone out for a walk wearing blue jeans and had been mistaken for a Rocker and was forced to run, chased by screaming Mods. However, the most shocking and disturbing of all the stories was the young couple snogging up on the cliffs near Peacehaven. They were attacked and the boy thrown to his death off a cliff. The girl multiple raped. Gang hysteria is a very dangerous thing.

## The Bridge Game

During my last year at school when it was not possible to practise cricket I occupied myself playing bridge. The sixth form common room was a large pavilion some way away from the school. It was perfect for smoking, drinking, playing bridge and generally whiling away the boring hours of school time. When I got to college there were very few people that could play. I set about introducing this idler's pastime. Very soon, we had at least four schools of bridge going on throughout the day which, I'm afraid, often meant lectures being less popular than they might have been. They couldn't compete with the hope of the perfect bridge hand.

One of the players was the president of the Student's Union. He was a great friend of ours but even his best friends would say he was pompous. One day we thought we'd play a practical joke on him using a James Bond Casino Royale bridge hand. We sorted the pack in advance and produced it after about thirty minutes of very competitive bridge. Mike was a very impressively large bearded chap who normally expressed no emotion. But I do detect the merest hint of a smirk when he picked up his hand. Mind you, with a hand like he'd got, he was entitled to smirk. We'd dealt him ace, king, queen of hearts, ace, king, queen of clubs, ace, king, queen, jack of diamonds and the king, jack, nine of spades. He was looking at eleven tricks out of a possible thirteen and that was with no help from his partner.

He opened a confident two no trumps. I bid three spades, his partner ducked and Mike bid three no trumps. I raised to four spades and my partner up to five spades. Mike went absolutely berserk.

"You're just being silly!" he shouted. "I'll go to five no trumps."

"Six spades," I replied, smiling at him as I called. "A baby slam," I added sarcastically, in case he didn't know.

"This is just being childish!" he moaned loudly. You could see his point, as he held virtually every decent card in the pack. "Six no trumps!" he snapped, and with that he threw his cards down firmly on the table as if to warn us that the joke had gone too far.

"Seven spades," came the reply from my partner. "We'll go for the major slam."

His face was as black as thunder. He literally seethed with anger.

"Double!" he roared.

"Redoubled," I called.

With that he just sat and shook his head. It was his lead so he banged down the ace of diamonds which I promptly trumped. I led back a heart which forced him to play his queen which was trumped in dummy. Then started the fun; dummy led a low spade. Mike had a choice whether he should put his king, jack or nine. He chose the nine and I won the trick with the ten. Another heart meant he had to play his king which was then trumped.

By now he was looking very puzzled. Back came a low spade, he put on his jack, I took it with my queen and lead back a final heart forcing his ace to be trumped. Back came the low spade and his king got axed. I led back a diamond which was trumped in dummy then led back a club which I trumped. And finally, dummy won the last two tricks with the remaining two hearts.

"All thirteen tricks, a major slam doubled and re-doubled!!" I said triumphantly.

Mike said nothing. He just sat still looking very white-faced. He just couldn't believe it. Mike was a very strong character. I'd acted with him in a number of plays so I got to know him fairly well but even I was not prepared for his sketch at the Christmas revue.

He was sitting next to our Principal, a pompous white-haired moralist who was constantly lecturing us on our sexual habits, yet was reckoned to be having a ding-dong with the college purser. This was rich for a man who accused a girl kissing her fiancé goodnight for being no better than a prostitute. Mid-way through the performance Mike got up, excused himself and went up on the stage. His only props were a telephone and a chair.

The sketch consisted of a conversation between Arthur Stewart, our Principal, and a Headmaster who had one of our last year students teaching at his school. The Headmaster was very North Country.

"Hallo Arthur, how're things?" he enquired. "Oh, sorry to hear that. Have you been to the doctor, you mustn't be shy about these things you know." Much laughter from all the hall.

"'Ere, I've got one of your students 'ere, Arthur, and we 'aving a few problems. You see, I put her in charge of stationery." Much giggling from the hall. "Well, she's changed things a bit so we can only have pens and paper etc. on Tuesdays and Thursdays." Much laughter from the hall.

"Oh, you do it that way at Brighton? Well, it's all very well, but she's insisting we got to be there between ten and eleven a.m. It's causing all sorts of difficulties."

69

That's exactly how it worked for us and none of us liked it. Much laughter. Mike went on with a number of other risky jokes based on college procedures and then came to his final all singing and dancing finale.

"'Ere, while you're on the phone Arthur, there's something I've been meaning to ask you. You know that men are allowed into the girls' rooms for an hour only at lunchtime? Well, isn't that a bit odd?" Very loud laughter.

"You and me, Arthur, we're men of the world, aren't we? Tell me, what can they do in an hour that they can't do so in two hours? Once they know they've got the opportunity, haven't they?" Laughter and much giggling.

"Oh, I see. They can't do it twice. Fair enough!" Much applause and laughter. With that, Mike walked off the stage and re-joined the Principal for the remainder of the concert.

One of the best things about Brighton was the drama. I've always loved live theatre and to have a superb theatre like the Royal on my doorstep was a special treat. The Theatre Royal was a major preview theatre and we saw many of the West End productions a week or so before they hit the big time. Sometimes this meant we saw the changes that helped to make them more attractive to the audience.

Just before I started taking Cath out, I took Sandy, my previous girlfriend, to see Kenneth Williams in Gentle Jack. It was a fairly serious play about Jack in the Woods and Mr Williams was trying not to be beyond our ken. In theory it should work but his popularity was very much based on 'Round the

Horn', 'Just a minute' and the Carry On films. The audience had come to hear him say, "Nay, nay! Stop mucking about!" in that camp manner of his and were not inclined to be serious. He let slip just once and the audience burst into applause and it was fairly obvious that the production had a problem. A week later I took Cath to see it on one of our first dates. The play was now a comedy and very much beyond our Ken. It entered the West End to rave revues and did very well at the box office.

Noel Coward was much in fashion and we were delighted with the performances of Michael Dennison and his wife, Dulcie Gray. It does seem amazing, thirty years later we still go to watch them in the West End or Chichester and we thought they were ancient at the time!

Meanwhile I myself was a notable Thespian, starring in several college productions. The most amazing one was written by one of our students about a loony bin. I was, needless to say, a major loony and the dramatic moment when one of the inmates being bullied by the sadistic guard hung himself. At that point a folk song is being sung and the words fade out: "sun never sh..." and at that point the swinging corpse shadow plays across the stage. It was a moment of pure theatre. The audience were silent. Then all the scenery fell down upon us. It took us thirty minutes to get it all back again and by that time the play was lost. It was a pity because it was a good play.

In one of my other parts I was the Defence Counsel in the black comedy 'One Way Pendulum'. You know the one: the chap decides to teach sixty speak your weight machines to sing the Messiah. He also murdered a lot of people, telling them jokes before he kills them so they would die laughing. I was the Defence Counsel trying to persuade the jury it was a very laudable thing he did and how kind he was to actually think up new jokes so they would actually die laughing.

My final speech was about seven pages long. It all went well until the final night. I was approaching the end of this mammoth speech and before I knew what had happened I was back at the beginning again. A horrifying prospect of going right through the ten minutes again and so I had to ad lib. As most of the audience were asleep by then, I don't think they noticed.

I never really could understand the purpose of teaching us about distant customs from South Sea Islands. I suppose there is a relevance of knowing that young men stick conch shells on the end of their private parts and dance around and they oil themselves with grease and you can slip into the tents, huts of young girls, and not be caught as they run away. But really, growing up in Western Samoa and growing up in West New Guinea, as written by Margaret Mead, did seem to be a little bit unnecessary but then, some educationalists probably thought it was important that we should know all about conch shells.

We produced a play to take the mick out of Margaret Mead. We were a lot of sophisticated natives watching television and eating decent food but when the jungle drums suddenly come to tell us that Margaret Mead is coming, with that we get rid of all the trappings of civilisation and revert back to being tribal. Margaret Mead arrives, we do all sorts of strange dances and rituals, she writes it all down, gives us lots of money, goes away and we get out the television sets again and get back to normal.

We had to black up for the part. The first night we blacked up all over. I don't know what they gave me to use but it took me nearly the rest of the next day to get rid of it. We refused to black up totally the next night and we only went on with black tops and wore trousers. We had a particularly good chant. We all gathered round, glared at the audience rather like a New Zealand Hakka, shouted, "Embor-ah!" and the reply was "Ge-zing-a." This went on louder and louder to a final crescendo, it was quite impressive really. Unfortunately, it appears both words are filthy words in Swahili and one of the audience that night happened to speak Swahili very fluently. He complained and we were removed from the revue for the following night. I don't think the lady who was very keen on Margaret Mead actually enjoyed our performance much. I think she thought we were actually getting at her. How could she guess?

## Extra-Curricular Activities

After our heroic draw against the Sussex second eleven, I became friendly with one of the players. He was a strange chap who'd become very religious after being involved in a rather bad car smash. He actually had been driving. One of his friends, a passenger, and a very famous cricketer had actually lost his eye. I always thought he was riddled with guilt and I suppose that's a very normal reaction. His problem, he would lecture the other Sussex cricketers about their disgusting morals. A habit which didn't make him over popular nor did it help his career.

Robin had decided that I needed help with my bowling and had volunteered to coach me. Shortly after Cath and I had got married, we returned to Brighton by coach to visit Cath's ex-roommate. It was disastrous for many reasons.

College attracted all sorts of people, some were very nice, some complicated, some discontent, but there were very few like Roger Lewis. He'd worked out the perfect sex seduction technique. It was crude and yet very effective. He claimed that he had a very short time to live and that he'd injured his face by poking it up out of a tank and getting caught by a tree while on an army manoeuvre in Germany. He certainly did have a damaged face but I'd always doubted his dying story.

In my last year he had the room above me in the hotel I'd been moved to in order to get away from the depression of the landlord that had gassed himself in Happy Valley. During the time I was there, Roger had worked his way through dozens of silly girls, all trying to 'comfort' him. Very few lasted very long with him. At his worst, he would actually throw them out of his room after the sexual act had been completed. With one rather innocent girl he had apparently, according to his own boasting around the college, worked his way through the Kama Sutra. It was bad enough what he actually did to the girl but by boasting to all and sundry about every disgusting detail I thought he was the pits. Even worse for me, the walls and floors in the hotel were not sound-proofed and the noises I often had to put up with were very embarrassing, but at least I didn't know the girls personally.

That particular day, we arrived at Patsy's flat late in the afternoon.

"Hallo Cath," squealed Patsy. "It's great to see you. Obviously marriage suits you."

Patsy was a small dark-haired girl who worked as a dental nurse. I was surprised at her appearance. She seemed much more tarty than I remembered her and her make-up was certainly over the top.

"Hallo Tony," she said as she kissed me.

"I want you to meet my boyfriend, I think you know him already though."

With that Cath and I turned toward the living room door. To my amazement, Roger walked out.

"Tony and Cath, this is Roger."

"Yes, I know," I replied rather quietly. "We were in the same hotel last year."

Roger looked as revolting as usual. Why on earth any girl would want to get mixed up with him I just couldn't guess. But then, women were an eternal mystery.

"Good to see you, Tony. Getting enough are you?" he enquired with a dirty leer in his strange Welsh accent. "Patsy and I sure are, aren't we, love?" Patsy looked slightly embarrassed as he smacked her bottom. "She's great, boy. Can't get enough, can you?"

Yes, he was the same old Roger. The sort of chap you could take anywhere at any time and know he'd let you down. Cath and I found all this slightly embarrassing, particularly as we knew of his reputation. Admittedly, I knew rather a lot more of it than Cath did. We decided to go out for a Chinese meal that evening, but it was not a success. Roger seemed to be touching Patsy all the time; sometimes fondly but, more often, lewdly. During the meal they sat together and, judging by Patsy's face and the movement of the table cloth he continued his open philosophy on sex into the actual meal. After coffee we walked back to their flat and Roger continued his lewd behaviour. We were pleased to say goodnight at last and retire to our own bedroom.

"God, that was so embarrassing," whispered Cath, "he's an animal. Why on earth does she let him humiliate her like that? I'd see him in hell first!"

"Well, you know what his reputation is. I've actually known him throw a girl out of the room immediately after he'd finished with her leaving her to get dressed in the corridor of a male hotel! He treats women like dirt and the amazing thing is, how many of them like it." I kept my voice low because obviously we didn't wish to be overheard.

"Well I don't understand them," continued Cath, "but at least we're away from them till the morning."

This, as it turned out, were famous last words as the walls were very thin between us and their room. The noises coming through were something from the worst pornographic film.

"I think you spoke a little quickly there!" I giggled.

The creaking of the springs continued but the animal grunts getting louder and louder, culminating in a piercing scream which we assumed was from Patsy.

"Well, at least we can, hopefully, get to sleep now," I said.

A few minutes later, the banging started and the wall started moving. Back came the grunts, groans and other assorted animal noises. The performance seemed to have lasted for eternity.

"Perhaps that's what they see in him," said Cath naughtily, "pity I didn't bring a tape recorder, I could have made a fortune from this!"

We never really worked out whether it was done on purpose to shock us, or whether it was the usual nightly ritual. One thing we were sure about, we didn't want to spend any more nights there.

The next day we met Robin and we all decided to buy a car and go to Cornwall. We looked round all the cheap garages and eventually came across an Austin A80 with a new gold seal engine. It cost the princely sum of fifteen pounds and even at that price we were worried. We took it for a second opinion to another garage. The chap looked at us as if we were mad.

"Well, reckon the gold seal engine must be worth more than fifteen pounds," he chuckled, "you can't go too far wrong!"

So, we decided to invest in the car which had obviously previously belonged to a farmer. Well, to be honest, it looked like he kept his chickens in it. Robin asked us if we could stop in Maida Vale. He wanted to meet a friend there so we arranged to meet at nine o'clock the next morning. If anything, the sexual adventures of our friends were even worse that night. With all the practice he had, he must have been better than James Bond!

We left early the next day, picked up Robin and headed to London. Cath actually hadn't passed her driving test so Robin, as the qualified driver, had to always be in the car. We plodded up the road and eventually found Robin's friend's address; a large, luxurious, white, imposing house in Maida Vale. As it was about lunchtime, Robin suggested we all went to a local restaurant. The friend turned out to be a very beautiful Indian lady, wearing an exquisite silk sari. Cath was rather embarrassed to offer her a lift in our ex-chicken run. If she was surprised, she hid it very well.

The restaurant was virtually empty. The only other occupant sitting close to the door. We chose to sit at the far end of the restaurant.

"Introductions are in order," began Robin. "Princess Borate, these are friends of mine, Cath and Tony Buckingham. They're both young teachers. Cath and Tony, this I have the honour to introduce you to Princess Borate, wife of the Narob of Rangadoo."

"Delighted to meet you," I replied, "it's not often we meet a real princess. How did you get to know Robin?"

"Robin and my husband played cricket together at Oxford and we had the pleasure of his company for a year at our palace."

The princess was small, dark, and exceptionally well groomed. Her brilliant blue silk outfit contrasted with her dark skin and her gorgeous green eyes.

About her neck she wore a necklace of dull green stones, which I suspected were uncut emeralds. She had that great air of confidence that wealth gives you.

"So, you wish to help young people?" She spoke in a pure Oxbridge English accent and had the sort of voice that inspired confidence. "Have you always wished to teach?"

"I suppose so," I said, "but in all honesty, I don't know a lot about other opportunities.

"Teaching is a very worthwhile profession. We need many more teachers in India. Perhaps one day you might come out and help us with our young people?" She smiled and took a sip of the house wine that Robin had ordered. It was obvious from her face that it was not quite the quality she was used to but she made no fuss.

"Are the people in India as poor as the newspapers lead us to believe?" asked Cath.

"Oh, yes indeed!" replied the princess. "Oh, we often feel could we do more with our million a year allowance from the government. But we do, obviously, have our position to keep up."

A million pounds income and people literally starving on her doorstep. It all seemed dreadful to us but we politely said nothing and listened with ever-widening eyes to her stories of India. As it happens, we were not the only ones who were interested in her stories. The other customer had gradually moved tables until he was actually sitting next to us at an adjacent one.

After we had finished our meal, we ran Princess Borate back to her luxury London house, one of a number she apparently had around the world. Robin spent a further twenty minutes with her inside while we waited in the car. When he came back, Cath enquired: "You look very pleased with yourself, Robin! Good news?"

"As it happens, yes! Very good news. I've been invited to India," he replied.

"Will you go?" I asked.

"I don't know, I'll certainly have to think about it."

For the next couple of days Robin fussed round our flat. He was very concerned that I didn't exert myself before my cricket match on Saturday. It was my first for the Bedford Club and, surprise, surprise, I'd actually been picked for the first team. I really didn't expect it and was determined to try to do well.

"You mustn't do anything physical the day before a match," Robin lectured me. I was, at that time, moving furniture for Cath.

"I suppose I should do it myself," replied Cath. "I'll just put the wardrobe on my back and shift it that way!" I think Cath was going off Robin slightly. However, the final straw was just before we went to bed that night.

"Remember, no sex tonight! It's very important to keep all your energy for tomorrow."

"Perhaps I should move out the night before all matches?" Cath asked sarcastically. "So as to remove all temptation. Could of course sleep in the bath, I suppose!"

Robin seemed put out. "I was only thinking of your game," he said.

The match itself was at Stanmore. It was an all-day game and I actually got the honour of opening the bowling at the common end. I desperately wanted to do well for two reasons. Firstly, to thank the Bedford lot for giving me the chance and secondly, to impress Robin as I really thought he could help me with my career.

Some days are good and some bad. This one was a peach. The catching of the Bedford players was brilliant. Every mistake by the Stanmore batsman was punished and I grabbed six wickets in the first part of the morning's play. With the very last ball before lunch, and with the smell of hot potatoes drifting over the ground I lengthened my run up and roared and grunted as I hurled down the last ball. It was all a big con as I actually held it back so it was very slow. The poor batsman, thinking of his lunch, fell for it hook, line and sinker. He played too soon and the ball plopped on his pad.

"Howzat!" I roared, jumping up and down waving my arms. The umpire thought for a long time and then finally raised his finger.

"The only doubt I had," he told me as we walked off to lunch, "was whether it would have enough pace to actually knock off a bale."

I looked for Robin to hopefully get his praise, but he was nowhere to be seen.

"Excuse me," I asked a Norwood player, "I had a friend with me: brown hair, stocky, well-tanned, about twenty-six. Has anyone seen him?"

"He's gone," came the reply. "He asked directions to the Underground station, took his case out of the boot of your car, and left!"

"Oh great!" I exclaimed. "That's perfect!"

Robin had obviously worked it all out; a Tube from Stanmore to Maida Vale and then probably stay with the Princess until they went to India.

"Cath? We've got a bit of a problem. Well, a big problem to be more accurate."

Cath was obviously very surprised. As I'd only just been clapped off the field she expected me to be in a different mood altogether.

"What's up?" she asked.

"Robin's up or, more correctly, Robin's beated off to his precious Princess. The problem is, we've got a car and no licensed driver at Stanmore and we've got to get it back to Bedford."

"God, he's a pig," moaned Cath.

"Well, we can't do anything now. Let's wait until the match is over and see if anyone will travel back with us."

I asked around but nobody with a licence wasn't driving, so it was back to the drawing board. Although I was very pleased with my debut, seven for thirty-four against a good London side, I was very concerned how we were going to get home.

"Come on," said Cath confidently, "I'll drive and you act like the confident driver next to me. Anyone looking will assume you're taking me out for a lesson."

The drive back that evening was one of the most traumatic I'd ever experienced. When you want a policeman there's never one to be seen, but that night they were out in strength. It seemed as though every one of them knew our secret and was just waiting to pounce. I needn't really have worried. Cath was a very good driver and we got back safely, leaving the car in the car park.

"There goes Cornwall," I said as we dug into a delicious packeted paella. Still, it was a long way and we hadn't really got the money.

"But it would have been nice," added Cath, wistfully.

I dreamt that night of further glory with Bedford. Unfortunately, my dreams were short lived. The regular opening bowlers were available for the next weekend and despite my seven for thirty-four, I was dropped to the second eleven. What a come down!

# CHAPTER 4

## *Romance*

*"Love and Marriage, love and marriage*
*Go together like a horse and carriage."*
*– Alma Cogan*

John had wanted a car for as long as I could remember. It was always difficult travelling backwards and forwards from Knebworth and so his need was probably far greater than mine. At the same time, I suppose I'm not really a car sort of person. I drive a car. I enjoy owning a nice car. I don't really care about it that much, I don't polish it, cherish it, I don't lust after new models. As far as I am concerned, a car gets me from A to B, whereas for many people, a car is almost like a girlfriend!

We decided to buy a car between us the first long, hot vac. back from college. It was long before the days of MOT and death traps were available for incredibly low prices. We took the researching into buying an expensive motor very seriously. After all, if you're going to invest up to £15 on a car, you want to make sure it's really good.

I use the phrase 'death trap' in its literal sense. These cars in many ways were not fit to leave the field they were parked in, let alone travel on the road. It was amazing the variety of scrap on wheels that we were offered!

Eventually, we were told about a car that was for sale, that was in our price range, and had been owned by Goofy, an acquaintance of ours from school. We traipsed around to Chells to have a look at this car and both of us fell in love with it from the start. It was a 1930s Hillman convertible and it really did look like a million dollars. At some stage in its career it had obviously been a very expensive car and ironically, had I still got it now, it would be an even more expensive car. But to us, it was the most beautiful thing we'd ever seen. We haggled a bit on the price. We thought £15 was a bit steep. Eventually we agreed to pay £12 10s; £6 5s each.

It was already taxed for a couple of months which would see us through the summer. I didn't drive and the insurance for John to drive third party only was fairly cheap. I must say, our status was raised considerably; turning up to cricket matches in our own sports car! After all, we had cleaned it, polished it, and made it look as if it had come straight from the show room.

John very much wanted to take it off for a holiday and, as I was pining for Cath (she was away in distant Scilly, and, in my imagination, being pursued by armies of handsome young men), I had nothing better to do and we decided that we would head off west to the surf city of Newquay, Cornwall. On the way, John wanted to go in to Torquay where we had a college friend who we wanted to look up. We planned our journey carefully as the car really wasn't up to great speeds, and it was not very sensible to travel at night as the headlights were not only rather dim but John couldn't reach the switch, which was on the floor nearer the passenger than the driver to dip them, so I had to do it for him from the passenger side. It would appear that when we dipped the lights, all they did was spin round and point into the hedge, thus temporarily blinding the driver. Taking all these minor points into consideration, we decided that it would be better to break the journey and look for a Bed and Breakfast somewhere on the first day.

I can remember the excitement as we packed the car early one morning and headed off from Stevenage on a cross country route, eventually to pick up the A303 down to the West Country. We hadn't gone very far when a strange knocking noise started; it was quite persistent and I have to say, sounded quite serious. It didn't seem to affect the car and so we pushed on. Eventually after we'd done about twenty or thirty miles we stopped for petrol. A charming old man came across to us while we were filling up.

"My word, my word!" he exclaimed. "Do you know I had just such a car when I was first married, in fact, I went on my honeymoon in one. Oh dear, oh dear, it brings back memories. Wonderful cars, these. They don't make them like this anymore!" he said, walking round the car with a loving expression in his eyes. "I suppose you know the big end's gone, don't you?"

"The big what?" said John, puzzled.

"The big end," he said, "it's gone, you know. You can hear it clearly, I knew as soon as you drove up to the garage."

"Big end," I said, "is that serious?"

"Where are you going?" he said.

"Oh," I said, "down to Cornwall, we're going to Newquay."

"Oh no, not terribly serious," he said. "Drive very carefully."

We thanked him for his advice and we set off. We didn't realise he was being kind, at the time, and the big end was fairly serious in fact, so serious that the engine could seize up at any moment. But then we were very young and looking forward to a marvellous holiday.

The noise got worse and worse, and eventually we went into a garage somewhere on the outskirts of Torquay.

"Yup, your big end's gone," said the mechanic.

"What's to be done?" I asked hopefully.

"Well, I can tell you where to go," he said, "when you go out of the garage you turn left and you go on down there until you see a signpost to Ratcliffe. You turn right there and then left at the roundabout. Just down there on the right, that's the place you want. You'll see it clearly."

We thanked him for his advice and drove off, following his directions, to the place that would solve all our problems. He obviously had quite a good sense of humour as what we found was a scrap yard! We certainly weren't going to leave our beautiful car there amongst all those ruins and so we pulled out and went to see John's friends in Torquay.

Their father had some knowledge of engines and explained to us that the big end could go at any time but at the same time there was no reason why the car shouldn't go on for thousands of miles making that horrific noise. Working on the basis that we only really wanted a car for the rest of the holidays, we thought we'd take the chance. So the next day, bright and early, we pushed off down to Newquay.

We found a nice little hotel at a reasonable price, settled in, and that evening I phoned Cath. It was probably a mistake because obviously she'd had such a good time in Scilly that she was having second thoughts about our relationship and we had a bit of a row on the phone, in fact we had rather a large row. The net result was that at the end of the phone call, I hadn't got a girlfriend. Now for some men this might be a trivial event. For me it was very serious, as far as I was concerned, Cath was the only girl in my life. She had often asked me how I was so certain and I've never been able to put my finger on it. Somehow it just seemed right and was for keeps. It was also devastating to be so far away and not be able to do something about it.

I moped around for a number of days, ruining John's holiday. It's not helpful when picking up girls on holiday if your friend is a manic depressive! The final straw was one evening when things had gone for most of the day, we went to the pub and John got, to say the least, plastered. As I mentioned, I didn't drive and I did find it embarrassing, and slightly scary, when John drove home standing up! I honestly don't think it was a way you should drive a car. It didn't look right, even in my slightly intoxicated state!

The inevitable happened: while this was happening, of course, John turned a corner on to a road and had an accident. He struck a very new, and obviously expensive, car. The driver was furious. The impact had thrown John back down on to his seat and before he could get out, as the least drunk of the two, I went out to deal with it. The man was furious.

"I'm going to make sure you pay for this," he raved, "you're not going anywhere and I'm going to call the police and you're going to be in really serious trouble. People like you shouldn't be allowed on the road."

I had to admit he had a good point. There was no way that John should have been driving, in the state he was, which was obviously confirmed by the fact that he did insist on standing up while driving. I saw ahead a chain of events which would result in John losing his licence and, who knows, even prison? At that point, however, a knight in white armour came to our rescue.

"'Ere, mate. Why were you driving on the wrong side of the road?" he enquired rather belligerently.

"What do you mean?" said the driver of the posh car. "What do mean, driving on the wrong side of the road?"

"Well mate, look where you are. Look! You're not on the right side of the road, are you? You were driving on the wrong side of the road, weren't you?"

"Well, what of it?"

"Well, if that car had turned down the right side of the road, which he did, he'd have had no problem would he? The problem was that you were coming on the wrong side of the road, weren't you?"

I looked, and yes he was right: the car not only was on the wrong side of the road, it was virtually in the gutter on the wrong side of the road! If he'd been driving on the right side of the road there would have been no question of an accident.

"Well, shall we get a policeman, mate?" said the bystander. "I think they'll be very interested in the way you way you were driving. I'd have said it was dangerous. The police will probably charge you, I shouldn't be surprised!"

With that, the driver of the new car backed away, muttering something about: "There's not too much damage really, I suppose. I think what we'll do is we'll just call it quits. We're both in the wrong, I suppose and it's a bit late at night and, anyway, I'd like to get home."

He hadn't got back in the car when John, who'd been struggling to get out for some time, managed to wrench open the door and stagger out. Just as the driver was about to get back in the car, John shouted: "Here, what about my paintwork? You've scraped all the front of my car!"

The other car drove away. I thanked the witness for helping us, managed to calm John down who, in his drunken state, was convinced we should have sent for the police and had the man taken in charge.

The next day, nursing our hangovers, we discussed the situation.

"It's no good," said John, "you're a total misery. We've got to sort you out. How about going up to Birmingham so you can see Cath? Will that help?"

John was a very nice man: to drive from Newquay to Birmingham in the middle of his holiday was a lot to ask and I was very grateful.

"I'd love to go," I replied, "but it's a bit much, isn't it? I mean, it is your holiday."

"Not much of a holiday while you're like this," he said. "I'll make a bargain with you, I'll take you up to Birmingham, you see Cath, stay the night with my cousin and then we'll go up to Scarborough. You're always telling me what a lovely place it is. You can show me what it's like!"

"No problem," I replied, "you'll like Scarborough, and the Yorkshire girls certainly like Southern men so you'll have a wonderful time!"

I was very excited at the prospect of seeing Cath but apprehensive at the same time. What if it went wrong? What if she didn't want to see me again? I would be even worse company for John, but then I couldn't really contemplate defeat, I had to be successful.

We 'big-ended' our way up to Birmingham at a steady thirty to forty miles an hour which took us rather a long time. John had arranged that I should stay with his cousin and I phoned Cath and arranged to see her the next day.

We went off to Stratford-upon-Avon. It was a little bit awkward to start with as both of us seemed to have nothing to say, but there was a will to talk and gradually, as the outside influences disappeared and we were back to just ourselves, things began to work out. I always think that our marriage was saved on the banks of the Avon, that hot summer day. We walked, hand in hand, watching the swans, the boats and gradually the magic, or whatever it was returned and I think at that time we both knew that we didn't want to part. As we lay, snogging on the grass that summer afternoon I was the happiest man in England!

The next day, as promised, John and I set off for Scarborough. The car sounded much, much worse. In fact, it was almost unrecognisable as the car that had come up from Newquay.

"What's happened to the car?" I asked. "It's bloody awful!"

"It's not my bloody fault," snapped back John, "it's my bloody cousin's fault. He taunted me how awful the car was and what a wreck and how could I be seen in such a dreadful car. I told him it could do sixty or seventy miles an hour if pushed. Well I pushed it: I don't think it really did the car much good but it shut him up!"

I would imagine it did! The thought of travelling sixty to seventy miles an hour in this bone shaker was quite horrific. I don't think I'd fancy it!

We'd got off to a very bad start in the morning, we had to drive and didn't make very good progress during the day which meant we had to go on in the dark, something we hadn't really reckoned on. I had to work overtime operating the dip switch, though to be honest I don't know why I bothered; the lights were so dim I can't imagine that anyone would notice having them full in the face but John was insistent that we did it properly.

We eventually got into Scarborough late in the evening and managed to find ourselves a hotel and made plans what to do for the next day. Privately I realised that I had a little bit of a problem: I didn't want to let down John because he'd been so kind but at the same time I didn't want to be disloyal to Cath. I'd always found it easy to get on with girls as friends. I was never short of chat, it was just that I didn't really want let in anything get out of hand. At the same time I'm sure that Cath had snogged the odd friend of hers in Scilly and so perhaps it wouldn't be too much of a bad thing should I have the odd kiss.

The few days that we had in Scarborough went very quickly. We had one major shock as we parked the car after having a very enjoyable day up at Robin Hood's Bay. We'd met a couple of girls at the hotel and taken them out for the day to the beach – all fairly proper – and had returned them safely to the hotel before parking the car which was some way away. As John parked there was a very loud bang.

"Oh shit!" I said. "The bloody big end's gone."

"Yeah, it certainly sounds like it," said John, kicking the wheels in disgust. "We'll have to get somebody to have a look at it in the morning."

We trudged wearily back to the hotel wondering what we would do and if it was possible to scrape enough together to buy another cheap car. More likely we'd have had to either hitch or get a train back which was not very encouraging.

The next morning we went to a local garage and a mechanic came out to see our car. He chuckled when he looked at it and suggested that if he put a match to it would save all our problems. He gave it a good look and started to laugh. It was not, apparently, the big end but an electrical fault. The bang we'd heard was some form of electrical explosion and the wires were in a pretty disgusting state but for a few shillings he managed to sort out the problem and get us back up and running. In all, it was a very lucky car. At the end of the holiday, we managed to coax it back to Knebworth where it finally gave up the ghost.

We got the scrap merchant to come out to see the car in the drive as we couldn't actually get it to start again. An unpleasant-looking man arrived, looking like he'd drunk far too much, having a very red face and exceptionally red nose. He looked at the car and then at us and then back at the car.

"Waste of time coming, wasn't it really?" he said. "Not worth the bother. No good to me really. However, if you pay me ten pounds I'll take it away."

"Pay you ten pounds?" said John furiously.

"Well, take it or leave it. It's not much good to me but I'll do you a favour. Ten pounds: that's my final offer. Cost me that getting it back to the scrap yard."

"Well in that case," said John, "I'll put a match to it. It's virtually all wood anyway. There won't be much left after I've burnt it. We'll be able to deal with the rest ourselves."

"I shouldn't do that," said the scrap man, "it could go up like a bomb if you've got petrol in the tank."

"Oh, don't worry about that," said John, "we'll drain that first and the oil. We'll take it away from the house. But I'm not paying ten pounds, that's final!"

We argued for some time and eventually the scrap man decided that he would take it away for nothing. I often think of that car. If we'd have had the sense or the money to be able to put it into a store, it would be worth tens of thousands of pound now. But then, who's to know the future?

Shortly after that I returned back to my everlasting holiday: my college. I'd managed to repay my enormous overdraft courtesy of the potato lark and the council labouring, and left myself with a very large balance for the following term. As a second year, I'd also managed to get myself a much better single room in my digs which were in a hotel close to the seafront.

It was a very strange place. My first room was rather like a coffin; it was very small and benefited from free gas! All the other students had to pay for their gas using a meter but my room was allowed free gas. The reason for this was fairly obvious: there was such a strong gas leak in my room it didn't seem fair to charge! This meant I had to have the window open at all times even in the worst winters. It wasn't a nice room. In fact, I think someone described it as a steaming pit!

Still, it was convenient for the college and, as there were something like fourteen of us living in the hotel, it did make for quite a good team spirit. The landlord was mad. I'm not just saying that as an expression; he was mad! He had a large family and I really felt sorry for his long-suffering wife. He really was looking for something different. In fact, in my second year he actually joined the college as a student as he thought he'd have much more fun there! He encouraged the students to wild excesses. We became known as The

Lewds. Although I joined in occasionally, I did not get involved in their worst excesses as I was too busy going out with Cath.

Cath, by now, had moved into a hotel in Hove and so I used to see her home and then walk back along the seafront or, if I was lucky, catch the last bus. Whenever I got back to the hotel in the early hours of the morning I was always prepared for the unexpected. Water fights were the norm. There was nothing unusual for me to walk in and have a bucket of water thrown over me from the top floor of the hotel! Needless to say, it wasn't meant for me, it was meant for somebody else who'd scuttled out of the way!

More bizarre events were when I came home and found one of my fellow students stark naked in a bed in the middle of the street with barely enough cover to cover his main essentials. Another time the whole group were in the street singing carols to the neighbouring hotel. That wouldn't have been quite so bad but for the fact that it was mid-May! Another time I arrived to find the Gas Board and gas fitters in: it appears that they had been doing press-ups on the gas pipe and had broken it!

The hotel was dirty, and stunk of urine as the small children seemed to wee anywhere. The food was appalling, however, both Cath and I have very happy memories of that hotel for the thousands of hours that we spent finding out about each other, talking, kissing, playing records, setting the fundamentals of a relationship that has already lasted thirty-three years.

Towards the end of my second year two tragedies occurred. The first was our landlord, mad as ever, with a very sick sense of humour took himself in his car up to Happy Valley, parked right outside a large sign saying 'Happy Valley', and then put a rubber tube from his exhaust into the car and gassed himself.

The second, which was one of the most traumatic moments of my life so far, I had a phone call to say that my father was seriously ill and had been rushed to hospital and I should return immediately. I got as far as Brighton station when I got an announcement: could I go to see the Brighton Station Master. He had the awful job of telling me that my father was dead. I managed to get back later that day and had the awful job, myself, of phoning around family and friends to tell them about our sad loss.

Apparently, he had been operated on at least six times, the surgeon having to operate blind because there was so much blood. My mother afterwards was to confide in me that she prayed that God would do the best thing for him as it appeared that he had been seriously brain damaged during the operation. If he had recovered, he would have been a total cabbage which, for such a bright, intelligent man would have been absolutely awful.

For my mother, it must have been like the end of the world. It must have been obvious to her that Cath and I were destined to get married, probably at the end of college. My sister was already away from home with children and Mum was left in a big empty house after giving up everything for the last seven years to look after my father. It had been a traumatic time for her. Ironically, during that time she had damaged her body so much, pulling my father up and down, that she herself developed arthritis towards the end of her life which totally crippled her as well. However, she took everything in her stride. She was a tremendously strong and competent woman. Having witnessed the struggles and pain of both my parents, I can only hope that I will be half as strong when my time comes.

It wasn't to be long after my father's death that Cath and I decided to get engaged. We searched the jewellers' shops in Brighton extensively for an engagement ring and eventually, practical as ever, we found in a back street jewellers behind the bus station, a zircon (a manmade stone something like an aquamarine) which Cath loved. Even though the ring cost only a few pounds, Cath has treasured that ring all her life, always rejected the chance of upgrading to a better stone. I can still remember the excitement of choosing the ring and the thrill of Cath putting it on and feeling that I was another step nearer to marrying, to me, the most wonderful girl in the world.

I couldn't really face the prospect of going back to the 'lewd' headquarters for my third year. After the landlord had killed himself it was a very depressing place and so I moved out to another hotel but unfortunately, as I was now a new boy, I had to share a room, something I had never done in my life. I managed to put up with three roommates in that year.

The first was a very sad young man who was convinced that everyone was having a wonderful time in those swinging sixties with the exception of him. He was somewhat eccentric; he dyed his shirts purple. At the time, all men wore white shirts and a purple shirt certainly made him stand out! He moaned incessantly about how he'd never made love to any girl and everyone else was at it all the time. I tried to tell him that many people exaggerated the state of their love lives and he shouldn't worry about it, but he wasn't to be reassured.

Eventually he was caught with the college 'bike'. She claimed he had lead her astray. Bearing in mind that she had probably been led astray a hundred times at least, it did sound rather funny. One couldn't really imagine anyone believing it. Unfortunately for this young man, the college authorities did believe it and he was summarily expelled. It seemed ironic to be expelled for sleeping with a whore, but then life can be very cruel.

My second roommate was the most depressingly miserable person that I'd ever come across. I christened him 'Happy'. He had been a bank clerk but had found the bank a sordid, dirty place. People apparently told dirty stories and made awful suggestions. He was a very pure young man, He had thought that in the company of teachers he would be surrounded by purity and decency. It didn't take him long to find the error of his ways and he became very, very depressed. I don't think he lasted more than a month or so before he decided he was living in Sodom and Gomorra. He went off, hopefully to find a pure place. As far as I know he's still looking for it! At least he was no bother as he went to bed at about seven thirty at night, got up early and spent most of his time working.

My next roommate was the exact opposite: a strange extrovert who went to bed stark naked with the exception of a red bobble hat which had a very large burn in it where once he'd thrown it on to a light and not noticed and the electric lamp had burnt through it. He also had the unfortunate habit of coming in at around about three every morning which wouldn't have been so bad but I was in the middle of my final exams and, as I'd done virtually no work throughout the three years, I was hoping that, miracle upon miracle, I might just be able to scrape through the exams and I didn't need the added disadvantage of no sleep!

In order to try to stop him, Cath and I devised a haunting tape. We spent a very enjoyable day making up rattling chains, groans, moans and anything we thought was frightening. I set up the speaker so that it was right by his bed and waited for him to come drunkenly back from his evening excesses. As soon as he lay down on the bed I started this grotesque tape running. The effect was amazing, I think he thought he'd got the DTs. He leapt out of bed and ran screaming down the corridor. Luckily for me, for the next few days he stopped drinking and came home early and tried to be more serious. This had the desired effect because it saw me through to the end of the exams. As far as I was concerned, after that he could easily drink himself into an early grave as long as I didn't have to pay for the funeral expenses!

With exams, we had been somewhat lucky. Our Education Lecturer, which probably was a misnomer, as we hardly ever saw her in three years, had realised at the last minute that she had, perhaps, let us down. A few weeks before the exams, a lecturer that I had some respect for, came to deputise for her as she had again had a problem. Her problems were quite varied: on one occasion, apparently, she sat down on a deckchair and killed a kitten. This upset her so much that she couldn't come in for two weeks! Her marriage would appear to be on the rocks, but at the same time she was a marriage guidance counsellor!

Anyway, the lecturer asked us what we would like to revise. We said we had quite a good scope as we'd only ever done two topics: play and learning. He thought we were joking and when he found that we were serious he became very worried. It appeared that there were slightly more topics that we should have covered, probably about twenty! He must have had a word with her because she panicked and brought in some ideas of questions for us to think about. Unfortunately, she'd forgotten to bring her glasses so she got one of the students to read out the questions.

It didn't take him long to realise that these were not examples but that what he had in his hand was the actual exam paper for that year! He indicated to us that fact and, obviously, we all talked through the questions very seriously and made sure we could answer the three or four questions that were needed to get a good grade. It all seemed too good to be true, and of course it was. Our results were so good that there was an enquiry and the papers were cancelled. Instead we had to submit four essays.

Four was a bit of a problem for us because we'd only ever done two: play and learning and so, at the end of our college life, while everyone else was having a good time, we had to settle down and do two complete new works! I don't know why I bothered really because it took a lot to fail in those days. One of the reasons why our educational standards are so low is because we allowed so many second and third rate teachers to pass when they should have been expelled. I've often thought, I wouldn't want many of the people I trained to with to come anywhere near a child of mine!

Exams apart, it was a blissful summer. Cath and I were very much in love. Brighton had all you could want: an excellent theatre where we were regulars, wonderful restaurants, plenty of cinemas and, of course, at least one or two excellent dances a week. I was enjoying myself as captain of the college cricket team. I'd got involved in college drama. I was in the college bridge team and I'd even miraculously got into the college basketball team so, in all, I was having a ball!

The one worrying aspect was what was going to happen at the end of the college term. If Cath went to Birmingham and I went to Stevenage I was convinced that our relationship may not last. It was asking an awful lot, particularly as I knew me: I'd be playing cricket every Saturday and Sunday which didn't leave a lot of time for travelling to Birmingham. I suggested to Cath that we should get married immediately we left college. She thought about it for some time and then agreed it was the most sensible option.

We didn't have a lot of money and, obviously, it would be quite a struggle to start, but then we wouldn't be spending a fortune on travelling backwards and forwards. There was no problem with our relationship. We knew each other so well. Three years at college seeing each other in the best and the worst possible light meant that there was very little that we didn't know about each other. We thought we'd exhausted the rows but then if you have a real, proper relationship, I don't think you ever stop occasionally rowing. I believe a relationship with no rows is not really a proper relationship.

The problem was, where did we want to live? I had very strong views as cricket, to me, was the most important thing in my life other than Cath. I wanted very much to play minor county cricket and still secretly had the ambition that someone would discover me and I would end up playing for a proper county team. I knew it was a dream, I knew it was highly unlikely but then, dreams are the things that keep us all going.

We applied to Aylesbury and Bedford. We both got jobs in both towns, the difference being that in Aylesbury Cath was offered a language post in a grammar school and I was offered a nothing job in the back of nowhere, ten to fifteen miles away from Aylesbury. In Bedford, I was offered a star job and they would take Cath as well. Cath, very decently said that it was better that the man should take the best job because he was going to be the bread winner and so we accepted the jobs in Bedford.

The following weekend I went over to Bedford to find us somewhere to live after we'd got married. I was very young and naïve and knew nothing about renting – or, for that matter, Bedford itself with the exception that it had a superb cricket team which played on the London Conference circuit. Obviously there were important things in life, like cricket, and cricket, followed by cricket and, I almost forgot, cricket. Coming from Stevenage, I had always thought of Bedford as a large town. I was therefore apprehensive, given the task of finding suitable accommodation for Cath and me, particularly as we were to be married in a month or so. It didn't take long to find the way the land lay.

"Rented accommodation, sir? Dear me, no!" said the superior young man in the first estate office. He managed to make 'rented' seem like the plague and as for his 'sir', it sounded like an insult.

"We do *sometimes* have flats," said the old lady in the next, "I remember, last year we had a lovely one. I'll take down your details, just in case."

She at least was kind, even if her message was very depressing. After all, we were getting married soon, not next year.

"No, no, no, I'm afraid we don't. Sorry," came the next reply.

I was beginning to get worried. I had assumed I would have been given dozens of superb flats to view during the day. Things, however, brightened at the next office.

"You're in luck!" smoothed the young man in the next office. "I've got the ideal thing for you."

"Oh, thank goodness!" I said. "I was getting desperate."

"Oh rather! But your troubles are over. I've got a delightful terraced house, just north of Kettering," he continued in a rather smarmy way.

"Is that close? Because I can't drive, and neither can my wife-to-be."

"No problem!" he reassured me. "Excellent bus service to Kettering."

"But I don't want to go to Kettering! I'm teaching

in Bedford."

"You'll need to get into Kettering to catch the bus into Bedford." He spoke very slowly, as if I was a retarded child. I began to have a few doubts.

"Is the bus service good from Kettering to Bedford?" I asked.

"Oh yes! Every hour," he replied.

"What about the bus to Kettering?" I added

"Probably the same, but we don't usually go that far north."

"That far north? How far is it, two or three miles?" I asked hopefully.

"Oh no! Thirty or so, but it's good roads."

"I haven't a car and I can't drive. We both have to be at our schools at eight thirty!" I shouted in desperation.

"Well, no need to be rude! I was only trying to help. I admit that you would probably have to get a bus at about five thirty, but it's a nice journey," he added hopefully.

"No, I'm sorry, I really don't think so. Anything else?" I hopefully enquired.

"Sorry, nothing!" he snapped, shutting his file abruptly, somehow making me feel that I was being very unreasonable. I was getting to feel very depressed and hungry so I had a frothy coffee in the coffee bar in the arcade. After paying, I saw a notice board crammed with those little cards, you know the sort of thing, 'Small crocodile for sale. Needs new owners having eaten its last.' Or 'Gardener wanted urgently' which was next to 'Garden work wanted' which always seemed to me a bit of a waste of effort. Why didn't they get together and save sixpence a week? There was, however, no flat for renting, but I did notice a Bed and Breakfast for ten shillings a week. I noted down the phone number and continued with my flat hunt. I visited office after office. Some were rude, some were polite. Some tried, some didn't, but by four that afternoon, I was really getting to the end of my tether. The last agent I tried turned up trumps. I could have cried. They were the agents for a new conversion, which had only just come on the market. It was four flats in a converted school. Three had already been let so I grabbed the last one – at least I grabbed an option for a day to give me a chance to view it and make up my mind. The very helpful agent ran me round in his battered Morris Oxford. Despite the fact that the actual flat was virtually a ruin, I took it as I was assured that it would be ready in time for our needs. I agreed to rent and signed the contract straight away. I floated happily out of the office as if I was in air. It was already six o'clock so I rushed back to the bus station and caught the bus home. It was only as I was sitting on the bus going past Henlow, that I realised that I had also been supposed to find myself digs for the two weeks early teaching I was going to do at the end of June and the beginning of July. Then I remembered the card I had seen in the arcade. I still had the number. When I got home, I phoned and booked myself in.

*Not a bad day's work*, I thought.

I had become a bit of a star at Stevenage Cricket Club at last, and had been enjoying the status of opening bowler. Some days I even got the choice of ends, which as every opening bowler knows, is the final accolade. My closest friend and deadly rival at this time was John Ridgwell, fondly known as Woggywell. He had recovered from a disastrous accident when at school, and despite doctor's advice not to play he continued with all his favourite sports. John had been a megastar at school – Captain of cricket, hockey tennis, Victor Ludorum, Deputy Headboy, etc., etc. School suited him and he certainly suited school. I wish I could have said the same about me. I wish! Mind you, at least I wasn't expelled like the future Headboy, who took to drawing obscene pictures. It was amazing as he had always been the goody-goody of the school. However with John it was a different matter. He even entered the shot-putting at the school games at the last minute because he needed the points to win the Victor Ludorum. I must admit, I wasn't very pleased to come second in my only event! This, however, was before the accident. He was cruising to his first ever hundred. He was ninety-six not out when he hooked the ball straight into his eye. It was not a pretty sight. Our stupid games teacher asked him if he wanted to carry on to get his hundred. Luckily Justice Pigshit was there.

"Are you mad, man!" he thundered. "This boy's going to hospital now!" He rushed John off.

All seemed well and John returned to continue his glittering career. It's funny, in life, how events change when looking backwards. What appeared to be a triumph at the time, was in reality rather sad. John came out to bat in the nets one balmy June evening. As I said, he was a hero as far as the majority of the boys in the school were concerned and needless to say had a large fan club. A crow always watched him in the nets and to make things even better that night they got a double – the captain being bowled out by the best bowler, a contest worth watching. It was shortly after the shot-putting incident that had so annoyed me, anyway our friendship was very much based on rivalry, most male bonding is. I lengthened my run and put one hundred and fifty per cent effort into the first delivery. The result was, to say the least, impressive. I removed the off stump and strung it up to the net. This was more than satisfactory; the batsman had to fiddle with the stump to remove it from the netting, hence humiliating himself even further. The boys clapped. I felt good. John didn't. The next delivery removed his middle stump with a similar result. I should have realised that something was very wrong with John, but at the time I assumed, big-headedly, that it was my class bowling. The next ball he stopped, but the fourth ball put the off-stump back in the netting again. With that John decided that he'd had enough. It was, in fact, the first indications that John had lost the sight of his right eye. As I said, in retrospect I had achieved nothing. All I did was gain some cheap glory.

John changed enormously after that, as a person he probably became much nicer. Sports suffered while he learned to adapt to one-eyed sight. I t was a measure of the man that he scored his first century for Stevenage with only one eye. Our rivalry continued, but was much less intense; I always reckoned he turned to bowling to get even. In reality, he needed to become an all-rounder because he couldn't rely on his batting as he had on the past. The annoying thing was that he bowled very quickly. He wasn't a good bowler and not in my class but he was very effective and he had that magic thing called luck. It seemed to me that during that hot summer, just before I got married, that I did all the hard work getting out the top order batsmen, then John would come on and bowl at the tail-end and frightened the life out of them! I'd get four for sixty-five and he'd get four for six. I wasn't to have known that those three years at Stevenage were to be my happiest years of my brief cricketing life. One of the tragedies of life is that you don't actually know how much you enjoy things at the time and we always think they'll go on forever.

"Have you packed your case yet?" called Mum from downstairs. "You ought to be getting off if you want to settle in your digs."

She was right of course. I was due to start teaching the next day and hadn't really thought about packing.

"Can you do it for me?" I asked, knowing she would.

"Put out on the bed the clothes you want and I'll find the case."

I knew she'd do it. She'd do anything for me and I was mean enough to let her. My father had become crippled with arthritis. It started when he was fifty and had got steadily worse. I have a job to remember him other than as a very old man and since I'm now older than when he first collapsed, it's all become very sad. He wasn't ever an old man, just a man suffering with so much pain that he looked old. However, since he had died a year earlier, Mum had really only me – that was when I was back from college and not out staying with friends. In many ways I was a rotten son, in others a good one. But I did take advantage of her. Then, as Cath has since pointed out, she probably enjoyed being useful.

I grabbed my case, kissed her goodbye, and hurried to the high street where I just managed to catch the bus. As I walked to my digs, I noticed I hadn't actually chosen the best area of Bedford. In fact, it looked more like a slum. Well, what the hell. It was only for two weeks. I knocked on the battered, unpainted and slightly rotting door with rising apprehension.

"Oh, come in, come in..." mumbled an old lady, dressed in a cardigan three sizes too big for her which had seen better years – too many of them to count! "Just in time!" she added. She opened the door, and I realised she meant for a cup of tea. The room was small and full of odd-looking people. It could have been a tramps' convention for all I knew. I sat on a non-too-clean chair and eyed the cup suspiciously. I was also aware of the smell, and it wasn't roses. I was forcefully reminded of the popular dirty joke going around:

Landlady to the Guest: Have you messed your pants today?

Guest: No!

Landlady: Are you sure you haven't messed your pants today?

Guest: Definitely not!

Landlady: There's a horrible smell. And I think you have messed your pants.

Guest: Oh! You mean yesterday!

I admit it's not very funny — but it sure smelt in that room. I waited for about twenty minutes and then begged my leave.

"I'm very tired," I assured them, not wishing to appear a snob. Heaven forbid! "It's my first day tomorrow, so I'll need a good night's sleep."

"I'll show you the room," replied the old landlady.

She led me up the stairs to a small room which had three beds in it.

"You'll like it here," she said. "All my gentlemen like this room!"

After she'd left, I unpacked and thought how nice it was to get away from those awful people. Call me stupid, it never crossed my mind what would happen next. About eleven o'clock, two of the worst men, including the smell, arrived for bed. I was sharing a very small room with two tramp lookalikes. It would have helped if they snored in unison, but each had its own distinctive snore. I found it impossible to get any rest that night. I was up early the next morning and was introduced to Jock, a fellow guest.

"Jock, this is Tony. He's a teacher," droned on the old lady. "Tony, this is Jock. He used to be a soldier."

Introductions over, we tucked into our breakfast.

"Why, you're not in with them smellies, are you?" asked Jock.

"I'm afraid so," I replied.

"Did you sleep?" asked Jock.

"No. Not a wink," I wearily replied.

"Mrs Jones! Tony didn't sleep last night. And him

being a teacher. I told you they snored. Have you no other room?" he demanded.

"Well," she replied thoughtfully. "There is the box room, with a small bed..."

"I'll take it!" I answered quickly, thinking anything was an improvement on the awful night I'd spent.

"Well, that's settled!" said Jock. "Come out shooting with me tonight! You'll enjoy it! That is, if you've got nothing else to do?"

I was grateful for the offer, and I set off to school in a more cheerful mood than I thought possible.

School was very easy. It was only really just observing and learning the ropes, so I was looking forward to my evening adventure. I didn't know much about guns, but Jock's looked very large to me. We trudged miles into the country while he told me about himself.

"I was good in the army, but the bastards didn't appreciate me," he said aggressively in a strong Glaswegian accent.

"Oh yes? Why was that?" I enquired politely.

"Oh, I was in Cyprus. They said I liked killing too much. I ask you! Isn't that what being a soldier is about?" His voice by now had become fairly hysterical.

At that point, he saw a rabbit behind me. He fired immediately over my head, next to my ears. The noise was deafening. The rabbit twitched in pain, jumping up and down in a frenzied, agonised death dance. I noticed his face. His eyes were wild. He was grinning with excitement and sweating. He walked over the rabbit and finished it off with the butt of the shotgun.

"They said I was a natural killer and lacked discipline," he continued.

"When was that?" I asked.

"At the Court Martial. They threw me out. They said I was lucky the Cypriots didn't charge me. All I was doing was my duty."

While he was talking, he managed to mangle a couple more rabbits.

"Do we take these back to Mrs Jones?" I asked, thinking rabbit stew would be an improvement on the meal we'd had the previous night, which was a bit of 'hunt the meat'.

It reminded me of another stupid joke

Waiter: How did you find the steak, sir?

Diner: Under the lettuce leaf, eventually.

"Nah, I don't bother. I just do it for the sport." He was literally shaking with excitement, sweating and not looking at all stable. I began to have a horrible thought. *When does he say 'Right I'll count a hundred and I'll come for you'?* After all we were miles from anywhere and he was a self-confessed psychopath. Stupid really, but I was very glad to get back that night and was amazingly busy at school for the next three nights!

Box was the right name for my room. The bed was very small and the room was dirty. If I'd been older and more experienced I would have moved out. Mum would have paid for me to stay at the Swan if I'd have asked. But I was proud and very young.

Friday came and I packed and returned home for the weekend. Unfortunately I developed a flu-type bug

113

and amazingly couldn't return for the second week!

I was very uptight about the wedding. After all, I'd never been married before; John was to be my Best Man. My mother agreed to lend us her car so John could drive me up and we were to stay at his cousin's the night before and he would get me to the church on time. I had a magnificent stag evening at Stevenage Cricket Club. I will never forget it. As I walked by the fruit machine I said to John: "I think I'll have a gamble, who knows, I feel lucky."

I put sixpence in the machine and won the jackpot!

"You jammy bastard," said John, "there can't be many people who make a profit out of their stag evening!"

I had to admit that it was a good omen. A couple of days later we were driving off to Birmingham. John enjoyed driving my mother's new Corsair and was very aggressive in the way he drove. It was, however, unfortunate, that the car he cut up so badly on a roundabout approaching Birmingham just happened to be my brother-in-law, who was bringing the family up to the wedding. I can remember seeing the horrified expression on my mother's face as she saw her car virtually force them off the road! My mother was never very lucky and it was even more unfortunate that the wedding guests decorated her car so enthusiastically, particularly as we weren't going to use it. We were catching the train to go to our new home in Bedford. We couldn't afford a honeymoon, because as young teachers, we wouldn't be paid until the end of September so we had to get through ten weeks with no income.

It's a strange thing about weddings, funerals, family get-togethers: it always ends up in aggression! My Aunt Phyllis, a very strong character, couldn't find the hotel to change in so she ended up changing in a field with her son-in-law shouting out to her: "Hurry up, you silly old fool! You'll be done for indecent exposure!"

My mother's sister and her husband decided to stop for lunch in Stratford, obviously had too good a lunch because they missed the church service completely and ended up with endless recriminations all through the reception. As time went by we've heard of more and more squabbles, arguments, problems that actually occurred at the wedding. To be honest we were totally oblivious to it all. We spent most of the time giggling and, in fact, had hysterics during the actual service itself!

After the reception, where I managed to slice Cath's finger while cutting the cake (how nice of them to give us a double sided knife!) we eventually escaped to the station where we could start our married life first at the Swan Inn, Bedford and then, after the weekend, in our new purpose-built wonderful flat. We were very careful to ensure that we had no confetti on us when we got on the train. We didn't want to be embarrassed at the hotel so it was unfortunate that just before the train departed a young couple rushed into our compartment followed by guests who threw confetti everywhere including all over us. It was even more unfortunate that when we arrived at the Swan and opened our case we found that it had been well doctored with confetti which went everywhere in the room, which made sure that everyone there knew that we were on our honeymoon.

It was very thundery and hot that evening. We strolled across to a Chinese restaurant and toasted our future life together, and looked forward to seeing the flat which, of course, Cath had never seen, in the morning.

That night, we were to be entertained by the combined choirs of most of the rowing clubs in Great Britain. Bedford had won the Cup at the Regatta and the celebrations went on until morning. I had no idea just how many verses there were to 'Diana, Diana show us your leg!' We laugh when people say, "They're playing our song, dear." We could never ask any band to sing ours!

"Oh my God!" I exclaimed when we got to the building. "It doesn't look like anything's happened since I was here last!"

It was indeed a sorry sight. There was no way that we could move in to the flat. There was obviously an enormous amount of work to do; I was horrified. There was no way we could stay at the Swan either, it was far too expensive so we had to find alternative, cheaper accommodation. Having had experience of cheaper accommodation in Bedford, I was obviously rather depressed. I didn't fancy sharing my room with two tramps and Cath as well.

We went to the estate agent the next morning and expressed our concern.

"I've just been round to the flat and nothing's happened."

"Yes, I'm terribly sorry about that," said the estate agent, "it appears that they've got behind."

"When will it be ready?" asked Cath, hopefully.

"Well, it's always difficult to say," he replied slowly and pompously.

"We do need somewhere to live now," she added. "We've only just got married and we're homeless."

"Well, I'll have a word with the builder. He's an awkward fellow but he might be reasonable given your circumstances."

The next day we moved into a boarding house in the same road as the flat. We had two rather small single beds and a rather dingy room. Not the best of honeymoons. At the same time we started helping to get things ready in the flat. The big problem was that the builder quoted for every job and got them all, because he was so cheap. He tried to juggle what limited resources he had.

"You've really got to do more about this," I said one afternoon, "it's disgusting, we're never going to get in."

"If you keep complaining I'm going to remove my boy," he said, adjusting his hat to the back of his head. The trouble is, that's exactly what we had: a boy, doing a man's work where there should have been a number of men. You shouldn't moan, I've got people living in a tent up at the back of their garden."

"Well, at least they're not paying rent," I said, "we're going to run out of money if we're not careful. We need this flat."

"I reckon you should be able to move into the back room some time later this week."

With that, he disappeared, leaving the boy to do

the work. We did, in fact, move in to the back room while they continued with their work. They took great delight in arriving at six thirty in the morning, putting the radio on, bellowing honeymoon jokes into our room, but gradually the flat took shape. I wouldn't exactly say it was well converted, in fact, I'd go so far as to say it was exceptionally badly converted.

# CHAPTER 5

## Learning the Game

*"Learning the game, learning the game,*
*We're only learning the game."*
*– Buddy Holly*

"Mr Buckingham, you'll be in charge of the stamp club this year," continued Frances William Groves. "You'll also share responsibility for drama and the folk dance club. Mrs Dugdale will be in charge of drama clubs and Mr Gunning, as usual, in charge of the folk dance.

I had a mental vision of the very stolid John Gunning dressed in leather and a Tyrolean hat with a feather, doing the Bavarian clap dance. Nice idea, but I couldn't quite see it. I was sitting at the time in the staff common room during my first ever staff meeting.

"Mr Buckingham will also be the stage manager for the school play," added F.W.G., our distinguished Headmaster. To be honest, he looked out of place as a small school Head. He was a very dapper dresser and very handsome in an elderly way, or so I was reliably informed by the female members of the staff. He certainly was very charming. He had thinning white hair, always wore a smart blazer with some sort of impressive badge. He probably bought the blazer with the badges but he certainly looked the part. This was always paired with a striped tie, giving the impression of a public school, however I had my doubts, possibly minor, but I bet he was a grammar school grub just like me. His light grey flannels were always immaculately pressed, his shoes shone so you could use them for mirrors. When F.W.G. told you what to do you didn't argue; he had that sort of personality.

"Who ran the stamp club last term?" I asked, thinking it would be useful to find out how it ran previously.

"Nobody," answered F.W.G., "you'll be starting it."

As the meeting continued giving out the various duties and responsibilities that really didn't concern me, my mind wandered to what I should do to start a school stamp club. In reality if I could have gone back to my CV I would have left out stamp collecting, after all I hadn't collected since I was about fourteen or fifteen. My stopping stamp collecting coincided with the discovery that not all women were called Mummy! From then onwards I couldn't waste money on stamps; cinemas, drinks, taxis, all cost far too much money. It also occurred to me that I had not seen a stamp shop in Bedford and that would make collecting very difficult. Still it was a *fait accompli* so I had to make the most of it.

I didn't worry about the stage manager's job. I had already found out that the F.W.G. Groves production followed the end of the eleven plus exams. It was actually a fantastic idea; as soon as all the eleven plus papers were finished the entire fourth year switched into The Production. All the scenery and costumes were produced in-house. The children also ran the booking office and F.W.G. wrote the play so as to include the maximum number of performers.

However, that was not until June. As for running a drama club I could see no problem there, however, a folk dance club was another ball game completely. I didn't know a single folk dance so that should be fun!

Actually, the folk dance club proved to be very easy. All the keen dancers joined and I used one from my own class to virtually run my lesson for me. Luckily the club knew about ten or so dances so I bluffed my way through two years of Brickhill as a dance teacher. I also found out later John Gunning worked the same scheme; he'd continued with the dances he'd picked up from the previous dance teacher. Life after all was one big con!

The drama club was much easier and in fact I had to stop taking on new members as I had a continuous stream of fourth year girls wanting to join. It certainly helped to be a young man in teaching!

As far as the stamp club was concerned I had been correct in my feeling that there was not a stamp shop in Bedford. The inaugural stamp club meeting attracted a large audience of about three dozen members. To start with, they showed their collections. It was a bit like *déjà vu*; when I was about eight or so a relation came over from New Zealand who was a keen and knowledgeable stamp collector. When I proudly showed him my collection he slowly and carefully went through the albums, treating them as if they were very valuable.

"You've got a very interesting collection," he drawled slowly in that nasal way that Kiwis speak, "trouble is, you're collecting everything. You can't do that – the world is too big. What you ought to do is specialise. Just take Great Britain and perhaps the Commonwealth."

"But what will I do with all the other stamps?" I demanded. "I've got thousands that don't fit in with what you say I should collect."

Neither of us knew it at the time but his answer possibly changed my life forever.

"That's easy, you swop, sell, barter them for stamps you need." He told me confidently.

He was right it was easy. I used them to build up a very good Great Britain collection. I even started buying collections and breaking them up. I took out the stamps I wanted and sold the rest.

At the tender age of eleven I teamed up with a friend, whose initials were CD, and we formed the ABCD Stamp Company. We had quite a good business going. We stencilled ABCD Approvals on our books and had customers throughout the grammar school, including sixth formers. Our best line though was a special sixpence (2 ½p) packet. A hundred stamps as they came from old collections, boxes, packets. We promised they were never checked for catalogue value. We guaranteed at least a pound's worth as far as the Stanley Gibbons catalogues were concerned. This wasn't hard: all stamps were catalogued at threepence so a hundred stamps would be three hundred pence or one pound five shillings (£1.25). It's the same today: all stamps have a minimum catalogue value at 5p. It's actually a handling price. In reality all cheap stamps have no value.

I actually heard of an old man in New Zealand who found out the half cent stamp was catalogued at fifteen cents. He saw a very easy way of making money so he bought up the entire New Zealand post office stock and then toured small post offices buying theirs. Eventually, after spending over ten thousand dollars he tried to sell them. At this point he found the flaw in his scheme; of course nobody wanted them. What on earth would you do with hundreds of thousands of half cent stamps? The New Zealand Post Office wouldn't buy them back and eventually a dealer took pity on him and paid him seventy percent of what he paid so he lost three thousand dollars rather than making the fortune he thought he was going to make.

In a small way the same thing had happened to me as a youngster. At the time the General Post Office was experimenting with black graphite lines on the back of stamps. It was all to do with postal mechanisation. The experiments were not completely successful and so the stamps were discontinued. One evening, however, when I was at the stamp club news came through that rare errors were being bought from the penny stamp machines. The two lines were supposed to be on each side of the stamp but on these rare errors both lines were on one side. The meeting closed abruptly and we tore into Stevenage to try and get as many pennies as we could so we could stuff them into the machines to get these rare stamps out.

We must have managed to get hold of every penny in Stevenage from the off licences, the pubs, bus conductors and anyone who might have a penny must have seen a strange scene to people who didn't know what we were doing. Today the tuppeny stamp with that error is worth about £60; the penny, however, is only worth about ten pence. Still, the post office got rid of all their rubbish and at a very good price.

In order to help my young collectors I made up approval books in a similar way using my old catalogues. I was putty in the hands of the new generation of collectors. 1966 was a boom year for stamp collecting, prices had rocketed since I gave up. My swops went very quickly and at bargain prices. Of course, when I tried to replace them I found out the truth. However, at least it got things going and forced me to find ways of buying stamps. It also rekindled my interest in stamp collecting.

I had certainly landed on my feet at Brickhill. I loved everything about my job. In those mild autumn days the stroll to school was a treat. The major part of the walk was through a tree lined park, round the misty lake which appeared on those early mornings to be hiding Arthur's sword. The skies are very blue during that time of the year and the ever changing beauty of the russet colour leaves as they prepared for autumn made the walk even better. Occasionally I took a little bread with me and stopped to feed the now dowdy winter plumaged mallards. They enjoyed the bread even though at that time of year their larders were normally full of Nature's goodies.

Being young is a fantastic advantage in teaching and I was very popular throughout the school. Also, judging by the admiring glances I got from the grammar school girls I could also be popular there. Not surprising really: I was barely twenty-one and they seventeen or eighteen.

My class itself was a delight to teach; you never forget your first class and I can still name most of them today. You can't have favourites of course, but you wouldn't be human if you didn't like some more than others. In some ways throughout my teaching career I felt sorry for those I liked for I often bent over backwards to be fair which meant I wasn't particularly fair to them. But then it was all new and I was rapidly learning to teach; something unfortunately, sadly, missing from my training.

The class loved drama and in particular putting on plays based on fairy stories. I thought they were very good and when I was asked by one of my favourites if they could put on a play for the school I agreed, and got carried away with their enthusiasm. Written invitations were sent out to all the classes and by the time of the grand performance we were, in my opinion, brilliant!

The play itself was an amusing story of lies, treachery, murder, deceit, theft, extortion, bribery, death and mutilation – you know, the usual sort of fun that you get from a fairy story. The entire school enjoyed the show, the clapping was loud and enthusiastic and it seemed to me that we had had a fantastic triumph.

"Mr Buckingham," began F.W.G. ominously, "may I see you in my room, *now*?"

I assumed, after such a triumph, I was to be congratulated on my excellent work and so I entered his study in very high spirits.

"Sit down," he snapped. "What the hell do you think you're doing?" he shouted. This was not quite what I had expected.

"Putting on a play, sir," I explained.

"So that's what you call that rubbish, a play?" he continued, obviously very angry.

"I, er, I thought it was good, and, and the children enjoyed it," I said stubbornly.

"Of course they enjoyed it," he said, "they got twenty minutes with no work."

"It was good, wasn't it?" I said.

"What makes you think you have any idea what's good or bad? On what do you base your opinion?"

He was right of course, I honestly didn't know what the standard should be.

"Did you not think you should have asked permission before you disrupted the entire school?" he continued, now in a more sarcastic style. "It might have been nice to invite me as well."

Oh God! Had I forgotten even that basic decency?

"Next time, that is if there is a next time, use your brains, you're not a child any more. You must be more responsible."

I felt a complete fool. I didn't think, I just acted as

if I were the only person involved. Even more serious, I had to pass my probationary teaching year and upsetting the Head was not a good way to go about it, particularly as I respected him. I knew I'd let him down.

"All right, wigging over," he said, "would you like a cup of tea and perhaps a cigarette?"

As I drew in the welcome relief through the cancer stick he continued now in a more friendly way.

"Look, I know you didn't mean any harm but standards are important. Drama in this school is the best in the town and I want it to continue to be so." He paused and then continued with his carrot. "By the way, I'm hearing good things about you round the school. You've settled in well and I'm pleased with you."

He was a clever boss. I learned much from him. Never just tell anyone off if possible, always have something to praise. So they take the points and don't just resent you. I was very fortunate to start my career with this tough but kindly head teacher.

If I had landed in heaven as far as my job was concerned, Cath had gone down to hell. The probationary year for a young teacher is very important. This is where your confidence is built and the foundation for your future teaching career is constructed. Cath drew the St Trinian's of Bedford. In fact I would go much further; Silver Jubilee Girls was so bad that St Trinian's would probably take it as an insult to be compared to them.

The main problem was the head teacher. To put it mildly she was distinctly odd. All businesses, schools and institutions depend on the top. A good leader can make the worst place bearable, a bad one can make even a good place hell. This Head would rate high in a table of all time bad Heads. The girls were very tough but at the same time could be very loving. They hadn't got a lot in life.

Cath started with 2C as her class, which consisted of all the worst British in as far as academic prowess was concerned and a large range of various non-English speaking ethnic groups: Indians, Pakistanis, Greeks, Turks, Italians, Slovenians, West Indians, Russians, Poles, Hungarians, just to name a few. What brought us into context was that I had *the* immigrant of Brickhill in my class. She was a South American called Daniela, whose father was on a job-swop programme with a large American company called Texas Instruments. Brickhill was in the prosperous north of the town.

It makes things difficult if you have to teach a class who can't speak English but how on earth anyone should have to be made to teach them French I'll never know. But as Cath was a language teacher she had to go round the school attempting to interest them in yet another language. At the same time she was asked to teach Geography (a subject which she hadn't taken since she was about fourteen), Music (a subject which she had never taken), and Religious Instruction. That of course was one of the joys of teaching in secondary schools: during your first year you very rarely got to teach your own subjects, you taught those subjects which the more experienced teachers didn't want to teach. At the same time you had the worst classes as again the regulars take the best, leaving the newcomers to teach the difficult ones.

It didn't help also that Cath was a nice, decent, innocent girl. I know it seems hard to believe but, just thirty years ago, sex wasn't rammed down your throat all the time. Most of the rude 'X' films that we sneaked in to watch as teenagers are now so tame they are shown during normal hours television. I remember well the best sex film I saw. It was called 'Naked as Nature Intended'. It was actually a naturist film promoting nudism. In reality an excuse to show breasts (wow!), naked breasts on the cinema screen! Needless to say it was a very popular film and most of the school went to see it, probably many times.

We also went to see that disgusting, filthy French 'X' film called 'The Red Balloon'. Unfortunately for us the cinema organisers had assumed that as it was French it had to be 'X'. In reality it was a rather whimsical film about a small boy's red balloon. Life could be full of disappointments for a red-blooded teenager in those days.

We didn't swear in front of ladies or on the street and, needless to say, girls didn't swear. 'Bum' was a very rude word. Mind you, as Dylan was saying, times they were a-changing.

Much of what went on at Silver Jubilee Girls was a quick education for Cath. For example, on going to her first French lesson with 3D, the previous teacher asked her to do her a favour. Apparently she had not collected the last bits of work from the previous term and wanted Cath to collect them for her. When Cath asked 3D to bring up all their French letters the class went absolutely berserk. You can imagine how she felt when she found out what French letters were! She was also furious and of course it didn't help her discipline as a new teacher.

One evening as I was preparing my approval books for the stamp club Cath came in with a puzzled expression on her face.

"What's a cunt?" she asked, puzzled.

I honestly thought I'd heard her ask what a cunt was. No, couldn't be.

"Do you mean cant?" I asked.

"Of course I don't mean cant," she replied. "Is it a very rude word?"

"Well, yes one of the worst you could use. Why do you want to know?"

"It's the Reverend Jones, he teaches in the next hut to me. He's a sweet old gentlemen but every morning when I arrive at school written on his door or on the blackboard or on the wall is The Reverend Jones is one, so I had to keep clearing it off but I ought to know what it means."

I explained that the girls were technically wrong but continued rather embarrassedly to tell her its full meaning. Mind you, I also found I was ignorant of the meaning of blue words myself. I used the word 'twat' in the staffroom one day and got a five minute lecture on its meaning. Ironically, I didn't know it was a rude word.

In my attempts to find stamps to buy I had discovered a large stamp auction house was based in Bedford. It held its auctions in a London hotel but I could view and be part of the professional world of stamps just by going to the offices in Bedford. The auction was run by a jovial public school chap called Warren Smith. He seemed very old to me but was probably only in his mid-fifties.

It was obvious that Warren Smith loved stamps. As I was to find out during my stamp career most stamp dealers liked nothing better than chatting about their love of stamps. The tragedy was that society didn't reward them for creating a way of life that provided them and their family with a home and subsistence. These decent collectors were not, and didn't want to be, business people. All they wanted to do was to play stamps. Unfortunately society is suspicious of what it doesn't understand so it loads enormous bureaucracy on them as soon as you become a dealer, and working full-time you're swamped with regulations: rates, VAT, tax, restrictions on what you can do and what you can't do. It's the same for all small businesses but for the dreamers who pursue their hobbies it seems far worse. If you send for a plumber who will charge you an arm and a leg for the call, stamp dealers will often spend a whole day travelling to see a collection and then valuing it and not charging a penny. Collectors will spend hours in stamp shops drinking free tea, eating free biscuits, stopping the dealer from working and then spending less than a pound and even then, asking for a discount.

Warren Smith was no different. He was kind, helpful and always ready to give me a lesson on aspects of Great Britain collecting. I loved going to his musty rooms; they were a veritable treasure chest. The best stamps and covers were kept secure in special books. In the beginning I wasn't interested in those, I couldn't afford them. What interested me were the miscellaneous lots. Here there were hundreds of old albums of all sorts and colours, collections built up painstakingly by collectors who in many cases had died or lost interest. Nobody could really check all of these so Warren Smith would estimate a value. Obviously he was a very knowledgeable philatelist but it was very easy to miss a gem. Or perhaps it was something that he didn't even know about.

Experts look carefully through collections hoping to spot gold missed by the auctioneer. As there would normally be more than one expert, all sorts of fun could be had at the auction. It was not unusual for a collection to be sold at twenty times their estimate but on the other hand sometimes they went for half. The real bargains however, could often be found in the boxes, suitcases, packing cases and carrier bags. Very few dealers could be bothered to spend hours going through these accumulations. This was the nearest the stamp collector got to the Californian gold rush. They were perfect for my stamp club; the chance for the children to get stamps at ridiculously cheap prices and for me to have some fun. I spent many happy hours in those dusty offices and would then work out what I could afford to pay for the lots, leave the bids with Warren Smith and wait until after the auction to find out if I was lucky. That again was a bit of a lottery, you never knew what was going to happen at the auction but it was fun the following Monday to go to his auction rooms, pay for the purchases and excitedly take them home to start my own personal treasure hunt.

Our flat, although wonderful as far as our social life was concerned, was not a great success otherwise. It had been very badly converted and our kitchen, which had previously been the boys' urinal, never seemed to dry out. Worse still part of our bedroom was directly underneath the toilets of one of the flats above us. The occupants, a boring old couple, proved to be very regular in their habits so we were awakened every morning at 5.30am in the most unsatisfactory manner. Even worse, nasty stains appeared on the wall directly behind our bed. We'd also found out that we were living in the brothel district of Bedford. This explained why there were so many large American cars parked regularly in the street.

Liz and Carl, our next-door neighbours, however, were great fun. Liz was an extremely beautiful but scatter-brained English girl who had married an American GI based at the Intelligence Centre at Chicksands. The flat was their first home together and their lack of experience occasionally showed. Liz was always at our door begging sugar, coffee, flour. Sometimes I felt the excuse was genuine but often I felt she just wanted an excuse to talk. I believe she was very lonely.

When they first moved in neither of them fancied cleaning the floor which was covered with builders' mess. They found what they thought was an excellent solution: they put cheap carpet wall-to-wall throughout the flat. Needless to say, the sharp stones worked their way through the carpet so it looked a little odd. It was also never advisable to walk in that flat without thick-soled shoes.

They had a little boy called Jimmy; he was

approaching four and I am sure eventually he learned to talk. At that stage however, he existed on strange noises which both Liz and Carl understood fully. "Wah, wah wink," he would call, and immediately he would get a drink.

He was also a dab hand at throwing Coca-Cola tins at objects around the room. He'd been trained by Carl; he was an expert. The trouble is, every so often he broke things and then got into trouble. This seemed a bit unfair as he'd always been encouraged to do it in the first place.

In a similar way Carl liked him to fight. It was a bit like John Wayne; teaching him to be a man. Most evenings they'd have a little spar and then Carl would have a drink. One evening Carl was back from the station late and we were sitting having a cup of coffee with Liz. As Carl arrived little Jimmy punched him very hard below the belt. He had been trained well and it was a very painful blow. Carl took this very badly and shouted at Jimmy and gave him a good hiding. Apparently he didn't see the funny side of it – I can't imagine why!

Very early on in our relationship Liz asked us round for a meal. It was bizarre. Carl liked steak so Carl, Cath and I had big steaks. Liz didn't like steak so she'd bought herself chicken. Jimmy didn't eat either so he had a pork chop. The table was literally groaning with food. We had a choice of four or five different ice creams for pudding. It was however, the beginning of the month. By the end of the month Liz had run out of money and Carl was having to eat baked beans. Within a short period of time he took over the catering and did all their shopping at Chicksands.

Although there was no stamp shop in Bedford there was a sub-post office that sold some stamps. It was on the far side of the town and had taken me quite some time to find it. I regularly checked it out to see if there was anything I wanted for my own collection and it was here I met a middle-aged American collector who was particularly trying to buy a set of stamps from South Africa depicting animals. The sub-post office didn't really have much of a range of stamps and it was extremely unlikely that they would have had the set in the first place, however I did have a set, part of my old collection as a boy which I was now selling.

As we left the post office I told him I had a set and if he wanted to buy it would cost him one pound ten shillings. He was very tempted, it was a very good price. However, he seemed a little bit nervous about it all. I suggested that he came back to our flat and I'd show him the set and if he thought it was in good condition then obviously he'd buy it and if not it didn't matter. He prevaricated for some time but in the end his desire to have that set was too great and we went back to his rather flashy American car and he drove me back to my flat in Goldington Avenue.

As we approached I realised I hadn't got my front door key so I'd have to go in through the kitchen. The chances were that the kitchen would be in a bit of a mess, in fact it was almost certain that it would be as I was supposed to have washed up and I knew I hadn't. Cath would not be very happy if I took a guest through this messy and rather unpleasant room and so I asked him if he would wait and I would go through the house and let him in the front door.

When I got into the road again he was standing some way from the flat looking very worried.

"Don't you want this set?" I said. "It's just inside."

As if drawn towards a magnet he moved towards the flat. But again seemed reluctant even to come into my door. I couldn't understand it, to be honest I thought he was a bit odd and wondered if I wanted him in in the first place. Was he some kind of nutter? Just at that moment Liz came out of the flat next door.

"Oh, hallo sir," she said, "what are you doing here?"

"Why hi, Mrs Rickerman, do you live here?"

"Oh yes," said Liz, "Carl and I have been here some time. This is my next door neighbour, Tony. Do you know each other?"

"Why yes, he was trying to sell me some stamps."

"Oh stamps, he's always on about stamps. The flat's just full of them," said Liz. "I didn't know you were interested though, sir."

I was beginning to get the idea that this middle-aged American was not only an American soldier but obviously one of high rank. He relaxed enormously once he saw Liz, came in and had a cup of coffee with me. He was delighted to buy the set of stamps and in fact came back on other occasions to buy other sets and to talk about stamps.

He was, as I was to find out, not just an officer but *the* officer, the commanding officer of the station. RAF Chicksands, which was RAF in name only, was the American control centre for Intelligence in Western Europe. The man held a very key responsible position and obviously thought it was some form of attempt to lure him into a honey-pot situation. He was not the sort of person that would be tempted by loose women or drugs or drink but then as they say, every man has his weakness and for this Colonel the weakness was stamp collecting. How lucky for him that I was not a Russian spy!

Just after half-term Cath came back from school one evening, again puzzled.

"Do you know, I really can't believe it," she started. "I've got a whole load of Bedford schoolboys hanging about outside my classroom. They've got a different half-term to us and they seem to be waiting for my girls. What on earth would those public schoolboys want with my girls?"

"Well, Cath," I chuckled, "they want extra lessons and it's not the intellectual prowess of your girls which interests them, they don't want to be stimulated by academic conversation but they do want to be stimulated in other ways. It's all part of the lessons of life and they want to learn about the birds and the bees!"

"I hadn't thought about that," replied Cath, "should have done really. Anyway, I won't be about Saturday. I've got to go and help at a hockey tournament; for some reason Silver Jubilee girls have been entered."

"Don't worry," I said, "the district team's playing away. We're off to, I think, Barking for a game of football. I'll be gone most of the day too."

As it turned out, when we got together for a meal that Saturday evening, both of us had amazing stories to tell. Cath couldn't stop laughing while she told me about the hockey tournament.

"You couldn't believe it," she said, "it was an absolute farce. Why on earth they allowed Silver Jubilee to enter I'll never know.

"With the first match the umpire tried to keep discipline. The Silver Jubilee girls would insist on swinging their hockey sticks like clubs which of course is against the rules. It's called 'Sticks'. The umpire blew the whistle and called 'Sticks,' the Silver Jubilee girl replied, 'No it f***ing ain't,' and carried on.

"This was the pattern for the rest of the tournament. The Silver Jubilee girls terrorised all the other schools and actually won the tournament. However, they have been told they would not be invited again; they would not be welcome! It really was the most extraordinary thing you've ever seen. I was embarrassed to be anything to do with them."

When she had finished her story I told her mine, which was just as bizarre.

We'd gone up to Barking as usual in a number of cars, most of them driven by parents, got ourselves organised and were met by the opposing teacher. He was an extraordinary chap; he looked like he'd escaped from a prison. He was a real 'cor blimey' Cockney and was obviously very enthusiastic about football.

The game started and it was not to be a game for the squeamish. Barking's idea of football seemed to be to pole-axe their opponents as quickly as possible and it was not unusual if two boys were running for the ball to see a fist come out and strike the other boy, knocking him to the ground. Needless to say, the fist came from Barking and the boy that was felled was from Bedford.

The whistle was rarely blown, the teacher appeared to like the game to flow. Despite that we weren't doing too badly, in fact we should have been a goal up. Our centre ball kicked the ball hard and high over the top of his opposing number and as he played it the forwards set off so that we had forwards between their defence and the goal with nothing to stop them. The centre half however, had other ideas. He jumped an incredible height, caught the ball and then kicked it up the other end. We waited for the whistle to blow for the free kick but not only did it not blow but Barking scored from that deliberate foul. Our parents were furious.

"It's a disgrace," they said. "What on earth are you going to do?"

To be honest I wondered what Roger would say to the team at half time. It was so blatantly unfair and the violence that our team had been experiencing was something I'd never seen before in my life. Roger calmly looked at them and listened to their squeaks of protest.

"Sir, did you see what he did? Look at this bruise."

"I got bashed on the head!"

"Look, I've got a great cut there, he knocked me down sir!" and so on.

Roger calmly said, "Well, there's very little I can actually do but I can give you some advice. The only thing you can do is exactly as they are doing. Forget the rules. You have to play the game their way and do to them as they are doing to you. Now I want you, Smythe to come off, I'd like Castionello to go on." Castionello was a very big Italian.

"Now Castionello, you see that chap there, the one who's been causing so much trouble, well I don't want him to get the ball very often. Do you understand me? I want you to mark him and when you to tackle him, make it very hard so that he knows he's been tackled."

"All right Mr Mallows, you can count on me," said Castionello with great determination.

When the kick-off came again, the game changed and became exceptionally violent. Our boys retaliated and the game became more like hand to hand fighting. Very early on Castionello clashed with his opposite number; the boy went down on the floor and the ball ran away in a different direction. Castionello waited, looking at the ball and looking at the boy on the floor.

*Oh dear,* I thought, *he's thinking of going and finishing him off on the floor.* It was clear what was in his mind but he obviously thought better of it and continued to chase the ball.

We managed to equalise eventually and, at one all, the game ended, a travesty of a football match. The teacher rounded everyone up together and spoke to them.

"Well lads, that was a really good game. Not physical like when we played New Ham last week."

I couldn't believe it: not physical?! It had been the nearest to all-out war I had seen on a sports ground in my life. And what on earth was the game like at New Ham? Did they bring chainsaws, machine guns and machetes? The mind boggles. 'Not physical' – I've never forgotten those words.

Young teachers were paid particularly badly in those days. I think we got about thirty pounds a month and we couldn't exactly rush out and buy furniture for our new flat. We had discovered, however, a place where we could buy furniture at a very reasonable price. It was called Peacock's Auction Room. Not only was it where you could buy furniture at a price you could afford, it was also an entertainment in its own right. We had to start to learn the coded warnings given in the catalogue or in the actual spiel by the auctioneer. For example AF (something you had to be careful with) meant 'As Found', in other words it was probably broken, riddled with woodworm or missing some vital bit. The other remark we rather liked was when the auctioneer said, "Needs slight attention." This would almost certainly mean that whatever it was would be absolutely useless once you'd bought it.

We bought all sorts of things in the auction room. If we'd have been able to see into the future we should have bought far more. Victorian furniture which now sells for a small fortune was literally being given away in those days. In fact, quite often it was chopped up for firewood. We ourselves broke up a most beautiful linen press, something I've always regretted.

We did have one bizarre experience at the auction. We liked a small ornamental table made of mahogany. It was very attractive. The problem was that with it was the most hideous bird cage.

"I'd like the table," I said to Cath, "but what on earth will we do with the bird cage?"

"Ugh, it's horrible," said Cath. "Wouldn't want that anywhere near my house. It's probably full of fleas as well."

I explained my problem to a helpful old porter who immediately explained how we could do it.

"Well that's no problem is it? You buy the two and you leave the bird cage in here for the next auction. Simple isn't it?"

Yes, I suppose it was really. Funny thing is I'm supposed to be intelligent. So we bid for the two and I think we got them for about one pound ten shillings. We left the bird cage behind and the following week it fetched two pounds. Funny old world isn't it?

We weren't quite so lucky with a chest of drawers we bid on the following week. We'd allowed ourselves to go up to two pounds. I didn't like the woman I was bidding against; she had a very red nose and was rather unpleasant, and she looked at me very strangely.

Well it wasn't just the chest of drawers, this was war. We quickly reached two pounds and I continued, I wasn't going to be beaten by this red-nosed lady. Eventually, much to her disgust I won and got the chest for just under five pounds. When we got it home however, we found it was riddled with woodworm. It was in an awful state, we certainly didn't want it in our home.

We put it back in the auction to be sold the following week. It managed to make one pound ten shillings. At least I learnt a very valuable lesson; when going to auction set a price and do not ever exceed that price, and certainly don't ever become embroiled in a personal battle with someone else. This is a sure way of losing a lot of money. As we hadn't much money we couldn't really afford carpets or linoleum, in fact when we were looking for floor covering we asked for cheap, like cheap, covering for our floor.

The swarthy Italian salesman said, "I see, you want cheap like-a brown paper," which has become a family expression.

However, it appeared we couldn't even afford the brown paper so we took to the staining the floorboards. Staining, however, has to be done in a very careful way. It took quite a while for the stain to dry and therefore it was important to remember to paint in the direction you wanted to go. For example if you were doing the living room. You either painted it at night and went into the bedroom and then came back out when it was dry in the morning or painted it in the morning and went to work and came back to tread on it in the evening. It was important you worked out the best strategy for your particular staining.

Above us lived a very nice couple called Brian and Jen. They also had a problem with flooring and quite admired our staining when coming for coffee with us one evening. It particularly appealed to Brian as it was of course very cheap. The only problem was that he hadn't worked out the technicalities of when to stain and how. He stained his living room floor late one evening away from the bedroom. Just as he finished he realised to his horror that he was stranded on the wrong side of the room wanting to get to the bedroom but the floor was soaking wet. With no carpets noises came through the flats very well and I still remember his shouts of anguish all those years ago.

The other embarrassing thing about no carpets was that Brian and Jen also were very regular in habits. Friday night was nooky-night. At times we thought the bed was going to come through the floor. We realised then why it was important to have carpets in flats, nothing to do with appearances, it was just for common decency.

During the spring we decided it was time to look for our new house. I had a very firm idea of the sort of house I thought I should be living in. Unfortunately my pocket had different ideas. It appeared that I couldn't quite afford the big detached house with marvellous gardens, it was more the shack by the railway track that was my mark. At the time we were very lucky; the housing market was in the middle of a great big slump. There had been a major boom in the early sixties and like all booms had resulted in a crash. Houses just weren't selling. We were the rare commodity that all estate agents were looking for: the cash buyer. As we tried the round of estate agents this time the reaction was totally different. We were treated like royalty. However, one young man was far more of a businessman than the others.

"You know it's very difficult getting an idea of what's available just looking in our windows and looking through the brochures," he said one Friday evening just before they closed. "I've got a much better idea, why don't we go out tomorrow in my car and I'll show you everything in your price range?"

We were very grateful, we didn't of course realise that in doing so he was creating a bond that would probably ensure that we buy a house through him. He was excellent though. We drove round and round the town and through the villages. He showed us house after house after house. If we expressed an interest in a house that wasn't on his books he was quite prepared to show us that too and try to do a deal with the other estate agents should we want to buy it. During these pleasant days we became great friends, so much so that that summer I played cricket for Bedford Estate Agents even though of course I wasn't an estate agent. Mind you, neither was the jeweller who kept wicket for the estate agents, having previously kept wicket for England. As with everything, even for estate agents, winning was everything!

We eventually settled on a Wimpey chalet type semi-detached house on a new estate in Bedford. It was a pretty house. It was virtually brand new with one bedroom, half a bedroom, and a strange cupboard described as a third bedroom, which became the headquarters of my flourishing stamp empire. There was a very large wild garden and the main room was what was described then as a 'through lounge' which had a beautiful green Wilton carpet and wonderful velvet curtains to match at either end. Unfortunately, the velvet curtains and the carpet were removed. We couldn't afford to buy them. Underneath was some horrible black thermoplastic tiles that looked dirty even when they had just been cleaned. It seemed such a shame after that beautiful carpet and curtains, but we felt very lucky to have the house at all.

"Actually, we only own the front door knob," I joked to Cath. "I've just had our mortgage statement. We owe more than we borrowed in the first place.

Cath was appalled. She hadn't bargained on the building society charging interest a year in advance.

Transport was a bit of a problem. When we first got married we bought a car in Brighton, called Bertha. Bertha was an old Austin A80 with a new Gold Seal engine. It cost us the princely sum of fifteen pounds but as neither of us had a licence it languished in a car park in Bedford for some time before eventually I gave it away to a passing student, much to Cath's disgust. As it was a charge car park I was getting somewhat concerned about the possible bill which might result from the local authority.

Cath, however, had been taking driving lessons from a disgusting thing called Dave the Rave. Dave the Rave was something straight out of a sleazy play about driving instructors. He was much older than both of us and was looking for an exciting way of life. He kept moaning about wanting to see a new face while he made love. Although he was a nasty bit of work he was in fact quite a good driving instructor and very shortly Cath had passed her test, so we bought a new car.

I say new in the literal sense, it was certainly new to us and it had been new to somebody else probably twenty or thirty years earlier. In fact it was an old Morris Oxford with the bar down the centre of the window. My father had driven a similar sort of car when I was a child. It had actually seen better days and to be honest in today's safety conscious world would not be allowed on the road. Again it was before MOTs had been introduced, death traps like our Oxford were allowed on the road all the time. We were quite happy with it until one day we took it to a multi-storey car park and got stuck on a steep slope for some time while people tried to find parking spaces. It was rather frightening; we sat still but the car gradually moved backwards, giving out horrific groans as it did. We realised at that point we couldn't continue driving this rust bucket; it was very dangerous.

We had, however, some adventures with it. The most famous of all was when it started making the most dreadful noise. We were very concerned; we took it to a garage and anxiously asked if they could do anything with it. The man listened to the noise and then looked at us and very seriously told us that we had a very big problem, however, it could be fixed. In fact he had just what it needed to make the car work again. We instantly asked what that was and he said, "Petrol." Apparently the horrible noise we could hear was the petrol pump pumping with no petrol to pump. As you can see I was a great engineer and knew all there was to know about engines!

Buying another car though was a bit of a problem, we hadn't got a lot of money and we didn't really want to buy another death trap. We eventually were recommended to a garage out at Wooton. We were told that the owner was sympathetic towards paupers like us and would try to give us a car that would actually be safe. We drove out to the garage and were greeted by a gruff man, dressed in dirty, blue overalls wearing a dark blue cap. His face was covered in grease as were his hands and he looked very tired.

"So you want a car that will work," he said in a gruff mid-European voice. "Don't we all? Everyone wants a car that will work and of course they want it cheap. That is so is it not, you want a cheap car?"

I explained that we were young teachers and yes, we did need a cheap car but obviously wanted one that was going to be safe.

"That is the problem, everyone want a cheap car. I have a few here. Maybe one will be good for you. The car we fell for, at least the only one we could afford, was a Mini van. It was so much newer than ours and looked in reasonably good condition. Admittedly, it didn't have any back windows.

"You can always convert it," he said, "however, it can cause problems. But at least it's taxed differently and it will save you money. He offered us thirty pounds in part exchange for our Oxford and as it was more than we paid for it we were delighted. We proudly drove away our Mini van as if it was a Rolls Royce.

The paintwork, however, was a bit scruffy. We decided we would paint it. We couldn't afford to have it properly so we would rub it down and do it ourselves. We got it all prepared and then painted it with red oxide to protect it from rust. It took some time to dry so for a few days we drove round Bedford in this rather strange-looking red oxide Mini van and then painted it black. We thought it looked rather good; of course you could see all the brush marks which people said was unusual as far as cars were concerned. We also remembered to change the description on the log book and sent the details up to the licensing authorities.

That Mini van served us very well. We drove backwards and forwards to Cath's parents in Birmingham on many occasions together with our small cat, Tweasel. There was no heater in the van so in the winter we made sure that we had plenty of warm blankets. It wasn't particularly quick but it was very reliable. We were very proud of it.

As well as a new car we of course had our new house. We moved in at Easter and promptly set about cleaning, painting, polishing. We were very much in love and so proud that we had our own first house. When we finished decorating it we invited Cath's parents down to stay and to show off the house. Everything was to be perfect. They were coming down after school on Friday evening but when we came home from school that evening it was very cold. It might have been April but, as my mother was always reminding me, it snowed on my birthday on the 28th.

"It's very cold," said Cath, "do you think they'll be all right?"

"I don't know," I said, "I'm feeling the cold already and it's going to get much colder tonight. There's not much we can do though is there?"

"I suppose not," said Cath. "I suppose all the shops are shut?"

"They will be by now, or by the time we got to them," I replied. "Wait a minute, what about the paper? Perhaps we can get something privately?"

We grabbed the local paper and looked through it and there, it seemed, was the perfect answer: "New oil heater. Unwanted gift. 17s 6d."

"That would be perfect," said Cath, "we used to have oil heaters at home. I know they work very well."

"Right," I replied, "let's phone up and see if they've still got it."

As luck would have it the oil heater was still available. We got in our new sparkling black Mini van and drove round to where the oil heater was up for sale. We quickly bought it and rushed back and turned it on. At that point they both arrived and we went out for a meal.

On the return it was like something from a science fiction film. It is hard to imagine that a house can change so dramatically within a few hours. When I opened the front door it appeared that I'd walked in to a devil's grotto. The whole place was black and filthy. Cobwebs of filth hung all over the hall and up the stairs and the smell was absolutely overwhelming. Both Cath and I could have wept. We couldn't believe something could happen so quickly. The oil heater was faulty and it had burnt its own fumes creating a black mess that engulfed the entire house. All the work we'd put in to decorate, all our efforts and all our plans had gone for nothing. We just couldn't believe it was possible to be so unlucky.

Luckily the bedroom doors had been shut so it was just possible for everyone to sleep. But I don't think Cath and I did much sleeping that night. The following day the visit was curtailed and Cath and I were left to clear up the mess. We contacted the insurance company and a loss adjuster came round to see us. He obviously felt sorry for us because not only did he help us with our actual claim, he also gave us some advice: "And what about those net curtains?" he said.

"Oh they're all right," said Cath.

"Are they?" he said. "Just touch them, will you?"

Cath touched them and they fell apart.

"I thought so," he said, "that normally happens."

By the time he'd finished our claim had gone up considerably. We also did a deal with him that we would decorate most of the house ourselves if the insurance company bought the paint and materials and they would pay for our main room to be professionally decorated. The nice thing was that once we'd finished we would be better off than we were before the accident. The only problem was we had to get three different quotations for this decoration.

We phoned painters and decorators from the paper and duly awaited their attendance. The first two were exactly as one would expect: men in white overalls, white caps, paint stains all over them. A quick look round and a reasonably quick price. Both of which were fairly similar. The third painter was something rather different. He arrived in an E-type Jaguar with an assistant. Neither of them were wearing overalls and he looked something out of Country Life. He went round talking to his assistant who wrote in a small notebook. We very much got the impression we had sent for the wrong decorator. When his estimate came in it was pretty obvious he didn't want the work; his price was something like seven times more expensive than the other two. *Nice work if you can get it,* I thought. Another lesson learnt in life: horses for courses! If you were decorating

Buckingham Palace I am sure he would have been fine but for a small semi-detached Wimpey house in Bedford the other two were just what the doctor ordered. Eventually we got the house back to normal. We reinstated the visit and vowed never to buy an oil heater for the rest of our lives.

I had started to teach cricket at Brickhill even though I wasn't responsible for games. Obviously as a keen cricketer I wanted to contribute and needless to say, John Gunning would never turn down a qualified MCC coach so I was given a fairly free hand during those hot summer days of my first year. As usual the stupid arrogance of youth was to catch me out yet again.

On one particular lunchtime, I was asked if I would bat against the star school bowler who, for an eleven-year-old, was particularly brisk. Without thinking I said, "Fine," and took my stance with no pads, no protection and just a very small bat; the size used for small boys. At this point I realised I was on a hiding to nothing. It is very important to keep up one's image; it wasn't going to be a very good image to see my stumps splattered particularly as I was supposed to be such a fantastic cricketer playing for Bedford. I decided on a course of action: I would bash the first ball as hard as I could and then say it was far too dangerous for me to continue and thank everyone for letting me have a go. This would have worked but for the fact that my aim was not perhaps as true as it ought to be. Sure enough I struck my ball: it looped high in the air straight through a greenhouse. Even worse, it went in one side and out the other!

There was a hush about the school field. The owner came out of his house, red in the face, spluttering and shouting: "What stupid person did that?"

I had to confess in front of about three hundred children that I in fact was the stupid person, and apologise.

"Well you should know better, a teacher. It's disgusting," he said, and wandered back into his house.

It wasn't necessarily an example to set to the whole school.

# CHAPTER 6

*"June is busting out all over."*
— *Rodgers and Hammerstein*

It was show time again and the F.W.G. production unit was in full swing. At the same time the famous June Fair was approaching.

"At least you've got your hair back for this year's production!" teased John. "What are you going to do this year to excite the audience? Chop off a hand and pretend to be Captain Hook?"

"Very funny, very funny indeed. You want to try that particular trick. I was lucky not to lose my eyesight!" I replied indignantly. "It also put me off smoked food," I added jovially, thinking I'd gone a little bit over the top

"Have you got all your stage directions and props lists?" he added. "We're just waiting for the usual nail exercise."

"Hmm, I thought you were joking last year. No! I'm going to insist on full details."

He got up, looked at me, chuckled, and then continued as he left the room: "IF I were you, I'd start training now. Are you any good with weights?"

With that, and still laughing, he left the staffroom.

"Any idea what he's on about?" I asked Nancy, who'd been listening quietly to our exchanges.

"I think he might be referring to the three netball posts which apparently represent the masts of the ship. Could also be referring to the three wheel beds in the nursery plus, of course, the chest of drawers and the various other furniture. I gather they're very heavy and rather difficult to move quickly."

She told me all this information as usual as I was an infant from her class, and laboured all the points extensively.

"Do they ever swop the ship to the nursery?" I enquired, hoping the answer would be 'no'.

She smiled. "Only about four times and, of course, you'll have the backdrops to change."

"Oh, God!" I exclaimed.

"No, he won't help, though you certainly will need a lot of help. Rather you than me!"

Nancy always reminded me of a slightly smaller Hattie Jacques. Very plump and extremely large in the bosom department. She always wore similar sort of dresses, normally a dowdy brown, and looked like she could do with a shave although, of course, it would be rather rude to suggest it. At least between them they had given me reason to worry and to start researching into other problems.

Peter Pan was the ideal F.W.G. story. A retarded twenty-something man tempts a sweet young girl away to his lair, pursued by a disgusting old man whose cruelty to dumb animals resulted with him being mentally disadvantaged. The sweet creature, it appears, was being force-fed alarm clocks when it snapped. It's had a guilty conscience ever since. It didn't actually own the alarm clock and has spent the entire production trying to give it back. For some inexplicable reason, a band of dancing Indians keep appearing, singing sophisticated songs such as "Scalp-um, ar gar gu-war!" You had to admit, they don't write them like that anymore.

However, the most extraordinary character of all was a fairy that hid herself mainly in chests of drawers, being the only object in the entire production big enough to hide her. I must say I often worry about the lack of morals of our child story writers. They seem to me to be dirty old men writing about their would-be fancies.

Although I was only the Stage Manager, I'd had much more of an impact onto this year's production. The star, Wendy, was one of my best from my first year class and her younger brother was in my present class. Many of the others were from my drama group so I felt much more involved than just back-room boy.

The June Fair was an annual money raising event organised by the Parent Teachers Association. Although we weren't expected to do much of the organisation, we were encouraged to do something. As far as I was concerned, it was a serious loss of a day's cricket but it wouldn't look too good if I went sick and then bowled well enough to get into the local papers!

"What are you going to do?" asked John as we walked up towards Games one afternoon. "I need someone to run the 'soak the teacher with a wet sponge' stand."

I'd seen that one last year. The poor unfortunate teachers poked their head through a hole and then the paying public, at a penny a throw, heaved wet sponges at you. Not my idea of a good afternoon's pleasure.

"I'd have rather thought Will would like that one. He loves to get involved, don't you Will?"

Will, who had been meditating, snapped out of it as he heard his name.

"Oh rather," he replied, "anything for a laugh. What do I have to do?"

"Oh, it's easy," said John. "I'll put you down for it. Well, what about you Tony?" he continued, hopefully.

"Well, I'll run a 'bowl the batsman for five shilling'. They pay a penny a ball and I'll take an off stump guard – it'll be money for old rope." *At least I'll get some practice*, I thought, as I said it.

As usual, the June Fair was hot and sunny. There were those that said that F.W. had done a deal with the devil because he was always very lucky with the weather. Mind you, there were also others in town, who thought he actually was the devil! Of all the paid-for attractions that day, the most sensational, the biggest and definitely the most popular of all with the small boys was Will's wife, Jen.

She arrived in a very fashionable crochet dress. As it was the time of 'burn your bra' feminism, she had conveniently left off her bra as it was very hot. She wore a very skimpy pair of briefs. The holes in her dress were very large and the dress left nothing, and I do mean absolutely nothing, to the imagination. It was the sort of outfit that would have encouraged the punters in Soho, and would have certainly earned the film producer an 'X' certificate, were it on celluloid. It was not the sort of outfit expected at a junior school fete!

Jen seemed oblivious to her mistake. She walked round slowly, showing herself to all and sundry as if in a haze, oblivious to the dirty sniggering all around from little boys of all ages. It reminded me of the Tom Leher's famous song which included the lines: "It was me who stepped on your dress, fah la-la,

The skirts all came away, I confess, fah la-la,

Revealing to all of the others to see

Just what it was that endeared you to me."

Certainly, by the end of the afternoon one knew what endeared Jen to a rather wet and soggy Will!

As for me, I raised nearly five pounds for the fund and only paid out one lot of five shillings. This went to a five-year-old girl. I reversed the bat and used the handle, it wasn't the best decision I'd ever made but it did make her day!

Billy Pete had been drinking more than usual. His lewd suggestions had become even more unacceptable. Obviously, someone or something had upset him and it would not be long before he confided to someone.

"Buggers had stopped my lunchtime practice!" he moaned as we were watching yet another century opening stand from the Bedford opening pair.

"Er, which particular 'buggers' are we talking about?" I asked, thinking it was hardly likely to be Bedford Cricket Club that stopped his practice.

"Ministry buggers! Bloody spoil-sports. Weren't

doing any 'arm whatever they said. Stuck-up load of buggers!"

"Where is this?" I politely enquired.

"Over near my work. It's the only place I can practise if it's raining. It's ideal, a complete indoor net. They say we might damage the planes. We never hit that far. There's normally plenty of room," moaned Billy.

"Planes? Aeroplanes you mean? What are you talking about?" I asked incredulously.

"Where they test them planes. Call it a wind tunnel or something. It's the ideal cricket net though!" he added.

Then the actual penny dropped. I'd read they were testing Concorde in the nearby wind tunnel. I could see their point; a cricket ball smashed into a hundred million pound prototype supersonic plane might be considered by some 'spoil-sports' as an unnecessary risk!

"Locked it all up," Bill continued sulkily. "Said they couldn't trust me!"

"Well, could they?" I asked.

"No, but that's not the point! They should 'ave."

We all chuckled, it was typical of Billy's logic and, to be fair to him, he joined in the laughter.

It was almost enough to start me smoking again. I was sitting in the staffroom joining in to a 'hate F.W.G.' meeting.

"All the sailors' costumes, all of them, are currently wrong!" complained Nancy. "They're the wrong period! Who cares, it's a school play not the Royal Opera! We're supposed to make them all again, completely new ones, it's just not fair!"

"Hmm, you should see the lighting plan," added John, "it's a nightmare! It's ten times worse than last year and that was difficult."

"I don't know why you lot are moaning," I said indignantly, "try moving those netball posts quietly, let alone the beds. My props fill the entire entrance lobby! I'm dreading one of the posts falling over especially if it hits someone. I'd rather have the singed eyebrow look any time!"

We all agreed it couldn't go on. The F.W. productions had to change, not that it bothered me, I was off to St. Joseph's next term.

The girl playing Tinkerbell was a very precocious almost twelve-year-old going on twenty! Her mother was a very sexy executive separated from the father and dating regularly. The girl was obviously treated like a younger sister and dressed and acted like jailbait. If I was casting for Lolita she would be the ideal choice. Despite her youth, she oozed a sort of innocent sex.

On the second night there was a bit of a cock-up on the lines front. Tinkerbell was in the chest of drawers and, unfortunately, the line that got her out was missed. She got stuck in the chest, missing all of her best lines. To say we were shocked with her extensive vocabulary would be putting it mildly. Her language would do credit to a rugby club very late at night! The only consolation was I doubt if most of the children understood her. At least, I hope they didn't! There was a funny side to it but, unfortunately, she didn't see it.

My team somehow managed to shift the extensive and impressive range of scenery and, as usual, the glowing red cigarette man had a major triumph.

Billy condescended to help me with my garden. He wouldn't bring his own rotivator because of the possibility of damage, but he knew somebody who would come and do it for me.

"'Ee don't know much about the area," said Billy. "So don't tell 'im."

"When will you be there?" I asked.

"'Bout ten on Saturday morning, I'll bring a load of topsoil with me. They're giving it away back at Clapham. Reckon you could do with some."

They both arrived on time with a very large and expensive rotivating machine.

"It's pretty rough ground," said Bert, a small inoffensive chap. "Now wonder you want it rotivated! This'll soon sort it out"

He took off his jacket, rolled up his sleeves, straightened his flat hat, pressed a button, and the giant rotivator sprang into action. The giant blades ripped into the clay and, as luck would have it, no damage was done to the machine and it quickly ploughed up our couch-ridden garden.

"You must be very proud of your machine," I said to Bert.

"Oh, it's not mine," he replied dryly, "I borrowed it from the Ministry."

Billy winked at me and put a finger over his mouth. In other words, "Keep quiet!" As Bert was loading up the lorry, I asked Billy what I owed.

"You just give Billy a couple of quid, you can buy me a few drinks after the game this afternoon. Lucky there weren't a car under your bit!" he chuckled.

I could hear his laughter as they drove off to return the borrowed machine. I couldn't help wondering what Bert would have done had it broke.

## Making an Exhibition of Ourselves

I was, as usual, putting together the orders that had come in during the day while I'd been teaching, when the phone rang. Cath answered it downstairs and called up to me: "There's someone on the phone from the Aldridge Philatelic Society for you."

"All right, put them on," I said. I took the phone. "Yes, can I help you?"

The voice at the other end of the phone was very Brummie.

"We have a meeting of the committee and they've asked me to invite you to have a stand at our exhibition. It was a bit of a toss-up between you and the Argyle Stamp Company, but they thought Benham would be more appropriate."

"When is this exhibition?" I asked.

"It's a week Saturday and the stand will cost you five pounds. It's a good event, you should do well."

"I know it probably sounds rather stupid," I said, "but, where is Aldridge?"

"Just north of Birmingham," came the surprised reply, obviously expecting everyone to know immediately where Aldridge was.

I'd never actually done an exhibition. I suppose it was a good time to start, particularly as we could go up and stay with Cath's parents which would mean we wouldn't have to pay for a hotel bill.

"All right," I said, "we'll do it."

"Good," he said, "I'll send you directions and the invoice. Look forward to seeing you."

I went downstairs to Cath hoping she wouldn't mind.

"I've just been invited to take a stand at the Aldridge Stamp Exhibition. Apparently Aldridge is just north of Birmingham. I thought we could go up and stay with your parents. It might be fun. Apparently it was between us and the Argyle Stamp Company. They chose us!"

"Who are the Argyle Stamp Company?" asked Cath.

"I've got no idea," I said.

As time went on I learnt that Angus Parker, who ran the Argyle Stamp Company, was one of the top dealers in postal history. The thought of him actually visiting the Aldridge Stamp Exhibition, let alone having a stand there, was quite amazing. Unfortunately though, the man's sarcasm was totally wasted on me.

# Five Thousand Stamps or Nothing

One big problem in getting our first day covers organised was to actually getting the stamps in advance. You could actually do it but you had to guarantee to buy five thousand stamps for each issue. It was all very well when there were five stamps in the set which meant you only need to buy a thousand sets. Occasionally, you got one stamp such as a ghastly issue for Ghandi in 1969. This meant we had to look for other ways of actually disposing of the stamps.

We came to an arrangement with a dealer in Sutton Coldfield that we actually bought his stamps, drove them to Sutton Coldfield for him, and drove back. Needless to say, we charged nothing for that service. We also similarly ran stamps to a dealer in Stevenage. We received no credit for buying the stamps, quite the contrary. We weren't even allowed to pay with a cheque. We had to go to the bank, draw out the cash and go across to the post office to get hold of our stamps. We then had the whole job of sticking them on all the envelopes and getting them off to the various places for post-marking. If they weren't into the post office by the end of the day of course, we didn't get the post-mark date and we lost our money. It was all very worrying.

It didn't really pay to be a friend of ours in those days. If you dropped in on us unexpectedly while we were sticking, you ended up sticking stamps with us. In fact, some of our friends were so good they actually came round to help us, and we even employed F.W.G's daughter on a regular basis to stick stamps. They became quite social events, sitting round our table and sticking the stamps and chatting about things in general.

On one occasion, I even actually had to take stamps into school to stick and got some of the better children to help me. But the Headmaster walked in on me and asked me what I was doing. I said it was a project involving timing how many stamps could be torn up in a certain amount of time, timing how many stamps could be stuck on in a certain amount of time, adding up the value of the stamps that were stuck on, thus making it into a mathematical project. Of course, it was a bit like craft because of the skill of placing the stamps in the right position. He told me he'd never heard so much bull and laughed as he went out of the room again! Luckily, it only happened the once.

The most exciting time in the early hours of one Saturday morning came after we'd been sticking from about four thirty onwards in the afternoon. I'd noticed that the gold on the stamp for the queen's head was getting very poorly printed.

"Have you noticed the gold on these stamps?" I said indignantly to Cath. "It really is appalling, they ought to do better than this, they look dreadful!"

The reply from Cath was quite interesting: "I haven't got any gold on mine," she said very quietly, "in fact there's no queen's head anywhere."

I looked, she'd already started tearing the sheet and it was quite right; the queen's head was missing off every single stamp. Such errors were rare and were worth quite a lot of money. Whenever I'd had anything good before there'd always been a reason why it wasn't worth very much. On one occasion, I found I had stamps printed on the wrong way up of the paper with the water marking inverted. I was very excited until I found out the entire issue had been printed like that and the only good ones would have been if the stamps had been printed the other way round which, of course, I hadn't got.

I decide I would sell them quickly because I was convinced that hundreds of others would turn up. Cath had already stuck six onto our own envelopes so we sorted those away in various boxes, hoping that the post office wouldn't notice them.

I phoned round the leading experts who dealt with errors and managed to get six pounds for each stamp which seemed to be a reasonable return seeing as the face value was threepence! We sold all of them with the exception of the ones that were on first day cover and these we sold for seven pounds fifty to collectors. Those fortunate enough to buy them did very well; today they're probably worth something like three to five hundred pounds each. But that bonus of six hundred pounds certainly helped Benham on its way.

"There's an international stamp exhibition at Earls Court," I told Cath excitedly. "I've never been to an international. Do you want to come with me?"

"Yes," she said, "might be interesting."

Luckily it was in the Whitsun holiday so we could go on the first day. The exhibition itself was mind-blowing. Thousands upon thousands of collectors walking round all the prestigious stands. Stamps on sale from pennies to hundreds of thousands of pounds. Dealers and post offices from all over the world were competing hoping to take the collector's money. I'd never seen anything quite like it. It was very inspiring to realise that so many people could make so much money out of my hobby. I was buying mainly to re-sell to dealers so I had to be very careful what I bought.

We came across one stand that looked more like a supermarket. It was covered with green luminous signs screaming 'bargain', 'sale', 'special offer', 'only available today'. It was run by a very distinguished man with white head and a white moustache, wearing a smart suit. I spotted quite a few covers I wanted to buy, if possible up to a hundred of each. Sometimes dealers didn't like to sell to other dealers so I diplomatically asked him: "Excuse me, would it be possible to buy a hundred of these ship covers with the Cutty Sark post-mark and a hundred of these art covers with the art on stamp post-mark? And there's a few others I'd like."

"I'm not sure, sir," he said in a very plummy voice. "I'll have to ask the owner." He went over to a rather flashy-looking, spivvy sort who was doing business on the far side of the stand. He explained quietly what we requested.

"What, cut me bleeding throat?" came the cockney squeal. He then came rushing over to us. "No, I couldn't give you any more discount, I'm giving the stuff already away. You know what I mean?"

"No, that's quite all right, I didn't want a discount, I'm happy to pay your retail price, it's very reasonable."

"Well, that's all right then. Yeah, you can have a hundred. You have to pay full price, all right?" With that, he went across back to his other customer leaving us to be dealt with by the distinguished assistant.

"I'm terribly sorry 'bout that sir, I hoped I could get you a discount but, as you see, he's adamant that you have to pay the full price."

"Don't worry," I said, "he's right. The price is very good. I'm delighted that he'll let us have a hundred of each."

We sorted it all out and paid for the covers and asked if we could leave them on the stand and come back for them.

As we wandered round, picking up the odd bargain here and there, we came across a stand which intrigued us. Although it was called Gainsborough Stamps, the owners were called Buckingham. Well, to be honest, De Vere Buckingham. Even more extraordinary was that the wife of the stamp dealer's name was Cath. With a 'K', not a 'C', but to have two Cath Buckingham's, both stamp dealers, seemed to be quite a coincidence. It appeared that the couple had only just become full-time stamp dealers. The husband, Keith, was an accountant and he'd taken the plunge. This was their first big exhibition. It was obvious they were short of stock and so I came up with rather (I thought) a good idea.

"Would you like some first day covers to sell on your stand?" I asked. "You seem to be a bit short of stock and we've got quite a stock at home which would probably be very popular here."

"That would be marvellous," said Keith, "how quickly could you get them up to us?"

"Either late tomorrow or the day after," I said.

The exhibition ran for a further nine days so it would be worth our while working virtually all night to get back to them. We finished our visit to the exhibition, gathered up our various purchases, and headed back to the station.

"This is quite a good opportunity," I said to Cath. "If they get that sort of number of visitors through, we could take thousands of pounds."

As soon as I got back home, I started preparing the covers for the exhibition. By now, I'd quite a good stock and it was ideally suited for a big exhibition as I had so many of each cover. I put together about twenty special offers and then made out two tarifolds of better covers. Tarifolds were like books to be displayed on the counter made of wire, displaying the covers through see-through plastic. I also made up other albums full of other covers priced up so, by the time I finished, the Buckingham would have an exceptionally good range of covers.

As I predicted, sales were very good. So good, in fact, that I was to become a regular fixture with the Buckinghams at stamp exhibitions for the next four to five years, broken only when we took our own stand there. I even was allowed to go and work for nothing on some stand on Saturdays, being allowed to pay my own fare and buy my own food. As you can gather from this, stamp dealing was, and still is, a very amateur game. Many of the people working at big exhibitions are just collectors working for the dealers just for the pleasure of being on the stand and perhaps a few cheap stamps or covers for their collections.

## Bidding for Glory

From the early days of the Warren Smith auctions, I progressed upwards to look at many auction catalogues and bid at auctions throughout Great Britain. Occasionally I actually visited auctions but this could be rather frightening. I regularly went to an auction in Birmingham where Cath could spent the day with her parents and I'd go in on the bus to Birmingham, visit the three stamp shops, view the auction, and then sit and bid.

It always amazed me at these auctions, by then I was writing cheques for thousands of pounds for my new issue stamps but when it came to bidding at auction it was something completely different. As my lot got nearer and nearer, I got more and more agitated, started to sweat, my heart started to beat so loud I was frightened that every single person in the room would be put off beating by this hammer beat smashing its way through my body. I was sure I was going to miss my bid so I concentrated a hundred per cent on what was going on. It was even worse when I had to bid twice in succession. If I got lucky with the first bid, I almost certainly lost the second one because in the excitement, I forgot to bid! Although I got better at auctions, there was always that feeling of great excitement and anxiety which I suppose added a spice to it all.

On one occasion I went to Birmingham and found a very unusual first day cover in a mixed lot. It was a George V halfpenny stamp on a postcard posted on the first day of his reign, but was actually post-marked Westminster Abbey, the site of his actual coronation and, as it was Coronation Day, it obviously made it very, very interesting. It came together with all sorts of weird and wonderful things and was estimated at twenty pounds. I thought it was worth a lot more and so was very pleased when I bought the lot for twenty pounds. I sold the cover very quickly for a hundred pounds and was told very shortly after that, that the post-mark alone was so rare it was probably worth two hundred pounds alone for any date, let alone on the first day of the Coronation which was actually held at Westminster Abbey. I think today that card is worth about two or three thousand pounds but I don't regret selling it as the profit from that and other buys helped to build my business.

We were not always successful at auctions. On one occasion I spotted a fantastically rare first day cover in an auction to be held in Reading.

"Cath. There's a Mulready first day cover at Reading in an auction."

"What on earth's a Mulready?" asked Cath, puzzled.

"Well, when Roland Hill introduced the world to the first postage stamp, the penny black in 1840, they also issued at the same time pictorial envelopes which could be used in the same way for postage. These were designed by William Mulready but never really caught on in the same way as the stamp did. They were all issued on the same day, the sixth of May 1840, and this is one of these envelopes actually postmarked on the sixth of May 1840!"

"Gosh!" said Cath. "It must be worth a lot of money."

"It is, but it's only estimated a hundred and fifty pounds. I'd like to go and buy it."

"Let's make a trip of it," said Cath. "Could we not stay overnight in a hotel?"

"That's a good idea, the auction's actually at a hotel so we could stay there."

I phoned up and booked us in so we could go straight after school on Friday evening to the auction and view the following morning. The hotel itself was a very modern one on a lake with a fountain in the middle of it. The room we stayed in was very posh, much smarter than anything we'd stayed in before, and after eating a really large English breakfast we went down to the auction room. I asked to see Lot 249, the Mulready first day cover. It was brought out proudly to show me. I looked at it and then looked again, and then looked again and finally asked the attendant over.

"Excuse me, can you tell me where the date sixth of May 1840 is?"

He looked at me rather superiorly, looked over and pointed to a blob which as far as I could see could be anything.

"It's there, sir, sixth of May 1840, if you look very carefully."

"Well, I can't see it," I said. "I've been looking for some time."

"Well, if you turn over you'll see that it's been written, the sixth of May on the inside by the person who wrote the letter, which obviously proves it's the sixth of May."

"Well, it might," I said, "but then again, it might not. He may have written it on the sixth of May but he might not have posted it until the ninth of May. Certainly, that squiggly splob doesn't say the sixth of May to me. I'd certainly not buy it, I've come all the way to Reading just to see it. Thanks for nothing!"

With that, I turned and Cath and I left. Rather a large expense with nothing to show for it.

Another time, there was a wonderful collection of illustrated envelopes produced for the 1890 Jubilee of Queen Victoria. It was estimated at between twenty and sixty pounds. I'd had it sent to me by post and thought it was absolutely fantastic. I would have paid up to seven hundred pounds for it and I was very confident that I could buy it. Cath and I drove up to Croydon to go to the auction. The auction was due to get very crowded and people came hours ahead to get a decent seat. We managed to get two at the back but otherwise there were very few seats left, certainly not in reasonable places. Just before the auction started, an old man came in and glowered to somebody sitting in the front row.

"I always sit here," he said in a very Jewish voice. "I've been sitting here for thirty years, young man. Can I have my seat please?"

The man sitting in the chair wasn't very keen on

getting up, knowing that he'd have a trouble getting another seat, plus the fact that he'd been there probably for two hours waiting for the auction.

"It doesn't say anything about it being reserved," he said. "I've been here for two hours."

"I always sit there, it's traditional. I've been sitting there for thirty years. I can't stand!" he added pathetically. "You'll have to move, I'm sorry, you shouldn't have sat there in the first place. If you're quick you'll find somewhere else."

The man still was not inclined to move and muttered: "Why don't you go and find somewhere else?"

"I can hardly walk, young man, I need to sit down now. That's my seat."

Reluctantly, the man got up, glared at the old boy and walked off. The old boy sat down and turned to the person sitting next to him. "And what about my wife?" At this, by magic an old lady appeared. "She needs a seat too!"

The other man put up no fight at all. He just glared, got up and walked off and the old lady joined her husband. I expect it was a regular ritual. They certainly weren't going to wait two hours to get a decent seat!

"It's better than television!" said Cath. "I thought it was going to be a boring day!"

We sat waiting for our lot; Lot 130. I waited with trembling anticipation. It's estimated twenty to sixty pounds, I could go up to seven hundred pounds. I wondered what I'd have to start with: thirty, forty, fifty? Or should I keep quiet and come into the bidding later? I didn't really get much of a chance to find out.

"Lot 130, I can start at nine hundred pounds."

"Nine hundred pounds!" I muttered to Cath. "It's only estimated at twenty to sixty!"

The bidding was brisk. It finally sold for sixteen hundred pounds. So much for my seven hundred pounds – another expensive trip for nothing!

The other funny thing was the unexpected often happened. I bought recently three lots from various auctions of the uncrowned king, King Edward VIII, first day covers. There were only four stamps issued: a halfpenny, a penny halfpenny and a twopenny halfpenny issued on the first of September 1936, and a couple of weeks later a penny was issued on the fourteenth of September. As he abdicated on the tenth of December, they were unusual stamps, although I suppose everyone thought they were going to be very valuable. There are literally hundreds of thousands of them about. They never really were worth much.

First day covers, though, were interesting but these envelopes were even more interesting because somebody had actually gone to Scotland to a place called King Edward, which was in Banff, and so, for a first day cover collector, they were very exciting. They came in sets of three: two first day covers and the abdication date, the tenth of December, also posted at King Edward. After I bought the three lots I received a letter from somebody in Hastings, who said that he'd been selling them and he had a few of them and would like to deal with me direct. We arranged to meet at the British Philatelic Exhibition at the Seymour Hall near Paddington Station. I had to go up to take my covers to the Gainsborough stand, as I'd done most times, for them to sell so I arranged to meet him in the bar.

"Hallo!" he said. "You must be Tony Buckingham."

"How did you know who I was?" I asked inquisitively.

"Well, there can't be many people carrying great bundles of first day covers around, meeting me in the bar, so it was a pretty fair guess."

Thinking about it, I was the only person with first day covers in the bar and so he couldn't go far wrong.

"You've been buying all my King Edward covers. I thought it would be much better to sell to you direct. How do you feel about it?"

"Fine," I said, "how many have you got?"

"Well, I did a count last night and these are the figures."

When he gave me the bit of paper, I just couldn't believe my eyes. The halfpenny, penny halfpenny, twopenny halfpenny first day cover: two thousand seven hundred and forty! The penny first day cover: fifteen hundred and sixty, the abdication cover: two thousand nine hundred!

"Well, it's certainly going to take you a long time to sell them at auction with this lot and the price is going to go down, you understand that, don't you?"

"Oh yes," he said, "I realise that."

"I couldn't possibly buy them all in one go either," I said, "talking a lot of money."

"I wouldn't expect you to. What would you like to do?"

I looked at the list. If I paid him five pounds a set plus bits and pieces for the odd ones we were looking at something like twelve thousand pounds, which was a lot of money in those days. My house had only cost four thousand pounds. It was roughly three times the price of my house but I was sure I could sell them.

"Supposing I gave you five pounds a set and guaranteed to buy them all over the next five years? I'll buy them in hundred lots. I'll take two hundred to start with which means you get a thousand pounds."

"Yes, that seems fair," he said, "I've also got one or two other things."

He produced bags of various used stamps, mainly George V which somewhat reassured me anyway, the only worry was whether they were in fact forged. Having all these stamps for the same period made it very much more likely it was all genuine. Over the next few years I bought the covers steadily and was amazed one day when in fact he told me it was the last hundred I'd had and that all the sets had gone. I was down to the odd ones. I could hardly believe it, I'd sold nearly two thousand sets in less than three years. Ironically, today the sets are very, very rare and you'd have to pay at least two hundred and fifty pounds for a set. If only I'd kept some for myself.

*

"It's always been the same," said Marie in her soft BBC English. "Young teachers want to have fun.

They're not serious. Every time we've tried to organise something with a serious note, it's been a flop."

"All they want is dances, pub evenings, theatre trips, parties, games nights. That's the sort of thing they'll come to. They won't come to anything serious, Marie's right!" added Dolly, her Irish accent contrasting strongly with Marie's English.

"Well, I think you're wrong," said Roland pompously. Roland was a very serious young man who'd started a new job in Bedford, coming from the nuclear-free borough of Greenwich. He was a typical leftie would-be intellectual. He wore a rather dirty check shirt, an old sports jacket, grey flannels and rather tatty shoes. He had rather tight-knit ginger hair, either not bothered to shave that day or he had the misfortune of his facial hair growing very quickly. He was, to be honest, a pain in the arse!

"There's so much we can do to help society rather than just waste our time with frivolous activities," he continued. "Just take Vietnam for example. We should be contributing, protesting, doing something to stop it. I think we should all go up to Grosvenor Square and lie down to make a protest." His eyes became rather wild at that point.

I looked round the room and just couldn't imagine any of our group protesting lying down anywhere, let alone in Grosvenor Square! We'd all seen the news and how the police moved those protesters.

"I don't think that would be a popular outing," said Doreen, our branch secretary. Doreen was a Welsh infant-teacher with striking long black hair. She spoke in the typical soft Welsh sing-song voice. "I'm certainly not interested," she added, as if we should imagine she was keen.

Doreen was a very ambitious teacher who undoubtedly would become a Head Teacher sooner rather than later. She was, needless to say, a very efficient secretary. Not that it would matter if she wasn't, there weren't many suckers who would take on the job at all. After her strong statement there was a strange silence. I thought someone should break it so I began: "Cath and I came across a fabulous pub the other night near Potton called the Rose and Crown. Anyone know it?" Nobody did, so I continued. "It had an old fashioned skittles table."

"What, with cheeses?" interrupted Joe in his gorgeously thick Irish accent. Joe shouldn't really be there except he was waiting for our bridge evening which followed as soon as we'd finished the formal part of the evening.

"Exactly," I continued, "I reckon an evening there would be very popular. Beer and skittles always goes down well."

How about May the twelfth?" said Doreen efficiently. "I'll put it down on the programme."

"What about the Foot-lights?" asked Dolly. "We've been there before and everyone enjoyed it."

"What's the Foot-lights?" asked Cath, who was a reluctant member of the committee. I didn't drive so she brought me. I was there as I could add up, hence they made me treasurer. It was a grand name but in reality, I lent the money for the events and tried to get it back again – not always successfully.

"The Foot-lights Review is in Cambridge. We hire a coach. It's actually the university drama group. A few years ago we saw Peter Cook, Alan Bennett and Jonathan King in 'Beyond the Fringe'. They were very funny." Marie obviously enjoyed it as her face lit up as she told us.

"Who was that tall man, last time?" asked Dolly.

"Oh yes, John something. John, John Cheese, was it? No, no it wasn't Cheese. Squeeze? No, not Squeeze. Something like that though. He was mad though, but he was very good."

"Right," said Doreen, interrupting. "Foot-lights it is. When's it on?"

"Early June," said Dolly, "I'll find out the date and we'll get together to organise it."

"Party time next," said Doreen. "We'll put one on, say, Friday the twenty-sixth of May, at our flat. We'll make it a bring a bottle party and we'll charge a pound to start the booze going. Can you collect the money, Tony?"

"Yes, of course!" I said, thinking, *Unless I'm very clever, I'll be down a few more pounds.*

"So we've got three events and the monthly bridge evening. We could do with two more," continued Doreen.

"Bat and Trap!" said Joe. "Why not have a Bat and Trap evening with some darts, say?"

"Make it a pub games evening," added Cath, "beer and games. We needn't say what games," she added naughtily.

Richard had just sat through all our fun things with

a look of disgust on his face.

"This is all very trivial. Surely we can have something with a little bit more meaning. There must be some serious teachers in Bedford."

He said this very slowly, probably because he wondered if we could actually take in what he was saying. "In my last society, we had a ginger group."

"Cleese!" shouted Dolly, excitedly.

"What?" asked Richard. "Cleese what?"

"No, John Cleese," continued Dolly, "that was the name. I couldn't think of it. Sorry!"

"A ginger group," Richard almost shouted, "was formed for serious discussion. At least you could try it. It met monthly like your bridge evening."

We all knew it would be a disaster but, who knows, we could be wrong? So we agreed to try it for three months that term. Richard was fairly pleased. He thanked us as he hurried off to his Young Communists meeting which he was due to attend next.

"He's a ball of laughs, isn't he?" I said after he was gone. "Who's going to come to be gingered up?"

"Perhaps he has lots of similar friends?" giggled Cath.

"They could all come and be serious! What a horrible thought." Marie had already set out the cards as she was talking. "Now, what about the important part of the evening: bridge!"

"I'll open the bottle," said Dolly, "Doreen, grab some glasses and let's have some music."

Very shortly we were all happily bickering over the cards.

*

Billy Pete was once again in the second eleven. He'd said a few things to the Captain which apparently had not gone down very well. It appeared the Captain didn't like to be told that he was talentless, witless, stupid, incompetent, hopeless, the worst Captain Bedford had ever had, ignorant, and apparently his parents hadn't got married before he was born. There were other home truths Billy had told him but, in all, it was enough for him to be dropped to the second team. Billy had taken it rather well.

"I suppose I shouldn't have made remarks about his parents," he said philosophically, obviously meaning all the other comments were fact. "Where am I batting?" he asked the Captain.

"You're in number three, Billy."

"Who's opening?"

"Jones and Hacket."

"Who's facing?" said Billy.

"Jones."

"Oh, that Jones! He doesn't give you time to get your pads on. Where are my pads? Quick, give them to me. I need them straight away."

"He's out!" came the cry.

"I told you 'ee never gave you time to get your pads on!"

Billy's pads were the most surprising pads I'd ever

seen. Most people had white pads. His were sort of metallic. They were almost antique. He'd obviously had them a long time. He strapped the pads on and rushed out to the wicket muttering about "That Jones, shouldn't be in the team in the first place. It's only because he has a large car." There was probably some merit in his remark. It was an away game, we had very few drivers and it was true: John Jones had a very large car.

\*

The ginger group was, as predicted, a great disaster. Richard turned up early with a large pile of notes of things he wished to discuss. The only other people that came were Cath, me, Doreen, Dolly, and Marie, and we were only there because we were on the committee and felt we should turn up. Without us Richards could have discussed in earnest the whole evening by himself. Despite the fact that it was obvious it was a disaster, he would insist on his meeting so we had to discuss the superiority of the East German educational system over our own, why we were wrong to help South Korea and why America were trying to create an empire in Vietnam. All the sort of things we couldn't wait to discuss after a hard day's teaching!

"When shall we have the next meeting?" he asked, ever hopefully, at the end of the evening.

"I think that could be very difficult," said Doreen, "I'm going out a lot in the next month."

"What about June the seventh?" he asked, ever hopeful.

"Ah!" said Cath. "Tony and I are going to the

theatre that night."

"What about the fourteenth?" he said.

Dolly and Marie immediately jumped up and said it was a Catholic evening which they had to go to. The amazing thing was, every day he suggested most of us had previous engagements. In the end he had to give up and agree it was useless, so the ginger group gingered out after one performance!

*

Billy was, as usual, holding forth under the tree on a hot Saturday afternoon.

"I've 'ad a threatening letter," he said in a conspiratorial voice.

"What sort of threatening letter?" asked Doc Heaton.

"'Ere, I'll show you." He pulled out a dirty crumpled bit of paper from his pocket and handed it to Doc. Doc Heaton straightened it out.

"Why, this is from the Inland Revenue. It just says you've got to go and see them."

"I don't want to see them," said Billy, "I've never seen them. I don't want to know about them."

"It's only about your tax. I suppose you're self-employed?"

"What I do is my own business," said Billy, "none of everybody else's business. Certainly not these people!"

"How do you pay your tax?" asked the Doc.

"What tax?" said Billy.

"Well, you must fill in some forms to pay some money?"

"No, I've never paid nothing. I work, I keep what I do!"

"Do you mean to say, you've never paid any tax?" I asked incredulously.

"No," said Billy, "never felt the need. They don't bother me and I don't bother them – till now."

"I think you'd better get yourself an accountant," said Doc, and wrote down a name and address and a phone number on a piece of paper. "I'd phone him before you go." With that, a wicket fell and Billy had to go out to bat.

"Do you think Billy's in serious trouble?" I asked the Doc.

"Hard to say, but I can't imagine he earns much. He doesn't do much, just scratches a living out on a bit of ground he owns over Clapham way. He's always available for cricket. He only spends money on drink. Who knows, he may be lucky?"

As it turned out, Billy was lucky. He apparently earned so little he was below the tax band. In fact, if he'd have wanted it he was even entitled to some benefits but Billy didn't want any help, besides, most of his income probably came in used notes which were used to buy the essentials of life, mainly booze. But then, that was only my guess. It was probably libellous!

"There's a most amazing advertisement in this month's stamp magazine," I said to Cath one morning over breakfast. "It has to be a con. But then again, I suppose it might be genuine."

"What's it all about?" asked Cath.

"Well, this fellow up in Northampton apparently was a war hero. He's been a stamp dealer up there for years and they're going to knock down his shop to make a new road and he can't afford another shop. His father was apparently a well-respected stamp dealer in Derby and he's been around stamps all his life. He doesn't think much of dealers but he doesn't wasn't to sell his stock to the trade, so he's offering it just to collectors at incredibly good prices, and they are good prices too! Very good prices. Mind you, he really does ladle it on. There's a bit here about he fought for king and country and all he got was shrapnel in the leg which gives him twinges of pain and now society are driving him from his love of stamps. It's all a bit flowery."

"It certainly sounds like a con," said Cath.

"Yes, I'm sure it is, but it's only up in Northampton. Why don't we drive up and find out?"

"Well, we've got nothing else to do, it's a nice day, and it would make a nice run. Why not?"

We got out the Silver Bird, gleaming and shiny, and purred our way up to Northampton. As it happened I had a customer in Northampton so I thought I'd start my enquiries with him. We parked the car and walked through the arcade where the stamp shop was. The shop, like many other stamp shops I'd visited, was an Aladdin's Cave. Piles of covers, boxes of stamps, row and rows of albums. It looked utterly chaotic – and probably was – but, for a stamp collector, it was paradise. Who knows what may be found as you searched through all those stamps?

"Morning Mr Whitehead," I said as I entered the shop.

"Oh, hallo Tony, how's business?"

"Oh fine, I've certainly got no complaints. Cover sales get better and better! How are you doing?"

"Well, not that good, to be honest. You get the people in, that's all right, but then they don't spend much. They hang around, go through everything and then spend a few shillings. You've got the best thing, dealing from home. You haven't got the expenses and if you have a quiet day you can just go out. I've got to be here all the time."

# CHAPTER 7

*"The whole world's a stage and each and every one of us must play a part."*

*— Elvis Presley, with apologies to W. Shakespeare*

Summer was now well set in. Crazy, lazy days when the majority of the school were looking forward to school trips, swimming in the school pool, the June Fair and of course watching the production of the year: the F.W.G. presentation of 'Hansel and Gretel' an everyday story of two scared children written by F.W.G. Groves, directed by F.W.G. Groves, produced by F.W.G. Groves, and of course with that well-known stage manager, A. Buckingham.

However, for the fourth years there was only one thing on their minds in the early part of that term and that, of course, was the dreaded eleven plus paper.

There was, of course, much talk at the time of how unfair it was for the children to have to do an eleven plus paper but in those days at least it wasn't just an IQ test which might well tell you the potential of the child, but it didn't tell in fact whether they were prepared to work at all, whether they were disruptive or whether they were going to cause problems at a grammar school. In those days, by taking four papers, two English, one Maths and an IQ paper, at least it seemed fair. The problem for us though, was that many of our children came from up-and-coming families on the new estates around us and the parents seemed to think that it was some form of insult to them personally if their child didn't pass to go to the grammar school. It obviously put lots of pressure on the children but then again, most of life is pressure so to a certain extent they were finding out reality at a very early age.

I can remember well the first time I sat in on an eleven plus paper to ensure that there was no cheating. One of the girls was sitting bolt upright with folded arms about twelve minutes after the paper started. They had been told that they must check their work thoroughly afterwards. I suggested to her that she should check her work. She looked at me straight in the eye and arrogantly said: "I've checked it three or four times, there's nothing more I can do."

I think this minor genius returned to our school about a year later and complained, on her visit, that she had done very badly in the biology exam amongst the others in her first year exams. We unfortunately took the bait and asked how badly she'd do. Her reply was 96%! And that was her bad exam!

As for the rest, they sweated away for their hour and went away full of dread or hope and waited patiently for the results to come out.

As was promised as soon as the exams were over, the F.W.G. production started. It really was something to behold: classes preparing backdrops for the stage, classes preparing costumes, rehearsals going on throughout the day. The business side sprung up:

posters were produced to sell the play, tickets were printed, and publicity was obtained from the local press. It was a very professional operation.

F.W.G. himself, was involved in the entire operation, checking every aspect and making sure that his machine ran like clockwork. After about a week, I was summoned, with John Gunning, to the Head's study where F.W.G. told me roughly what the stage manager would have to do. To be honest, I hardly understood a word he was saying. It was about green rooms and red rooms and this and that but John Gunning replied regularly: "Yes sir! Quite sir! Yes of course, sir! Yes, you would want that, sir. Yes, that can be done easily. No problem, sir!"

I was very relieved, at least someone knew what he was talking about. At the end of the meeting we had a cup of tea and a cigarette in the staffroom, I asked John to explain what had been said in the room as I hadn't understood.

"I don't know," he said, "you're the stage manager. I do know one thing though, on the day of the dress rehearsal he will nail up your instructions and you'll be surprised how long it is and how many props you need."

I thought he was joking. I should have listened more carefully!

On the day of the dress rehearsal F.W.G. produced the stage manager's list. It was, as John had promised, very long. He nailed it to the stage and went on with his business. I looked in horror, took it down and proceeded to put together all the props I was supposed to have had and to make a note of everything I was supposed to do. It was a very complicated procedure. The other thing I had learned from other members of the staff was it was best to get it right, this was an occasion when F.W.G. accepted no mistakes.

There was one small problem in the play that had taken some solving. There was to be a big flash and explosion when the witch appeared. One of the parents had come up with a plan of the utmost simplicity. He produced a tobacco tin and to it was attached a long mechanism which enabled me to strike a match in the tin, thus setting up a flash and giving the effect on the stage. This worked fine in rehearsal but on the first night the device broke. Thinking quickly, I took out my gas lighter, turned it up to full throttle, bent over and sprayed the flame into the box, thus causing the flash. The flames shot up and I screamed in agony. After the play it was generally agreed that the best moment was when the hideous face appeared on the stage at the same time as the witch. The parents were interested how we got the burning effect of eyebrows and the perfectly revolting face. Luckily it didn't take too long for my eyebrows to grow back and the minor burns didn't inconvenience me too much. The one thing I did know was not to lean over with my lighter for the next performance!

We also had a slight problem getting the smoke out of the chimney in the witch's house. The first idea of wet newspaper was not a great success. Not only was it a dreadful health hazard but the stench of wet newspaper was pretty appalling, it also had the effect of sticking in the throats of the actors which meant they were continually choking and sneezing which didn't really help the main performance!

We had to then obviously look for some alternative means; we turned to dry ice. Now dry ice, used professionally, can be very effective. It's the main means of getting smoke, fog or mist on stage but it does need to be used in moderation. In honesty, the people watching the second night's performance could have asked for their money back on the basis that it was very hard to see the stage, let alone the actual production. However, it did add an eerie quality to the whole production.

I had enormous respect for F.W.G., he was a great Head but then, as with all great people, he had his weaknesses. The major school production was certainly one of those weaknesses. In all honesty, he did take it rather seriously. I accept that you must aim for the best possible standard but there are limits! Throughout the whole production you could always tell where he was in the dark: a glow of a cigarette was continually seen as he worked his way through thirty or forty cigarettes per production. Every minor problem was a major catastrophe.

I was working closely with a young Danish teacher, who was on an exchange trip to England. One of our major jobs was to change the backdrops. I did feel that having twenty or so changes was unnecessary, particularly when a) we had to take them off the stage through the school, out into the playground, turn them round and rush them back and b) that he allowed us just under two minutes per change. He used a stopwatch and the curtain was drawn back on the dot, whatever the state of the stage behind. Apparently, in the previous production the year before, one of the young helpers had been stranded on the stage putting a tree on and remained on stage throughout the whole act trying to look like a tree! As it was a serious part of the play, it didn't go down well with F.W.G., but apparently was received very well by the audience!

F.W.G. was also very upset by the press reviews of the previous year. Apparently, they were very glowing about everything with one notable exception; they thought the children were brilliant, the costumes magnificent, and the scenery out of this world. The only comment that upset him was that they felt that perhaps with all that effort it might have been better to get a decent play to produce! As he'd written it himself, it seemed he was apparently very upset about the whole thing!

The production of Hansel and Gretel ran into a major problem. Willy (the 'W' was pronounced as 'V') and I ruined the whole production, at least on one of the evenings. We were getting ourselves in a bit of a lather about the backdrops. It was almost impossible to achieve the timing that was set, plus we had to remember whether to turn it to the left or the right, or in some cases upside down or the right way up. They were also about thirty to forty feet long and our problem was intensified by the fact that many of the actors were also milling about in the lobby and we had to clear them out of the way as we rushed out into the playground. One particular evening, we grabbed the back-cloth and rushed out before the act was completed. We didn't allow time for the crow to come and eat the crumbs that Hansel and Gretel had left for their trail.

"You ruined the entire play!" screamed F.W.G. at us. "The point that the crows eat the seed is so significant! Without this information the audience will miss the whole point of the play!"

He seemed very upset and distraught and we noticed that the glow of the cigarette after that got even more intense not that we really imagined that the audience even noticed or cared but to F.W.G. this was terribly, terribly serious. It was difficult to take our wigging seriously as the inclination was to giggle but that, I feel, would have gone done very badly! I don't think Willy could quite believe what was happening and so I took the situation in hand.

"Obviously, we're very sorry about it, Mr Groves, and we will ensure that it doesn't happen again – but hopefully it won't ruin entirely the production for the audience."

F.W.G. needn't have worried, the play itself was a triumph. The parents were incredibly impressed, the reviews in the paper were excellent. Once again, Brickhill had shown what could be done with primary drama.

I was always a very careful teacher. Cath always joked that I was like a mother hen worrying after my charges. But I was very aware that I was responsible for them and perhaps did take it a little bit too seriously. I had been a protected child myself and obviously, this was reflected in my attitude towards others.

One of the things that always worried me were balsa knives. I'd never been very good with my hands.

I was, to be honest, the worst do-it-yourself person you're likely to come across. My father had a very good theory: he believed that we should work at what we do well to create money to employ people so that they can do what they do well. My father was also not very good at do-it-yourself!

The problem with being a primary school teacher is that you have to teach everything. Creative woodwork was one of the subjects I had to teach and this meant teaching balsa-work and ensuring that the children didn't chop their fingers off with the very sharp knives. One particular Friday just after the school play, I was feeling particularly queasy. I had been out to party the night before and had probably drunk a little bit too much, probably, in fact, a lot too much. I did feel rather tired and ill by the afternoon and was certainly looking forward to getting home to rest over the weekend. I noticed, however, one of the boys trying to change a balsa knife blade and doing it very badly.

"Bring that knife here, Witty," I ordered. "Here, take this fresh one. I'll do that for you."

The last thing I needed on that sort of Friday afternoon was for a boy to have an accident. The class was divided into two. I took the boys for woodwork and we had a student, Suzanna, taking the girls for needlework. She was a competent eighteen-year-old with a big mass of dark brown curly hair, very much the public schoolgirl. Later on she'd be thought of as a Sloane. She was quite competent with her needlework and the girls all got on with her very well. I was sitting idly watching her performance, fiddling with the balsa knife, putting the blade back in when suddenly it moved rather quickly and I noticed a piece of my finger on the table and rather a lot of blood. I grabbed a handkerchief around my hand and went across to Suzanna and said: "I'm afraid I've got to go out for a few minutes. I'll be back as soon as I can but can you take control of the class for me?"

"Is there anything wrong?" she asked.

"Well, no, I've just got to leave the classroom for a while."

With that I went up to the office. They took one look at me and rang an ambulance and within a short period I was being rushed off to the General Hospital. Poor Suzanna, when the children asked if there was anything wrong with me seeing as I was just being led down the path to an ambulance and there was a piece of finger on the table and rather a lot of blood. That was the first inkling that she had that I had actually hurt myself.

It was a pity I hadn't had the sense to take the finger with me. They obviously may well have been able to put it back. Not only had I chopped off a piece of my finger but the blade had embedded itself in the second finger so I had both hands stitched up and was bandaged up in the most impressive way, creating an enormous white v-up to the whole world!

Poor Cath was phoned up at her school and told I'd had a serious accident and been rushed off to hospital. She immediately left, got into the Morris Oxford not noticing a trailer behind and reversed straight into it. She rushed to the hospital and of course was very relieved to find out that I'd only just simply cut my fingers rather than something far, far more serious.

Shortly after the balsa knife incident I was to be inspected to see if I was fit to be a proper teacher. Obviously, any exam is important but for an ambitious young teacher it was not a good idea to fail this probationary year and so I was very concerned that I would get an examiner perhaps sympathetic towards me and obviously hoped that F.W.G. would put a good word in for me. There were two of us to be examined. My examination came very early on. The examiner checked me giving out the milk and then left to go over to the other part of the school. The other teacher was not so fortunate, he spent the entire day with her and failed her.

Apparently I had passed with flying colours some time earlier and it was just simply having to go through the motions to actually visit me. I did at the time wonder how he could possibly tell I was a good teacher simply by seeing me give out the milk, not realising that technically pass or fail was very much in the hands of the Head Teacher. Again, I was grateful that I'd landed on my feet and started with such an excellent tutor.

During our first year, both Cath and I had become actively involved with the Young Teachers. The object of the club, society, group or whatever you like to call it was basically to provide a means for teachers to meet each other socially particularly as so many came from various colleges around the country and knew nobody within the area. Both of us got involved in the organisation of the club and concentrated on parties, outings and various sporting evenings ranging from Bat and Trap to bridge.

The members were a motley crew coming from all forms of teaching within the area and it was through this society that we met many of our friends in Bedford. Just before the end of that term one of the grammar school teachers had volunteered to organise a very large party to celebrate, for many of us, the fact that we'd survived our first year. He was a young physics teacher and it was no surprise to arrive at a very futuristic flat: he'd made much of silver paper and begged, borrowed or stolen large numbers of speakers which he'd linked up to the record player so he could provide absolutely deafening music. It wasn't, however, the futuristic theme that concerned most of us, it was the lack of carpets and the rather large use of a white substance round the edges of the floor.

"What's all that white powder?" I asked.

"Oh that, flea powder, we've had all sorts of problems," he replied nonchalantly.

Fortunately, once the party got going and the lights were low nobody really noticed the flea powder and hopefully didn't find their evening ruined by too much scratching on their return home.

He was a very strange character and as he got gradually drunker and drunker he confided to me that he had rather a serious problem.

"I'm in love," he told me seriously.

"Great," I said, "is the girl here tonight?"

"No," he said rather sadly, "in fact I couldn't invite her if I wanted to. She's one of my pupils."

*Oh dear*, I thought, *this doesn't sound too good.* The educational authorities somewhat frowned on teachers getting mixed up with pupils, and parents, quite understandably, don't necessarily like the idea either.

"Have you actually taken her out?" I asked, rather concerned.

"No, I just lust after her all the time," he replied wistfully. "I can hardly keep my hands off her in the classroom. It's very embarrassing."

"How old is this pupil?" I asked.

"She's seventeen, probably nearly eighteen now," he replied wistfully.

I began to see the problem: he was a young twenty-one in his first year teaching, barely out of university. She was obviously in the sixth form, probably the upper sixth, and in all fairness possibly old for her age. Girls often acted much older than boys which would mean that if they'd met each other, perhaps, in a night club in other circumstances it would be totally acceptable. In the present circumstances, however, the best he could do would be to forget her or simply to wait until she'd left school.

"She's the most beautiful girl I've ever seen in my life," he continued, "wonderful gold blonde hair, right down to her waist, beautiful blue eyes and such a super figure."

I must admit, she did sound rather gorgeous.

"She also has this wonderful Welsh accent, very soft and pleasant on the ear. I could listen to her all day. It makes teaching very difficult." He added sadly.

I really had some sympathy for him, it must be awful to be seeing, daily, a girl you would very much like to go out with, but could do nothing about it. He then started to cry which made things even more embarrassing. He'd obviously had far too much booze and was becoming very, very melancholy. Many of the young teachers who started their careers in secondary schools had found this close age problem, as far as the girls were concerned, very difficult.

Another friend of ours confided that he had learned one valuable lesson very early on and was happy to pass on the warning to all other young teachers. The problem was that he recommended you not actually go into a small cupboard by yourself. On his second or third day in, he went into a cupboard to get some notebooks and was followed very quickly by a girl that made it impossible for him to get out. Also he said it was a very difficult situation and he managed eventually to get away but made the mistake a few days later when another girl worked the same trick on him he realised at that point that it was not an accident. Obviously, it was something they enjoyed doing, embarrassing new young teachers. The big problem with a young teacher was that if they handled it badly and the girl complained, even if there was no substance to the compliant, everyone always thought badly of them: after all there's no smoke without fire. After listening to some of the stories from the secondary schools I was very grateful that I'd chosen to teach the younger children.

Shortly after the party we all sang that song which most teachers find so pleasant, singing, "God be with you until we meet again," which always indicated the end of a term and, in this case, the survival of our first year. The thought of an endless summer stretching out for seven weeks.

\*

"I've got a bit of a problem with my garden. I wonder if you can give me any help?"

I was talking to one of the stalwarts of the cricket team, Billy Peat. Billy was a rather short, squat, ruddy-faced man of about fifty-ish. He was extremely powerfully built and very rustic. He looked very much like Charlie Drake, the popular comedian at the time, and he worked on the land and certainly had an earthly sense of humour to say the least.

"Remind me where you live," said Billy in a very strong Bedfordshire accent.

"Mendip Crescent," I said, "up in Putnoe, the new estate."

"Oh yes, and what is it you'd like me to do?"

"I wonder if you've got a mechanical digger or something and could come and break up our garden. It's pure hell digging, and if I don't get something done I'm going to have to give up some cricket which would be serious."

He looked at me and then slowly shook his head.

"Oh no, I wouldn't take my digger up there. I've heard of someone who did; the problem is that the developers buried loads of cars under the gardens at the back. I'd be bound to smash my machine up."

It was certainly true that there was a lot of rubbish buried in our garden. It was thick, thick clay and I had been told that someone further down our road had dug up an old car. It certainly was amazing what you could dig up in your own garden. Rumour had it that the developers sold the top soil and then made the hole available for in-filling rubbish before they covered it up with clay again. It certainly wasn't the best soil or the easiest to work.

"But what about the couch-grass?" I said to Billy. "We've got awful problems with the couch-grass. What's more our next-door neighbour is doing nothing about his so as fast as we get rid of it our side it grows back through."

"Well, there's something I can do about that. I can give you some stuff to put down which will do the trick. You won't get any more problem from your neighbours. The thing to remember though, you must put it on at night."

"Does it work better that way?" I asked.

He started to laugh.

"Oh no, it's not the fact that it works best at night, it's better that no-one knows you put it on. You'll kill everything in their garden up to six foot away from the fence. You don't want them to think you did it!"

I thanked him for his advice but felt that, to be honest, it wasn't a very neighbourly thing to do. Besides that, I didn't really want everything on our side to be dead for six foot. After all, it wasn't that big a garden and we had already planted quite a few things ourselves.

*

Billy was not very happy on that particular day. He'd been dropped from the first team, something he took very badly.

"They said I was too old," he muttered, "too old,

me! They said I was past it. Past it? I'll show them!"

We were due to go off to a match in High Wycombe. I had also been dropped from the first team; in my case I had a slight problem of uncontrollable tongue. I tended to tell people what I thought and it certainly wasn't the way to succeed at the Bedford Cricket Club or for that matter, it seemed, anywhere else.

Billy, however, was very, very sad at being dropped. His whole life revolved around cricket and the thought that he would be excluded was something he took very badly. I travelled in the same car as him down to the match and he spent the whole time in the passenger seat moaning and muttering to himself. We stopped for a drink and, to my amazement, Billy refused all alcohol.

"No, I'm not having a drop. I'm going to show them this afternoon."

Now this was serious. Billy was as close to an alcoholic as you could actually get without actually being one. The fact that he refused a drink indicated that he was taking things very seriously. It was quite a long journey to High Wycombe, particularly when you stopped at three or four pubs on the way and on each occasion Billy refused to participate with alcohol, drinking a small glass of lemonade and muttering to himself as usual at the table.

When we arrived at the game, Billy immediately accosted the captain of the second eleven and insisted that he should be allowed to open the batting. Billy was not somebody you refused easily and so he was allowed to open the batting. It was obvious from the start that Billy was not to be moved. He batted throughout the whole innings scoring an amazing 130 not out. After the game, having vindicated himself to all and sundry, he returned to his basic habit of getting drunk. After many drinks in High Wycombe we returned to Bedford. To his delight, the first team had lost, which was unusual and he proceeded to tell anyone and everyone that would listen how, if he'd been there, it wouldn't have happened. As he sank more and more pints he became quite aggressive.

"I'm the strongest man in this club," he said, flexing his biceps. "I am, I am, I'm the strongest man in this club!"

"Course you are, Billy," said the crowd.

"You don't believe me! I'll show you! I'm the strongest man in this club!"

He then got down on his hands and knees and proceeded to do an amazing number of press-ups and various other exercises. Several drinks later he started calling again.

"I'm the strongest man in Bedfordshire," he cried. "I am, I am! I'm the strongest man in Bedfordshire!"

"Yes, yes, 'course you are Billy," said the audience.

"I'll show you," he said, "you wait and see!"

And again, he repeated his exercises, doing an incredible number of press-ups for a man of his age. He also managed to get hold of a beer barrel and did amazing things, lying on his back, picking up the barrel and rolling it on his feet. There was no doubting; he was very strong. He took a well-earned break and consumed many more pints and then started again.

"I'm the strongest man in England I am, I am. I'm the strongest man in England!"

Now, to be honest, this was going a bit far but at the same time no-one was prepared to interrupt or to point out that perhaps there were possibly others. Again the ritual was completed with Billy on his hands and knees performing what seemed to be hundreds of press-ups. Eventually, towards the end of the evening he passed out and was taken home by some of the team. I met him the following Tuesday in Bedford.

"Here, Tony," he said, grabbing me by arm and fixing me with a beady stare, "what did you buggers do to me on Sunday night?"

"Well," I said, "you had one or two drinks and performed a few physical exercises to impress us. Why do you want to know?" I asked.

"I couldn't walk on Monday," he said. "I couldn't even get out of bed. Never felt so bad in my life. It took me most of the day to get down the stairs. Still feel a bit queasy and I can hardly use my legs and I can't pick up anything. Next time I start to do things like that, you tell me to stop!"

I had a mental vision of me trying to get Billy Peat to do anything. I was a very tall and, I suppose, fairly strong person but I had a feeling that Billy could pick me up and snap me in half with no problem at all. He had worked on the land all his life and was enormously powerful.

"Well, I'll do what I can," I said to Billy, "but you can be stubborn!"

"I know I'm a bugger, but you must talk to me proper! I gotta go now I got business."

With that he hobbled off to into the Blacksmith's Arms.

The following week, F.W.G. summoned us all to a staff meeting.

"There has been a very serious complaint," he started. "It would appear that some of our children have grown up much quicker this summer than we usually expect. They are apparently up to sexual games behind the bank at the top of the sports field."

"What are they doing then?" asked John provocatively, grinning at the rest of the staff. "Not going the whole way I hope!"

"It's not funny, John!" replied F.W.G., trying not to laugh himself. The woman who has complained reckons that they are not far off it."

"It must be this hot weather!" said John.

"So much for sex education," said Nancy. "They are just experimenting with what they've heard. I always said it was a bad idea."

"So what do you want us to do? Are you going to make an announcement in the Hall after prayers?" he asked facetiously. "No sex on the bank!"

The upshot was that we all lost a couple of our break-times because we had to patrol the upper bank at every break. It was the first time I realised that young children could be so randy.

One hot, sultry afternoon in early August, both Billy and I were put back into the First Team. We were sitting around waiting our turns to bat.

"I'd better take my glasses off," said Billy, muttering to himself, "otherwise I shan't be able to bat."

We were sitting under a tree trying to get some shade, along with Doc Heaton and a few others, nattering about the world in general.

"What do you mean Billy, 'take your glasses off so you can bat'?" asked Doc Heaton interestedly.

"Oh, I can't bat in these glasses. I can't see properly with them."

"Why are you wearing them then?" inquired Doc Heaton.

"Well the optician said I'd gotta wear them, I needed glasses. Mind you I find it very difficult as I can't see as well sometimes with them as I could before."

Doc Heaton looked rather puzzled. "Glasses are supposed to help you," he said, "not hinder you. Come on, I'll give you a test."

He tore up a woodbine packet and proceed to give Billy a cheap eye test. At the end of it he proclaimed Billy's eyes perfectly all right.

"I wouldn't bother to put the glasses back on," he said to Billy, "but just to be safe, go and see Mr Jones. He's a friend of mine who runs an opticians on Kimbolton Road. He'll give you an honest test."

Billy found all this rather puzzling. "What do mean, an honest test, Doc? Surely, all opticians give you an honest test."

"Don't you bet on it," said the doctor, "they get paid when they issue new glasses, therefore it's in their interest to find you need glasses."

This certainly as a revelation to me. It never occurred to me that you would be given glasses simply to earn money any more than dentists would actually fill your teeth to earn more points or surgeons would operate on you simply to enhance their earning potential. It just shows just how young and naïve I was. As it turned out, Doc Heaton was quite correct. His friend confirmed that Billy didn't, in fact, need glasses, perhaps he's the only person in the history of eye tests to have been diagnosed using a woodbine packet!

To celebrate Billy, once again, took to his second hobby: the bottle! On this occasion, he turned amorous and made lewd suggestions to virtually any woman, regardless of age, in the pavilion. It didn't go down very well with any of the ladies but most of the married women could at least deal with it. One unfortunate was a young Bedford schoolboy who'd brought his new girlfriend to watch him play. He'd left her outside the pavilion while he went in to get her a lemonade and himself a light drink. Billy espied her, staggered over to her and told her in no uncertain terms what he'd like to do to her. Needless to say, when the young man came back he found his girlfriend had gone.

"Where's Delia?" he asked politely of Billy who was standing looking vaguely in the direction of the pavilion.

"I think she's gone," said Billy, "she seemed to get in a fluster and left quite quickly."

"Why on earth would she do that?"

"I think it might have been something I said," said Billy, as he shuffled back into the pavilion to get himself another pint.

Cath told me some years later of some of the things he'd said to her. It's always difficult to know how much leniency you should allow someone just because they're a character. I would imagine today, Billy would find himself in many court cases but then sexual harassment had not been clearly defined or invented.

Cath and I had become very good customers of an ironmonger in the High Street of Bedford. Firstly we'd obviously bought all our paint and brushes to decorate the house, and then of course we'd had to buy it all again to decorate the house after the oil stove had burnt up, ruining the house. We'd also bought all sorts of bits and pieces from this large emporium of household wares and we got very friendly with its owner; a delightful old man called Mr Lane. He'd become interested in my stamp stories of how I'd had to build up the business to help the children at the school. He was always interested in new business ideas.

"Why don't you sell your stamps here?" he asked me one day. "I've got plenty of room and you could have that little window out there in the street."

The little window was a display case that had been empty for some years but would be ideal to show off a few stamps and had the big advantage that it was actually on the High Street so it could attract a large audience.

"How much would you want?" I asked.

"Well if I didn't have to buy anything and it was

on sale or return," he said, "I'd do it for 25% commission."

This was before the days of VAT and there was no tax on stamps then so that seemed quite fair. I provided the stamps, he provided the space and the labour. It seemed to me a very good idea; I agreed immediately and rushed home to start preparing what little stock I had to put into his shop.

I wrapped up my first day covers in cellophane and priced them individually. The stamps were individually packeted and then put into an old coin album which made it easy for them to sell and easy for me to re-fill up again. I scraped together everything I had and gave it to the shopkeeper just before we returned once again to Southwold for our summer holidays.

This year we rented a caravan which was on a site very close to the sea and within easy walking distance of the Red Lion and, of course, we had the added advantage that we could drive there in our own car. Once again, it rained most of the time we were in Southwold but when you are young and in love these minor difficulties don't seem to matter. We had a lovely time and on my return I went into town to find out how things had gone in the shop.

"Where've you been, boy, where've you been?" called Mr Lane anxiously. "We've sold virtually everything you left with us. We need more stock."

I was amazed. The amount of money he had taken was way beyond my wildest dreams. He paid me my 75%. I immediately set to work to buy new stock. I had been buying stamps from a company in Fareham, in Hampshire, called the Connoisseur Stamp Company. It had a very interesting range of offers, particularly if you bought in quantity and was always offering three to tuck away for investment and in many cases the prices were very, very cheap.

It also had something else that appealed to me greatly; a scheme that you could buy over three months. It worked like this: if you bought £120 worth of stamps, you gave a cheque for £40 and then two further cheques for £40 for the following two months. I had used the scheme in a small way but this seemed ideal for me when I needed a lot of stock quickly. It was possible to visit them down in Fareham and I took the train and spent an enjoyable day buying all sorts of stamps and covers which I thought would sell back in Bedford.

On my return from Fareham I worked as late as I could into the night, preparing my new range of stock for the shop. I rushed it in the next morning and once again sales were incredible. There was no decent shop for stamp collectors in Bedford and stamp collecting was, at that time, on a tremendous high. The results were so good in that High Street shop in Bedford that I searched round and found a shop in St Neots and another one in Shefford and gradually, as people started to find out that I could provide first day covers for each issue, they asked me to get them for them regularly.

Very soon, I had over a hundred people buying from me for each issue and made about 6d per cover profit (which equates to 2½p today) so our profit per issue was £2.50 which added up to an amazing £12.50 profit per year. I realise it probably sounds pathetic, but you have to put this into perspective. Cath and I were earning around £30 per month as teachers and when you are clawing your way up the bottom of the business, you need every penny you can get.

One of the problems, in those early days, was to get the appropriate post mark to match with the stamps that had been issued. I soon learnt that Bedford, Bedford, Bedford, and Bedford was not terribly exciting, particularly when, for Christmas you could have Bethlehem, for Sir Frances Chichester, Greenwich and for the normal Machin stamps (they are the stamps that everyone uses on their letters with the head of the Queen which was taken from the great artist, Arnold Machin).

The first problem was where the cover should go and the second was getting them there. In some cases it was easy. I can remember Cath and me getting the train to Greenwich for the Sir Frances Chichester set. It was the beginning of our summer holiday and it was quite an exciting day out.

Similarly, when some stamps were issued for bridges, there was a special postmark in Bridge in Kent, which is near Canterbury; we persuaded a friend of ours to drive the covers down in his Jaguar. I doubt if the covers even paid for the petrol but at least we got the Bridge postmark. Things were not always so simple. We found an agent in Wales who could get us the Bethlehem postmark for Christmas. We carefully wrapped our covers up and sent them to him. He achieved the postmark all right but sent us a very abusive letter back, pointing out that newspaper was not the most appropriate way of wrapping envelopes. Didn't we know that the newsprint came off and would ruin them? What sort of stamp dealers did we think we were? I suppose the term was 'amateur but willing to learn!'

Possibly the most bizarre incident occurred somewhat later when I had become friendly with an old lady who was a sort of stamp dealer (the world is full of sort of stamp dealers, as we were to find out). She was always keen to be helpful and volunteered to go to Greenwich to take our covers to get a special postmark for the Cutty Sark. Cath was somewhat cynical about the whole operation.

"You're not honestly going to send Margaret to Greenwich with those covers are you?" asked Cath.

"Why?" I asked. "It's not that far – we did it."

"Yes, but we're slightly younger than she is."

"She's not that old," I replied.

"Have you looked at her carefully?" replied Cath. "I don't think she'll make it!"

"Nonsense!" I said. "She's stronger than she looks."

"She has to be," laughed Cath, "otherwise she wouldn't even make it to the house."

I had to say, Cath had got me worried. She did look rather ancient when I looked at her carefully and there were a number of boxes to take.

"Are you sure you can manage, Margaret?" I asked, kindly.

"Of course I can. All I've got to do is go to the post office at Greenwich and give the boxes in."

"Yes, but they are heavy and you've got to change trains in London."

"Oh don't worry," she replied. "Nothing's going to go wrong. Just give me the boxes and I'll be off."

"Admittedly, I couldn't do much else. I had to teach for the day. As it turned it out, Cath was almost correct in her gypsy's curse. Poor old Margaret had stopped in London to have something to eat and by the time she got down to Greenwich the post office was closed. Now this was very serious because in those days if you didn't get the envelopes into the post office before they closed, then you didn't get the first day post mark and therefore all my envelopes were worthless.

Poor old Margaret, she didn't know what to do. She sat down and virtually cried, and then, luckily for me, she had a brain wave. Trafalgar Square, she thought, they're open all night. So she managed to get back to Trafalgar Square in time to hand the covers in so that we got a London postmark. We told everyone we'd done it on purpose because of the port of London and it was a very good post mark. We did, I'm afraid, stretch the imagination a little bit! The ships cover with a London postmark today would cost probably a few pounds, with a Cutty Sark postmark £25! I was very lucky that Margaret was quick thinking and it was a great eye-opener to realise that one mistake could cost me my small fledgling business. In business you learn from your mistakes. I certainly took this lesson on board very strongly.

"I've an awful problem," I said to Cath one day. "I've got to produce first day covers for what's called regionals."

"What are regionals?" asked Cath, puzzled.

"Well, they issue stamps for Jersey, Guernsey, the Isle of Man, Scotland, Northern Ireland and Wales. They're not pretty stamps or anything like that, it's just really a token but they are new stamps and collectors want first day covers. The trouble is, they don't sell the stamps on the mainland, so I've got to do something about it locally."

"Yes, I can see your problem," said Cath. "You really need somebody in each area to do them. What about stamp dealers? Can't you look through your magazines?"

Isn't it amazing how the simple answer is staring you in the face but you're so busy worrying about it, you don't see it!

"Of course it's simple, there's bound to be someone!"

I looked through and found somebody in Scotland. *The chap who does our covers for Bethlehem in Wales will be ideal there,* I thought. Northern Ireland was a bit iffy but I managed to find someone in the end. Then I was left with the three islands. I suddenly came up with a brainwave.

"Wait a minute, they're all tourist places!" I got hold of some phone books and phoned hotels on all three islands and eventually found someone in each place that would do it for me. I was taking a tremendous risk as I had to send the money and the envelopes across to someone I had never met. But all three people sounded nice on the phone so I chanced my luck.

As it happened it all went well. It was amazingly successful. As it turned out it was even luckier than I could possibly have imagined. By this time I was advertising in a cheap weekly newspaper. I noticed one of my rivals was offering regional first day covers but I also noticed that he was advertising for agents in our trade magazine to produce the covers for him. Unfortunately for him, there had been a strike at the magazine headquarters and it was delayed by two months. As I looked at the two advertisements, an idea came into my head. *I reckon he's in trouble*, I thought.

I wrote him a nice letter saying I had noticed his advertisement for agents and realised that as the magazine was delayed it may well have caused him a problem. It was the sort of thing with first day covers that can happen which can be very embarrassing. If I could be of help, I would be delighted to. I had quite a few left over and obviously could provide them at a reasonable price.

I got a letter back by return of post. He was so pleased and in fact was in a mess. He'd sold quite a few and had none to provide to his customers. Not only did he order the regional covers from me, he decided that as I was so efficient and organised he would allow me to get all his covers for him in future which meant overnight the number of first cover envelopes that we had to get multiplied by four, and also discovered the joy of wholesaling in quantity. Suddenly we were involved in big money, big numbers and it felt good. The fact that it was small profit didn't really concern me at that point. Immediately I started writing to all the other dealers offering them my wonderful services. After all, I was on my way.

\*

It was one of those iffy days. It wasn't hot and it wasn't cold. When the sun poked itself round the various clouds it actually was quite warm, but when it hid again it turned quite cold. It was one of the days when you wonder what sort of clothes to wear. I also wasn't playing cricket, for a change. I wondered whether I should go out and do some couch digging; a prospect that didn't really appeal or perhaps we'd go out for a walk and have a drink. I was thinking about all these options when Cath appeared waving a newspaper.

"Did you know there's a special fair at St. Ives today?"

"You mean St. Ives with the seven wives?" I asked.

"Yes, as I was going to St. Ives, I met a man with seven wives, the seven wives had seven sacks and in the sacks were seven cats. The seven cats had seven kits. Kits, cats, man and wives, how many were going to St Ives?"

The answer, of course is one. The rest were leaving St Ives and we began to understand why!

"Isn't St. Ives miles away?" I said.

"No, it's actually not too far – probably about thirty miles. Let's go!"

It seemed quite a good idea and certainly an improvement on couch digging so we got out the black Mini van with no windows in the rear and drove off in the direction of St. Ives. Now, in those days, Cath drove (she had the licence) and I navigated. I always liked to take us round the villages and try to get the scenic route so instead of going up the A1 across that way, I took us across through Sandy Potton, Gamlingay, and on through Papworth, St. Agnes and Hemmingford Grey and into St. Ives. Somewhere around Hilton on the B1040, we got caught in some traffic. We sat motionless for a few minutes and I said to Cath: "Don't worry, it's probably just some traffic lights or roadworks. We'll be through in a few minutes."

About half an hour later, we'd moved just a few hundred yards up the road. We discovered we were in a traffic jam stretching all the way to St. Ives. Unfortunately, there had been quite a lot of publicity for the fair in the national press that day and it seemed that half of the country had decided to go and see it. We decided to abandon our attempt to see it that year and instead spent a pleasant afternoon wandering around the river at Hemingford Grey.

The following year we did make it to St. Ives. We went early this time. It certainly was a fair worth visiting, a very pretty place and to our amazement there was also a stamp shop. Now I've always been a sucker for a nice little stamp shop and obviously couldn't resist going in and looking through their stock. The old man running the shop told me he'd retired to run it some years earlier. It always amused me when many, many years later he came up to see us at Stampex, still a customer and still running his stamp shop twenty years after he retired! In many ways he'd got the perfect life; he only opened a few days a week, wasn't really bothered if he made much money as he got his pension. He actually lived above the shop in a very pleasant town.

All too soon the summer ended and once again we were back at school. Cath had managed to leave the concentration camp and had moved into the primary section and was now teaching in the local primary school, which was a very pleasant change for her. I was very superior; I was now starting my second year in the same school knowing most of the ropes, having established myself in the school the year before. Again, I had a lovely class and knuckled down once again to the routine, trying to get as many of them as possible through the eleven plus and at the same time making the teaching fun and trying to make it so that they actually enjoyed coming to school.

Once again, I was in charge of the stamp club and now ran my own drama club but had managed to get out of the country dancing, leaving it to a new teacher called Will who, even if he only knew one dance, would be an asset as I still really didn't know any and was very grateful to actually be out of that duty. But more about Will later.

I had also become very aware during my first year that my PE standard was not as high as others. Brickhill took PE very seriously. My memories of physical torture were just that. I was taught by an ex-army sadist. His principal means of enjoyment was to get us hanging on the wall bars. He used to strike the first one that fell down. Luckily for us, we had a tubby boy in the class and he was normally the unlucky victim. At the same time, it was pretty painful hanging there, desperately not wishing to drop and take the punishment.

Ironically, not long ago I read an article in *The*

*Times* about a sadistic bastard who had terrorised a class. It was so well written and so evocative of my own memories it actually could have been my school. When I looked at the name of the person who wrote it I realised it was my school; he was actually in my class. I hadn't really learnt much about PE but I had learnt about how to get out of PE. I was very good at illness and forgetting my various bits of kit.

It was not that easy then, therefore, to raise the standard of my own class without actually getting some extra help. I was lucky though because the kids had been well taught in the earlier part of the school and like most things I was able to follow along and pick up as I went. The one thing that did terrify me was the way they played with the ropes. They were amazingly agile, turning themselves upside-down and swinging, climbing to the top of the ceiling and back again. Being a natural coward, the sort of thing I wouldn't have done myself but at the same time I realised I didn't really want to discourage such adventurous behaviour.

One dreadful afternoon there, one of the girls who was brilliant at gymnastics, went up on two ropes to the top, swung upside down as she did so often. On this occasion something went horribly wrong. She lost her grip and fell. I was too late to stop her and the horrific swelling on her head was something that I can still remember. I was amazed that she wasn't dead. She was rushed to hospital and I can remember spending most of the night worrying if she had suffered brain damage, if would she ever walk again, and what if anything, I could have done to stop it. It really was the most dreadful feeling.

The next morning I came in dreading the worst. As I walked slowly towards the school a child skipped by me giggling and said, "Good morning, sir!" and then skipped on and rushed into the school, and it took me a few minutes to actually come to terms with the fact that it was the very girl I had seen rushed into hospital the night before, with a bump on her head the size of an ostrich egg!

I was talking to Nancy Barter in the staffroom the next day. She was always an excellent person to talk to because she was always sympathetic, gave good advice, and never made you feel as though you were stupid even if you were.

"It's a funny thing, Tony," began Nancy, "that with such an injury if you get a big bump it's much safer than if you don't. The real problem comes if there is no sign of a bump or bruise and it might mean it's internal and then it's very serious. Those awful eggs seem to go very quickly. I've had a few in my time," she chuckled, "but it's quite a fright at the time isn't it?"

"I should say. I honestly thought she was going to die! I've never felt so wretched."

"You'll have a few more like that before you finish teaching," said Nancy, "it's amazing what children can do!"

I must admit, the bounced head incident certainly changed me. It made me much more cautious and protective toward all the children. The horrifying thought of someone really badly hurting themselves, when I could have prevented it, was certainly key motivation to be much more careful.

The thing about accidents, you can't really predict when and how they're going to happen. One of my friends on the staff, Barbara, had a husband who worked in a nearby school. They'd had a problem with their football pitch for about six weeks and so had arranged to borrow ours.

They say things go in threes. Colin, a fellow sports teacher at another school, couldn't possibly have imagined three boys with broken legs in three successive weeks. The embarrassment he must have felt when the ambulance arrived each Wednesday to take away yet another of his casualties! It wasn't even as if the boys were rough. Obviously, it was just a matter of bad luck. I'm sure he must have started wondering what on earth he was doing wrong and even more important, how he could change it. I bet he was relieved on the fourth Wednesday when the games lesson ended and there had been no visit from the ambulance and no broken bones. I often wonder what the Head Teacher made of it. If you have never experienced teaching, you would have imagined the worst: that the poor chap was incompetent and perhaps the children were fighting, all sorts of dreadful things. The last thing most people would have imagined that it was simply a question of fate and bad luck.

As mentioned earlier, one of our new arrivals that year was a chap called Will. Now Will was the proverbial sixties swinger. He was very thin, rather short, and had a hippy beard and rather long hair. He giggled a lot and walked with a slack-hipped swagger, copied from the West Indians whom he greatly admired. His dress was always a little bit odd even when he was teaching but for his casual wear, he was very much into beatnik/flower power or whatever the groovy thing was at the time. His wife, Jen, was extremely trendy and her dress sense at times caused a great stir in suburban Bedford.

Will was very much of his time. He believed in freedom of speech, equality, racial harmony and that popular sixties cult: challenge everything! He believed that the boys and girls should be able to discuss and enjoy any subject. The idea was quite good, it was just the way Will went about it. One of the duties of men teachers at Brickhill, was to referee the House matches. Technically, we all refereed one and as we were all part of a different House in theory it made the system perfectly fair.

The game was watched by spectators from the two Houses playing and, obviously, the last thing you can say was that the crowd was unbiased. Will wasn't terribly excited by the prospect of refereeing a football match. For one thing, Will didn't believe in competitive sport at all, certainly not anything that was physical. His idea of sport was that you should lie around and meditate. In his case, I suspect, in private he smoked reefers which gave him the perfect floating sensation.

Will's game had been going a while when the incident occurred. Now depending on who you listen to, the ball entered the goal and left via a hole in the back of the net, therefore a goal was scored; alternatively, the ball narrowly missed the goal but entered the netting at the back through another hole and left the netting through yet a third hole. An interesting conundrum: should the referee blow for a goal kick and point to the goal kick spot, or should he blow for a goal and point to the centre?

There were only two options. The main thing was to make up your mind quickly based on your own judgement and let the game continue. Now this is where Will came into his own. He liked things to be perfectly fair, and loved discussion, but it was not necessarily a very good idea to start asking spectators what they thought had happened particularly, as I mentioned before, every spectator watching was biased in one way or another. After about fifteen minutes of lengthy discussion, John Gunning walked by, heard the dilemma, shouted, "Goal kick!" blew his whistle and told Will to get on with the game and stop mucking about. I think Will was prepared for further discussion but there was something about John's manner which made him realise that it would not be a very good idea. For some strange reason Will was never asked to referee a House match again!

Nancy was taking Service. She did this once a week; as Deputy Head and Head of the junior school, she had a very important role to play in the school. She'd been teaching the little ones probably far too long because she had a particularly sickly sweet voice she used for Service. But despite this very sweet exterior, Nancy was made of steel.

The Service started as always with a few notices and then on to the religious bit. She was just leading us with the Lord's Prayer in her usual sweet, little girl's voice: "Our Father which art in heaven, Hallowed be Thy name, Thy kingdom come... BROWN!" she bellowed. "You're talking! See me afterwards!"

She then continued the Lord's Prayer in the same sweet tone as if nothing had happened. Brown was dealt with afterwards in Nancy's usual manner. She liked to tell them what they'd done very slowly and, keeping time as she hit them across the legs.

"You nau-ghty lit-tle boy," she would start, each syllable with a leg slap accompaniment. "You must not talk in ass-em-bly," she would continue.

No doubt Brown wished he hadn't talked by the end because he would have had rather red, stinging legs when he went back to his class to continue work.

There was to be a parent teacher's meeting that evening. The thought did not excite me. If I could choose between watching the interlude on television for the evening or a parent teacher's committee meeting, I think I would have chosen the interlude. John always reckoned that the only good thing about the parent teacher committee was Mrs Kelly's thighs. Mrs Kelly was a reasonably glamorous parent, a little bit long in the tooth as far as I was concerned, she must have been at least thirty-two and to a twenty-one year old that looked a little bit like a Grandma! However, to John, she looked most attractive. She wore very short skirts that exposed acres of thigh. It was amazing how John always seemed to sit opposite her in the staffroom. It didn't seem to matter where she sat, he always seemed to be in the viewing seat!

However, something had dramatically changed since the last meeting. A television programme on BBC2 (where else?) had revolutionised breasts on the box. 'Casanova', a serial depicting lust, greed and sex was running every week at about half-past seven. The preview was the most erotic sequence of pictures I, or anyone else, had ever seen on television, and it was far better than anything I had ever seen on the cinema. 'Casanova' excited, and I do mean excited, the entire nation. There were no video recorders and we were rather disappointed that instead of having our weekly lust we had to attend this rather boring and mundane meeting.

However, ironically we were saved by the very same programme though, of course, no-one actually said this. Virtually every member of the parent side of the meeting cancelled for various reasons; other meetings, holidays, ill health and lots of other assorted excuses. It seemed that everyone wanted to see Casanova seduce yet another innocent virgin. Even John had to admit, it was far better than Mrs Kelly's thighs! It must have been rather sad for Mrs Kelly to realise that the secret of her sex success had now disappeared and from now onwards there were better shots on television!

It was always to be the same though, the most disgusting, the filthiest, the most lewd, the most violent, and the most tasteless would always appear on the cultural programme: BBC2. Cath always maintained that academics were randy old goats. I suppose BBC2 merely provided television programmes of the standard they wanted.

A few days later, Cath and I gave Will a lift back to his small terraced house in the back of Bedford. I don't know what I expected but certainly was a complete shock. On entering the house you immediately found yourself in the main room and your eyes were drawn as if like magnets to the fireplace. It was still reasonably warm and it was unlikely the fire had been lit since the late days of last winter. However, it was still full and ash spread from it like a creeping cancer. There was no carpet to be seen, it all seemed to be of the wall-to-wall ash variety. In this filthy mess were two of the dirtiest children I had ever seen, playing contentedly amongst the filth.

The room was decorated in an equally strange way. Will had taken home hundreds of gummed paper squares of various repulsive colours; the sort that infants cut out for mosaics and shapes. He had stuck them with no logical connection on the wall to give a rather bizarre effect. Hard to imagine a more hideous sight than hundreds of coloured squares of vile colours forming the complete wall of a house. On the opposite wall, Will had hung up a packing case with a piece of red string tacked across it.

"Do you like the painting, man?" he said enthusiastically. "It's to depict life entwined in red tape. Good innit?"

Certainly it was different, good, I wasn't qualified to say although probably it would have won a major award in the Turner prize at the Tate for being of a revolutionary design.

Jen offered us a cup of tea but, to be honest, we felt we hadn't enough time to stay nor had we got time to go to the hospital to have our stomachs pumped out from the resulting illness which I'm we would have got had we accepted. Jen was wearing a strange Eastern-looking garment of multiple colours, admittedly, somewhat dirty and appeared rather vague. The house stank of joss sticks which I imagined were burnt to cover up other smells that might have been more incriminating. As we left, Will had lit up a cigarette and was starting to giggle somewhat uncontrollably.

"What a way to live," said Cath as we drove off, "it's not much of an advertisement to make you want to become a free spirit."

Will and his family certainly were very odd, almost as odd as the more famous television family we enjoyed watching on our newly acquired shilling-in-the-slot television.

To be honest the shilling-in-the-slot television was not a great success. For one thing, you always seemed to run out of shillings at the wrong moment. The worst example was one evening we were watching a tense and thrilling film about a plane crash in the desert, the survivors besieged by Arabs. They were outnumbered, running out of water, running out of food. Would the rescuers get there in time? Would they survive long enough to be rescued? Would they be able to hold off the Arabs...? *CLICK!* The shilling ran out and we hadn't another shilling in the house. I ran out to the off-licence and ran back but by the time I got the shilling in the slot, the film was over. I've worried about those poor survivors ever since! Did they or did they not win through?

Every week, one member of the class won a prize for the most House Points they'd received during that previous week. I'd got my class system pretty well worked out by then. Obviously, the less able couldn't win points for getting twenty out of twenty but they could get points for improving their work; for the neatness and for other things around the classroom. I was pretty good at remembering who'd got what and how, so that I was guilty, I suppose, of cheating and trying to manipulate to ensure that the winner was not the same swot every week but a variety of deserving pupils and at the same time keeping the competition interesting.

Every week I would ask who'd got more than five or ten House Points and by doing so we would quickly establish who was the number one for that week.

"Anyone got more than five House Points?" I asked. Six hands went up.

"Anyone more than ten House Points?" Three hands went up including my selected winner for that week but there were two others who really speaking shouldn't be there at all.

"Anyone with more than fifteen House Points?" My preferred choice put her hand down and the other two beamed at me like Cheshire cats.

"All right, how many have you got, Mary?"

"Thirty-two!" came the giggling reply.

"And you, Susan?"

"Thirty-one," spluttered Susan, almost in total hysterics.

"Well done," I said almost incredulously, "how did you get all these points?"

"Mrs Barter gave us thirty for carrying her books," said Mary.

*Great!* I thought. Between them they'd mustered three House Points in the week, one good turn brings them up to record-breaking proportions. I tended to be very mean with my House Points but some other teachers had different standards. I was imagining that in Mrs Barter's class, the winner had two thousand eight hundred and forty. The system worked if you kept it to your own classroom but by having no universal standard for points the whole thing became pointless. I could imagine how mean I must have looked when I gave one of Nancy's class one House Point if they were used to getting a thousand for a good bit of work.

I thought I ought to have a word with Nancy to see if we could stop it happening again so I went over to her classroom. As I arrived she was instructing a small boy on the error of his ways. As usual the slap across the leg was matched with the words.

"On-ly don-keys kick!"

The boy was duly sent back to his seat while Nancy continued the RI lesson, the theme of which was 'God is Love!' She set them some work and then I told her my dilemma. She quite understood and promised to be a good girl and only give my class one or two House Points at the most. She recognised it was a problem and admitted she was rather generous with the points, but then the little ones did like to get lots of House points.

Teaching in the same block as Nancy was a firebrand of an infant teacher called Betty Brunt. I didn't really come across her much as the infant school was separate from the juniors. We, however, were very much involved in civil defence at that time. It was very much in the time of the Cold War and everyone was terrified that nuclear war would break out at any time. Teachers were obviously going to be very important with the aftermath of the slaughter and so we were taught what we should do and how we could become the responsible members of society after Armageddon.

We went to the first serious civil defence lecture where we were told by a rather pompous and self-satisfied man the things we must do. Firstly when we had the three minute warning from RAF Fyingdales on the north-east coast we should:

1) Run home as fast as we could.

2) Fill all receptacles with clean water; your bath, your sink, every jug, bowl etc.

3) Paint all your windows white.

4) Ensure all your food is well protected in a sealed food cupboard.

Finally, fill up as many sandbags as you could and seal off your doors and any other way of air getting into the house. Tape up your windows and finally get yourself under the stairs or into the cellar and await the explosions.

We listened solemnly to the lecture. I must admit, I couldn't take it terribly seriously. For one thing I couldn't possibly get home in three minutes let alone all the rest of the instructions. Betty Brunt was more forthcoming:

"Well, I'll tell you one thing, young man," she said, "I certainly wouldn't bother!"

"Oh?" he said, sarcastically. "And what would you do?"

"I'd drink a bottle of gin!"

"And what would you do then?"

"Young man, have you ever drunk a bottle of gin? I'd pass out of course. That'd save all the problems!"

"I don't think you understand the seriousness of this lecture, Mrs Brunt. It is not funny."

"No, I don't think it is. That's why I would drink my bottle of gin. Just out of curiosity, how long have you got to stay in the house after the explosion?" she enquired, somewhat sarcastically.

"About ten days we're told would be the optimum period," he replied.

"And how many people would be expected to have been killed in the first wave?"

"About 98%!"

"I see," she said, "and how long would the ground be contaminated after the bomb exploded?"

"About twenty years."

"I see, so you're supposed to live in your cellar, or under the stairs for about twenty years."

By now, she was beginning to get on top and was grilling him. He looked rather worried. The self-confidence had gone and his answers now were somewhat sheepish.

"W-w-well, I-I-I d-don't suppose y-you'd have to s-spend twenty years," he stuttered.

"Where would you get your food if all the ground is contaminated? What happens when you run out of the food you've got in the house?"

"Well, I-I don't actually know!"

# CHAPTER 8

## *Nuns are Human*

Nuns are human. I know this might sound a little obvious but that was the first thing I learnt as a non-Catholic teacher in a very Catholic school.

"You know, the people are so worried about us, they cross the road in front of us," murmured the delightful Sister John. "I suppose they think we'll convert them on the spot if they get near us!"

I found this gentle sister a delight to talk to – she was so normal, just like the girl next door.

"Trouble is," she continued, "they see us as some sort of religious freaks, not just people. To them we're just not human, we're nuns."

She continued while toying with the usual revolting school dinner, which could have been beef, could also have been lamb, pork, or some substance not known to man, or, in Sister John's case, nuns.

"We're no different from any other group. We all have our faults."

This was so very true. I didn't know what I expected – goody two-shoes with a halo, I suppose – but I was not prepared for the whole human range:

good nuns, bad nuns, devious nuns, stupid nuns, clever nuns, delightful, unpleasant, brilliant, sly, you name it, there was a nun to fit the description. My headmistress trained under Hitler with extra tuition from Doctor Goebbels. She was a fantastic actress. She played the part of a simple, fun-loving head who joked about religion and drank sherry. The truth was nearer the advice given to me later by Sister John while I was trying to get promotion and leave the school.

"Why not just get another job somewhere else? Don't even think about promotion," she advised after I had just been rejected yet again.

"Why should I?" I snapped. "I'm ambitious and I'm good. I just don't understand why I can't get a deputy headship. I know I'm ready."

"Oh Tony," she almost sang, "I'm not suggesting for a minute you don't deserve to get your job. It's just..." At this point she hesitated, but I was not prepared for the magnitude of the next few words. "You see, Sister Mary Benedict, *she's not a Christian.*"

In those few words she described the worst nun, the non-Christian, scheming, unpleasant boss. If it wasn't for the black and white outfit, we'd have all recognised her for the swine we all worked for. All this talking at lunchtime, however, wasn't helping me remove the laboratory sample that lay on my plate. It was all very embarrassing as we were meant to set an example to the children, particularly as we got free meals as technically we were all on duty. Being a man with a position, I took this duty very seriously.

"Don't throw your food at Smyth, Hobday," I called across the hall sarcastically. "He doesn't want it and it makes an awful mess."

Hobday was convinced we all had it in for him. The fact that he was large, with bright red hair, of course had nothing to do with it. He stuck out like the Post Office Tower in London, particularly when standing in Assembly. Perhaps he should have knelt, then we couldn't have seen him.

"If there's any food on the floor when I inspect later on there's going to be trouble, do you understand me?" Hobday understood probably only too well, it was well known I took football every lunchtime and the chance of me returning before late afternoon was remote. Still, I'd done my bit, felt virtuous, and in some ways I rather envied Hobday. I couldn't throw my food and get rid of it, could I?

The conversation turned to heaven which founded an interesting subject because, as a heathen, I wasn't even invited to the party.

"It's all right for you lot," I teased. "You've got free passes. I'm for the eternal fires. Mind you, it's so cold in my so called classroom, perhaps I'm on a winner!"

"Tony," retorted Sister Anthony, one of the very serious nuns, again a delight, but a little narrow in her interpretations for my liking, "you could go to heaven if you're very, very good. Not being a Catholic doesn't guarantee you will be excluded. There are some vacancies," she said reassuringly, obviously worried that I felt excluded.

"You don't really believe all that?" asked one of the new Catholic teachers. "Don't you think it's a bit silly?"

"Oh no!" replied Sister. "It's fact. You can't challenge that!"

Needless to say, the whole table did challenge. Just as I left, I decided to stir the whole thing up a bit more.

"I don't really mind," I said, "but I am a little bit sad that a Catholic mass murderer could get in but I'd have to queue and wait my turn!" With that I left for my daily football practice.

I hadn't really intended to spend all my free time coaching but it had become a habit. It all stemmed from my dreadful start as games teacher at St Joseph's. I had played football up to the age of eleven and then was forced to play with the wrong shaped ball and never took to ruby. Being a large boy I was naturally a second row forward. Now I defy any of you to enjoy shoving your face between two dirty, smelly bottoms! If this wasn't enough, they were often slimy with mud and smelt like an open sewer. Call me a wimp, all right, I'm a wimp, but spending most of the afternoon buried in heaps of sweaty bodies was not for me. Hence, when I took up my position as Head of Games, I didn't really know the rules – but learning on the job is my motto and I was sure I would learn very quickly!

I also had other problems.

Firstly, my predecessor had stitched me up very badly in two ways. Firstly, he'd given up on his fourth year boys two years earlier to play a complete third year team. This meant he played the same team for two consecutive years. The second year of course they were very, very good. They won two cups and got through to the quarter finals of the London Individual Schools Competition, the best ever for Bedford. This I could cope with easily – after all, it was only a game. However, after he knew he was going to Canada, he had drunk freely – *freely* – guaranteeing at least thirty boys places in the team next year. He got the beer. I got the problems.

"I pick my own team," was my stock answer as many a proud Catholic father learnt when they thought they could bully little Jimmy into the team. Winning is everything. Losing is not to be recommended. I didn't realise it was almost like mass murder to lose to a non-Catholic team. We got convincingly beaten in my first game as coach and nobody spoke to me on my return. In all fairness, I don't think it was as bad as it looked, but I did realise that winning was very, very important, not just for my everyday life, but also for my future career. So I worked and worked and worked.

The team was not particularly good but at the same time you wouldn't meet a nicer lot anywhere. This was perhaps their problem. Their other problem was that I didn't drive so we walked to nearly every match or caught buses if it was central. In one match I misjudged the distance and we force marched nearly four miles to the game. Not surprisingly, after taking a well-deserved three-nil lead we started to fade and only scraped home four-three. The other teachers remarked that my team tired very badly in the second half – not surprising, when you think about it!

In the late September of my first term, I found to my horror we had been drawn away to a village school twenty miles from Bedford. This involved two buses and a lot of walking. When we arrived it was like something from a nightmare. The pitch was full size with no markings. The goal was also full size but didn't have any nets. Their goal keeper was the largest eleven-year-old I have ever seen. I would imagine he was a rather backward fifteen-year-old who had been left behind in the village school. He may have been intellectually inferior but he certainly filled up the goal!

A rather asinine, white-haired old boy turned up carrying a strange object in his hand. I believe he thought it was a football. I was still young and innocent and thought, obviously incorrectly as it turned out, that the ball should have had:

1) A lace.

2) Some air in it!

After all it was as flat as the proverbial pancake. I told myself not to panic, thinking of the reception I'd get being beaten by a very small village school. No! We're a good-ish team! We can cope!

A few minutes later I decided that panic was the best answer. The ball had gone out of play up a small hill at the side of the pitch and the boys were still playing some twenty yards from the pitch. However, no whistle had been blown.

"Er – don't you think that's a throw-in?" I politely enquired. Unfortunately, the old boy was either deaf, or very devious, or perhaps both.

By now the village boys were approaching my goal. It seemed to me that it was wrong they should be coming from behind the goal. My brave ferocious goal keeper, Zelenski, dived and saved one of about six attempts played from behind the goal. The game was a nightmare. We eventually scrambled in a goal and never was I so relieved when the final whistle went some ten minutes early. The referee hadn't even got a watch. Whilst having a lukewarm cup of tea in his study come classroom, he confided in me.

"You know, we never actually entered the cup. We never have before. But as we got a home draw we thought, 'What the hell?' – particularly as you were the cup holders. After all, we didn't have to travel. It was no effort."

I politely enquired again about the size of his goal keeper, and for that matter, some of the other boys, but his deafness conveniently returned.

On the return journey, I did something that I have been ashamed of all my life. I was criticising the way the team had played and my tough centre half, a lad called McGoven, known to his team mates as The Governor, grinned at me.

"It's not funny, McGoven," I snapped, but he grinned even more. The grinning got me down. After telling him three times, I struck him. I learnt shortly afterwards that when the boy was embarrassed, he grinned. He couldn't help it. He bore me no malice, but I should have known better. The memory still burns.

"Will you come into my office for a few minutes, Tony?" came the command from The Evil Penguin.

I have to admit I never relished the pleasure of a royal audience. I entered the inquisition chamber and waited my fate.

"I've got two important things to tell you, so you'd best be sitting down." She spoke sweetly but then the female spider probably seems pleasant just before she eats her husband.

"Thank you, Sister. I thought the choir sung *very* well this morning," I added the compliment, knowing it would annoy her. The choir was brilliant, but the teacher in charge was not in Sister's good books. They had a very, very stormy relationship.

"Yes but they always look scruffy," she countered, knowing here she was on safe ground.

"Yes," I agreed, "but the sound was magic." The problem with Eileen, the teacher in charge of the choir, was that she had no idea how to polish the look to the choir. Most of the times the girls sat with open legs on the stage, giving all the music-loving perverts a double treat. However, I wasn't going to admit that, for once, I totally agreed with her.

"Two things I think you said," I added, as if I was in a hurry.

"Oh yes. We've been given a great honour. Bedford School want us to play them at football."

Now this was unusual. We were a state school and Bedford ranked in the national league of top public schools.

"What's brought this about?" I enquired.

"It's because they've heard we're so good. They want to test themselves against us," she said triumphantly.

"When is this exhibition match to be played?" I politely enquired.

"Next Tuesday afternoon – and you'll get a full tea afterwards."

"Full tea is it? Well the boys will certainly like that!" I was quietly thinking of the polite chatter over the table; I did not see some of my thugs, nice as they were, getting on with the likes of the sons of dukes.

"You'll be representing Bedford state schools so the boys must be on their best behaviour."

She said this very firmly and indeed I'd already started to worry. My yobbish centre half was known as 'The Governor' and the school chant was "Show 'em your boot Governor!" I somehow didn't think that this was quite what Sister meant.

"Now we come to the more important matter." She spoke slowly and very seriously. My heart sank.

*Oh what have I done now?* I thought.

"You know how short of money we are."

"Yes, Sister," I agreed, feeling a great sigh of relief. It was true, we were very, very poor. Church schools rely a lot on the diocese and we seemed to be very neglected.

"Well," she continued, "we're having the Canon in on Friday after school and we are going to insist on more money. You'll be staying for the meeting, of course."

I didn't think that I had any option and so I answered, "Oh, I wouldn't miss it for the world."

The sad thing was I had agreed to go out for a Bernie with Cath and it would make things tight, however I might be able to scrounge a lift as I would miss my usual school bus home.

"How are you settling in?" she continued. "Classroom all right?"

Now this was the lie direct. My classroom consisted of a part of the Dining Hall. We had no desks, only dining tables and cardboard boxes. To the right was the school hall separated by a glass wall. This meant that we put up with PE, Dance, Music, Drama, and anything else going on all day long. It was very noisy. To the left was the kitchen which provided an endless stream of interesting gossip and clanging noises. At the far end we had the swimming pool, which was at least quiet during the winter, but in the summer, the noise was incredible and of course we had to have the windows open because it was so hot. The pièce de résistance was behind my desk. The only thing that separated us from the corridor was another glass wall and behind this glass wall was the Head's office with chairs for waiting visitors. Above us was a giant ventilation dome which obviously was put in as a way of getting rid of the smells and problems from the kitchens. This meant that we had rain filtering through during most of the year and in the winter the snow actually came through and made our classroom very cold. Anyone who has taught will recognise the delight of such a room. It was therefore a difficult question to answer.

"Well, it's not exactly perfect, but obviously with the space problems I realise that we have to make the most of things," I replied diplomatically.

"But at least you have a small class. How many have you got, thirty-six isn't it? Well some of the others have fifty!"

"Yes, I suppose there is that," I reluctantly agreed. I would have liked to have added that some people might think that thirty-six remedial and problem children aged between eight and eleven would be a bit of a problem for 99% of all teachers and teaching fifty, relatively bright children formally would be a doddle by comparison, but I realised that it wouldn't be a good idea so I smiled and asked, "Is there anything more, Sister, as I am teaching in a few minutes."

I only got the free periods because as a non-believer, I couldn't teach RI. The young Irish teacher who drew the short straw to teach my zoo found it very trying.

"It's not that they are naughty," he confided in me one day in the staffroom when we were alone. "The problem is the questions they ask. I'm beginning to doubt my faith!"

He had hit the nail on the head. My lot might be the dregs of the school and technically brainless if you go by the academic tests, however, in many ways they were very able. My time teaching these 'rejects' I believe made me a much better teacher, business manager and ultimately a far better human being. However, I digress.

I left Sister's office worrying about the game with Bedford School. I felt like I'd been given a live hand grenade without the pin. After lunch, at the usual football practice, I called the team together as a special meeting.

"I've got good news and I've got bad news," I told them in a very strict way.

"Well, let's have the good news first!" bellowed Quigley, a long-legged greyhound of the wing. "I hate bad news," he added sheepishly.

"Good news," murmured the squad in agreement.

"Well, the good news is that you're getting a supper of sausage, egg and chips next Tuesday evening, completely free of charge!"

A great cheer erupted from the boys.

"What's the bad news then?" enquired Lowe softly. Lowe was the best footballer in the team, but yet only nine.

"You've got to play a football match first," I teased.

"What's bad about that?" came the general call.

"Who are we playing?" asked Quigley, in the sort of way that indicated that there could be a catch.

"Bedford School. And we're supposed to be representing Bedford and on our best behaviour."

The brighter boys began to realise the catch. We certainly were not in the Pearcy Road league for unpleasantness, but we were not a public school.

"I don't want any violence on the pitch. No swearing. And certainly no 'show 'em yer boot, gov'ner!'" I said firmly. "We want to be invited back next year. Got it?"

"You're sure we're getting sausage, egg and chips, aren't you, sir?" asked Zelinsky, who looked like he could do with a square meal.

"You'll get fed."

With that we continued our practice, which, to be honest, was definitely needed.

Friday came and the long-awaited meeting with the Canon. I had never known the staff to be so militant.

"He's got no alternative," stated Marie. "He *must* find the money. He's prevaricated for far too long. We can't go on like this."

"He knows it all right," added Dolly Cooter, Marie's close friend.

It was amazing to hear these meek and very pleasant teachers so angry. Apparently this money problem had been going on for some time and there was no getting away from it. The Canon was in for a very, very hard time. I did not envy his meeting.

"He *is* coming, isn't he?" demanded Christine, one of the younger members. "After all, he is already fifteen minutes late."

She was right. And it didn't seem that being late was an especially good idea, particularly when the whole staff were so angry. Eventually the Canon duly arrived. At this point I felt very sorry for him.

"Oh dear, oh dear..." he started in a delightful, quiet Irish brogue. "I've had the most awful day. You can't imagine. I've been up to St. Catherine's, the old people's home. You wouldn't believe the state it's in. Pitiful is what I call it. It's just falling apart. It really needs pulling down. But then, where do the poor old souls go? Needs a fortune spending on it. It's so very sad..."

At this point, he sighed wearily. He did look very tired and very old.

"Would you like a cup of tea, Canon?" enquired Sister, more kindly than she would have asked a few minutes ago.

"Och, would I! I haven't had a bite or drink all

day! So that would be very acceptable. Thank you."
He turned back to us and continued his sad
monologue. "You know, I had to go off to St.
Swithins afterwards. Poor old Father Brown, he's not
a well man, don't you know. Worry, I expect. Worry
over money. He's in a desperate state. There's
nothing like money worries to make you ill, you
know."

At this point, I began to realise we were up against
a master. I could see by the faces that he was winning
the battle.

"Have any of you been to the orphanage
recently?" he politely enquired. "I've just come from
there. I don't know what happens to the young. More
and more unwanted babies. They can't really cope.
They've asked me to provide the money for an
extension. They desperately need it. It would make
such a difference to the orphanage and I know if I
could, I would do it. But it's the same everywhere I
go. Everybody needs more money. I don't know
where they think I'll find it. It's so very, very
worrying."

At this point, he put his head in his hands and the
room became very quiet. Eventually, with theatrical
timing of superb proportions, he looked up.

"There I go," he said, smiling sadly at all of us,
"telling everyone my trouble and you wanted to see
me. What was it you wanted?"

Game, set, match to the Canon.

After an embarrassed silence, the staff managed to
bring up a few trivial points. Nothing of course about
money. The Canon dealt with them well, drank his

tea, ate a few biscuits and duly departed, I thought, looking a much younger man, and certainly smiling as he walked to his car. A man to be reckoned with!

I managed to get a lift most of the way with Marie.

"It's always the same," she confided sadly in the car. "He out-thinks us every time."

I had to agree. It certainly was an Oscar winning performance.

The morning of the big match was perfect. Beautiful, autumnal day. Blue skies, a slight touch a frost, but by lunchtime, the sun was bright. In all, you couldn't ask for a better day. My lot looked far smarter than I'd ever seen them before.

I remarked to Joc Quirk, who'd come with us to watch the match, "The bath's taken a bashing last night! Have you ever seen such clean boys? I always thought I'd got a team of very brown lads. Seems I was wrong!"

"They're certainly doing us proud," said Joe in his almost unintelligible Irish accent. "Will I see a good game!" he added.

I'd found this 'will I' very confusing at first.

"Will I clean the blackboard, sir?" asked Mab.

"I don't know," I replied, "will you?"

"Will I carry your bag, sir?" and on it went. An interesting Irish variation of 'can I'.

"I don't know about the game," I replied, "I just don't want any violence. You know I've outlawed 'show 'em yer boot gov'ner!' I don't think that's the sort of chant needed today."

Joe agreed. "You're right. If Sister hears of trouble, then you're in trouble. *Bad* trouble."

I was very aware of this as we marched towards the impressive entrance to the lower school. As we entered a band of delightful, angelic small boys walked in, dressed in light grey suits wearing caps and looking very smart. There was a murmur of giggling from my lads.

"We'll murder them! They look like sissies!"

I must admit, they didn't look like they could kick their way out of a rice pudding.

The changing rooms were very grand. Lots of space and the most important thing, as far as my boys were concerned, there were no girls to peek at them – a practice that thoroughly annoyed them, even when the girls were infants. You'd never believe the lengths they would go to ensure that nobody saw their private bits!

We marched out onto the pitch and I was amazed to see the size of the crowd. Hundreds of people – boys, teachers and parents. It was the parents that caught my eye, probably because they were mainly women, and mostly very attractive. This was the era of the mini skirt, and there were some superb vistas of leg and thigh.

"This was worth a visit, Joe," I whispered to Joe, who, although embarrassed, I noticed was getting his eyeful.

We lost the toss, and before they started, I reminded the boys yet again about best behaviour: "And remember: no 'Show 'em yer boot, gov'ner!'" The boys assured me they understood and so the game started.

The first thing that happened was one of the angelic little boys ran up to Lowe in order to tackle him and kicked him in the stomach.

"Well done, Piers!" shouted one of the attractive spectators. "That's the ticket!"

Within two minutes, Bedford had scored, both in the goal, and with various kicks all over my team.

"Knock him down, William!" shouted another mother. "Get stuck in!"

Some of the other shouts of encouragement were actually a little bit coarse. I hadn't expected this sort of situation. The angels had turned part devil, and they didn't seem to be playing the Marquis of Queensbury rules, let alone football.

The game became very one-sided, and my gentlemen didn't seem to be able to play against these rough boys. I watched in horror as McGoven, of all people, was clattered to the floor to the encouragement of, "Well done, Charles! Wonderful tackle!" This came from a delight in blue with acres of thigh showing. All these leggy charms, however, had stopped pleasing. We were losing two-nil and still my boys were not playing. Shortly afterwards it became three-nil. I really didn't know what to do to motivate the boys. It seemed to me there was only one thing I could do.

"SHOW 'EM YER BOOT, GOV'NER!" I shouted, as loudly as I could, in order to get over the yells from the home crowd. "*Go on! SHOW 'EM YER BOOT, GOV'NER!*" I repeated, in case one or two in Luton or Northampton hadn't heard it.

It was as if an electric charge had hit my team. The game changed dramatically. We managed to pull back to three goals all, then again we went behind. In the last seconds, just before the final whistle, Lowe scored and the game ended as a four-four draw. It was a wonderful result, considering we'd been three goals down.

Everybody shook hands and after a quick change the boys settled down to the promised sausage, egg and chips. The Bedford Head arrived – a very distinguished man wearing what looked like a Savile Row suit.

"I would just like to congratulate all the players. This was indeed a wonderful game. In fact, I believe it is the best I have ever seen here at Bedford. Both teams are a credit to their teachers and it's been a privilege to witness such a game. I won't bore you any longer and I hope you enjoy your supper. We look forward to seeing you next year."

He spoke in a slow, public school drawl and received a round of applause from both teams at the end of his speech. I felt a warm glow. Sister would be pleased, we'd get a return next year. After the last chip had been eaten and all of the pop drunk, we slowly marched back to the school.

"There not a bunch of softies, are they?" said Goggings. "They look it. But they played real hard."

All of the rest of the team agreed.

"You can't judge a book by its cover," I said smugly. "We've all learnt a valuable lesson today."

I thought quietly to myself how wrong I'd been. I'd honestly thought it would be a very easy game.

The following year, we did get our invitation, I didn't say anything to the team, we won five-nil, Lowe scored a hat-trick, the Head Teacher never appeared, and we were not invited back again.

The other thing that John Brown, my predecessor, had lumbered me with was as Ground Provider for the Bedford and District Football Team. Apparently, the team played at St Joseph's, and I had to unlock, lock up, make sure the pitches were marked out and organise refreshments. *Thanks a million, John*, I thought.

The manager of the team was a Welshman whose main distinction was: "I come from a village near to Llgwyngyllgogerychwyrndrobwllllantysiliogogogoch. His name was Noel, however it should have read Know-all! Noel had a very interesting selection policy. He listened to everybody – and I do mean *everybody*. A typical Noel selection would go as follows:

Noel is walking down the touch line watching the game, past me talking to Roger.

Me: I don't think much of the way Smith's playing on the wing. He really is poor.

Roger: Yes, I believe Jones would be a far better choice. He's much faster and has more control.

With this, Noel bellows: "Smith! Off you come, boy, at once! Jones! I want you to play on the right wing!"

A disappointed Smith went rushing to the changing room, probably to cry. Noel continued on his rounds. Roger then continued, "I know Jones will do well. He's my best boy."

Needless to say, there was a lot of prestige in getting a boy into the team so most of the 'advice' was suspect!

Noel would continue round the pitch, hearing snatches of conversation.

"Rutland! Off you come, boy! Cartlage, you go on now!"

Trouble was, once his selection procedure was widely understood, all of us couldn't help winding him up. Didn't do much for the team, but as far as laughs went, it was hilarious.

The other big problem with Noel is that he listened too much to football chat and rarely to anything else. He was friendly enough to ask Cath and me over for a meal one evening. It took us a long while to find the house, so we were slightly late when we arrived.

"Oh good!" he exclaimed in a broad Welsh accent. "Good of you coming, boy. We've been looking forward to it, haven't we, Glenys?"

Glenys nodded. I doubt if she ever got many words in. Noel was far too quick to give her much of an opening.

"Did you have a good journey? I suppose the traffic was bad at this time of night. What do you think of this room? We did it up ourselves, didn't we, Glenys?"

Again, Glenys nodded, while he continued faster and faster.

"I really appreciate all you're doing for the team, Tony. Your husband's a real sport. But I suppose you know that already, Cath."

Cath nodded.

"Is there anything you would like to do, or anything you don't want to do?" he enquired.

"Well, we don't mind most things," I replied. "With one main exception!"

"And what's that boy-o?"

"I can't stand being shown photographs of other people's holidays. It really does get up my nose." (We'd recently had a gutful at a relations house. It was a sore point.)

"Funny you should say that. We've got the projector all set up in the next room for a really good show!"

Both Cath and I laughed. We should have noticed Glenys' worried face.

"Could we not just have supper?" she asked in a delightful Welsh singsong lilt.

"Nonsense!" bellowed Noel. "They'll love the show!"

To be honest, two hours of pictures of Noel, showing his platform ticket of *Llgwyngyllgogerychwyrndrobwllllantysiliogogogoch*, wherever he went, was not the most exciting evening we'd ever spent. By the time we were allowed away from the sideshow, Glenys' meal was ruined.

"It's a bit dry, love," moaned Noel. "She's normally a much better cook," he confided. It wasn't very tactful. She smiled and apologised to us.

"I thought we would have eaten earlier."

"Oh, don't worry. We were late and obviously we must have mucked up your timing," said Cath, much to Glenys' relief.

"Now we can look at the Press Cuttings!"

Noel produced various scrapbooks which were full of local newspapers accounts of the man who came from *Llgwyngyllgogerychwyrndrobwllllantysiliogogogoch*. All accounts were accompanied by a photograph a Noel, holding up the same penny platform ticket.

"Well, you've certainly got your penny's worth out of that platform ticket," said Cath, rather sarcastically – unfortunately wasted on Noel. He took it as a compliment.

"I've got some more slides if you'd like to see them!" he asked invitingly.

If there was a choice between dining duty at school for a year and seeing any more of Noel's slides, I would have chosen the year's dinner duties.

"Tempting as it is, we've got to get home. Our cat is out and she's not very well, and it's a bad neighbourhood," lied Cath rather badly.

With that, we took our leave.

"I'm never going back there again!" moaned Cath in the car. "Is he normally like that?"

"No," I said, "he's just had a good night. Sometimes he's so good, he opens the boring for Bedfordshire!"

"Humph! Bedfordshire?" replied Cath. "He could easily do it for England!"

As with all females, she usually got the last word.

There was no difference on the Noel subject.

A bubble of excitement travelled round the school. Sister Mary Benedict had officially decreed that we were to have a school entertainment. All classes were invited to produce a piece of work and the show was to be in the form of a review.

As I had considerable experience as stage manager for the F.W.G. productions, Drama Club organiser and having annoyed F.W.G. by putting on my own class production to the school, I looked forward to the extravaganza.

My views were not necessarily shared by the whole staff.

"Waste of time," complained Chris, our loveable deputy head. "What is important is the eleven plus results, not pratting about with drama."

Dolly, the other fourth year teacher was similarly inclined.

"My lot don't even like acting," she said, "they would rather do an IQ test."

I found all this rather amusing as I knew the truth. The idea that any class would prefer an IQ test to drama was, to put it mildly, rubbish. The simple answer to their moaning was that they knew they were on a hiding to nothing.

So much would be expected of the top classes that they were in a no-win situation. Of course, on the other hand, nothing would be expected of my lot so I was in a win-win situation.

"I think it could be fun," I added. "After all there's more to life than work."

Chris and Dolly looked anxiously at each other. I don't think fun was the word they would have used.

"I've got some marking to do," muttered Chris.

"So have I," agreed Dolly, and they both hurried out of the staffroom.

I was left with Christine, my co-remedial teacher. She had the seven to nine year old problem children and her classroom was a corner of the hall. However she only had twenty-six in her class, but what a twenty-six!

"What are you going to do, Tony?" she asked.

"Well, I'm not going to load them with lines to learn, that's for sure. I'll do something modern with music, dance, mime and limited words. I've done something like it before and it will be good," I said very confidently.

"Yes, that sounds right. I thought I'd do a very simple mime play to music; something very gooey so everyone will say ahhh!" She giggled at the thought.

Christine was an excellent teacher. She wasn't appreciated by Sister Mary Benedict but then, like me, she was an unbeliever. I had no doubts that despite teaching the worst children on paper in the school, she would come up trumps. Meanwhile I had another problem to overcome. Apparently, before I arrived at St Joseph's, it had been decided that the remedial children should not join in the main games lessons. The idea was that if you weren't very clever, you could not play football. Obviously they had never listened to some of the star footballers being interviewed on television.

"Sister, I'm not happy that my class misses games." I had cornered her after service when Joe was losing his faith in my canteen-classroom.

"They don't have to miss games. You can take them out by themselves," she replied, as if this solved everything.

"What about the few that are good? It seems very unfair," I replied angrily.

"I doubt if they are up to the team," said Sister haughtily.

"According to Christine, Catherine O'Connor could easily make the netball team and I'm sure some of my tough lads could have a chance."

"Well, it's difficult," said sister. "The timetables have been done for this year."

"But not impossible," I challenged.

"Well, you'd better see Chris about it, but he won't be happy," snapped Sister, as she entered her study and slammed the door.

*I don't think that helped my career prospects*, I thought as I trudged to find Chris. I found him deep in thought in the staffroom.

"My next-door neighbour has run off with another woman," he said, though not necessarily to me. "Mary is a nice woman and she's broken-hearted. We had her round all last night. I just don't understand him," he added sadly. "They've got three kids as well. It's a tragedy. It's the same with so many then. They look at their wives and see an old woman and they want to replace them. They should look in the mirror more often and then they would see that they are old to.

He's a silly old fool."

Having got it off his chest, he sat down and looked at me. "Sorry, I'm just uptight about it. Can I help?"

Chris was a very easy man to talk to. He was very patient, extremely kind and it seemed to me, very intelligent.

"Chris, I won't go round the houses, I want my class to join in school games." I blurted my request out and waited for the arguments against.

"Why not?" replied Chris. "It seems only fair."

"Sister seemed to think it would be a major problem."

"Where's the problem? Joe would love to take the odd-bods so there is no problem with the boys. You have only got about twelve girls haven't you?" I nodded. "Well, Mrs Chang can take them, she would prefer it to the full class," added Chris confidently.

That's what I liked about Chris, an air of confidence and authority. He was more like the head than Sister Mary Benedict.

"When can we start?" I asked.

"This week," replied Chris, "I'll get it sorted."

Having solved the problem I felt very pleased, but thought I would add some insurance to the equation.

"I've got some very good news for all of you," I said to the class on my return. They all looked up hopefully. My lot didn't get much good news.

"Are we going to get a proper classroom," asked Paul, "with real desks?"

"Well no, but you're going to join the fourth year games as from this week."

Most of them were very excited, particularly Catherine O'Connor. This would probably mean that she would make the netball team. My football mad Celtic supporter from Glasgow was also very excited.

"Do you think that I could make the football team, sir?" He asked hopefully.

As he was only eight, it was unlikely this year but I had hopes of him for the future.

"Who knows Ravey, just keep trying. You know that if you're good enough I will pick you. Now, there is one problem; it's a trial. You've all got to behave yourselves, otherwise you will let me down.

"Whilst I'm on the subject of good news, there is to be a drama show for the parents this Christmas. All the classes are to enter and the best will be chosen."

"Well, that lets us out," said Sheila sadly, "we will never be chosen."

"Wait and see," I said, "I think you will. I'm a good drama teacher and you will be pleased with what we do, provided you are all prepared to work hard and trust me." They did trust me. I was their champion and they knew I would stand up for them. And they did enjoy drama.

The interesting thing about remedial teaching is that if you could find something to praise the children for so that they could feel good about themselves, then you could improve their overall performance by amazing leaps. I found drama to be the most impressive medium to work with, partly because I enjoyed taking it but also because there were no fixed rules. The children could listen to a story and improvise the words and actions. The results could be amazing. It was also nice to see them smile and for all of them to feel part of a team.

I chose for our entertainment 'The Magic Toyshop' – an old chestnut but an easy story to produce. Done well, it's very dramatic as the evil shopkeeper brings alive the various toys who dance to percussion and chosen music. It also includes effective but easy lighting and everybody could be in the cast but there would be no stars.

Unlike the bright children my lot had few inhibitions. They couldn't lose their dignity; they hadn't got any. This meant that they were capable of extraordinary work. Once we had mastered our performance, I was very pleased and rather smug.

I was worried about the new games arrangement. I didn't want it to go wrong and so I left the top team to practice skills under threat of death or maiming should they get up to anything. It was extremely unlikely that they would, as by now I had established myself as a minor god. It was not surprising really; I was twenty-four, and according to Cath, devastatingly handsome, and she wouldn't be biased, would she? I was the games teacher, and always cracking jokes.

I went first to Joe's mixed bag of wets, weeds and swots.

"How's it going?" I asked Joe.

"Well, as you can see, they can hardly kick the football. It's a doddle. I did have a thought though; do they have to play football? They might prefer other games."

"Use your initiative, Joe," I replied. "I don't see any of these playing for England, do you?" Chuckling with the thought, I moved on to the more serious second game. As one would expect it was going very well. There were no problems and Chris was coaching, refereeing and taking it easy at the same time. Sounds easy, but only a very good teacher could do it.

"Don't you trust me?" asked Chris cheekily.

"No, as it was my idea I just thought I ought to check."

At that point, someone kicked the ball the length of the pitch. In fact whoever it was almost scored.

"Who on earth kicked that?" I asked Chris. We both peered down where the ball had been kicked from.

"Which boy kicked that?" shouted Chris.

"It was me, sir!" replied a crewcut-headed, Spanish-looking boy.

"Good kick!" said Chris.

I watched for a few minutes and again the same boy kicked the ball with amazing strength.

"I'll have him next week," I said to Chris, "he looks interesting."

"You'll regret it," he replied, "he's soft as butter and scatty with it. He's a nice lad, but..."

The following week Navaro reported to my top game. He was very nervous and obviously worried.

"How would you like to play in the team?" I asked.

"What, now?" he replied incredulously.

"No, but perhaps in the future. You've got a very powerful kick and this is a big pitch. I could use you if, and it's a big if, you work hard and do as I tell you." I thought his eyes would pop out of his head.

"I'll do anything," he replied.

At last the day of the rehearsal and auditions for the family concert arrived. There had been a lot of talk about it in the staffroom while I was at football practice.

"I wouldn't get your hopes too high," confided Joe as we had a late break the day before. "They virtually have ruled you and Carol out."

"It's par for the course," I replied, "however I'll put money on the fact that we will be in the final show."

"I don't bet!" laughed Joe. "But if I did it wouldn't be fair. I don't think you've got a chance. Still, it's a pity. Your lot would love to be in it and they don't get much out of life."

He wandered off, leaving me to consider our chances. I was very confident, mainly because as my classroom backed onto the hall I had seen the efforts of most of the school. I'd also stood by the door and listened. Admittedly the children were very bright, but they did need to be helped with drama. It wasn't that easy. Either they get very silly or embarrassed and shy and mumble their words.

Sister addressed the audience from the front of the stage as usual.

"This will be a treat for all of us," she announced. "There are ten entries but only the best six will be picked for the main show. I expect best behaviour, otherwise I might disqualify any play whose class let them down." With that, she returned to her seat and the show started.

The two first year efforts weren't that good, but as one would expect, full of "Ooh, aah, isn't it sweet," type remarks. The second year efforts were poor. They were not gooey enough to get the 'aah' feeling. I thought it would be hard to justify either entry. Carol's class came next. Her young rejects were superb. They out-classed the first years, and in my opinion went straight through to the final, particularly if one judged their efforts by the applause. Three acts sure to go through, two failures, five to go with only three places left.

The two third year efforts were just about passable. They weren't good, but on the other hand they weren't bad either. Their fate would depend on the fourth years. My rabble were next. I had always been a showman, my class loved drama and threw themselves into it with great enthusiasm. The result was brilliant. At Brickhill, it would have been fairly good, nothing special, a good Drama Club presentation. However here, in the dramatic cultural desert, it was mind-blowing. I don't think they had ever seen anything like it. It was obvious that we not only qualified, but set the standard.

I didn't envy Chris and Dolly following us, particularly when I had seen their efforts. My opinion was proved to be 100% correct. Both plays died. They were dreadful. Both Chris and Dolly were brilliant teachers, but creative drama was not their thing. Sister was furious. There was much talk of no fourth year entry. Carol and I became stars. All of the staff were genuinely impressed. They knew the type of pupils we had and therefore understood the magnitude of our triumph.

I was appointed Head of Drama within days and took over teaching this subject to the fourth years the following year.

# CHAPTER 9

## *Winning Isn't Everything – but It Helps!*

*"Learning the game, learning the game,*
*I'm only learning the game."*
*– Buddy Holly*

My first year coaching the football team and been a bit of a disaster. For a start, one of the teams in the lead was being run by a non-teacher. Technically this was not allowed, however, nobody wanted to stop the boys playing football so nothing was said. The problem, though, was the coach was semi-professional. He'd played the game at a high level and his son was still playing professionally and occasionally helped him.

As far as the team was concerned, everybody agreed that they were very, very good. But that was as far as it went. The boys were very bad winners. They jeered at the losers and they were lucky, often, not to receive violence as their reward. Not only could they score goals with remarkable ease, they could also dive with the grace of ballet dancers and their game was a reflection of everything that was bad with the professional game. Playing Pearcy Road was not an experience I would ever forget.

In the two games we played them in the league, they scored nine and we scored one. As you can see, all very close scores! However well we played in the league, the best we could ever achieve was second place. Pearcy Road duly won the Sydney Black Cup and, as usual, were vile to the losers, losing even more friends in the north of the town. I just don't think I can imagine a more unpopular team.

Meanwhile, in the Cup we kept scraping home and somehow we reached the semi-finals, luckily avoiding our arch-rivals. How we won through to the final was always a surprise to me. We were not the best team but we were fit and Zelensky, our fierce Polish goalkeeper, seemed always in top form. Mind you, he got a lot of practice!

As expected, we were to play Pearcy Road in the final on the twenty-eighth of April. By this time, bad as I'd been throughout the year, I felt the boys had become very fond of me. All of us were very proud to actually have reached the final. Although I hadn't actually told anyone, Joe had let it be known that it was also my birthday. The team were annoyed with me as they had no time to buy me a card or even a present.

"What would you like for your birthday?" asked Zelensky.

I thought for a minute and then pointed to the Cup sitting on the table by the touch line.

"That's what I would like!" I shouted. "You couldn't give me a better present!"

With that, they went on the pitch and the game started. I'd never seen them play so well. Navarro, my shock player from the second game, was incredible. Every time Pearcy Road attacked, they ran straight in to him and he kicked the ball virtually to their goal, or up the wing each time. Half time came and it was still nil-nil. I don't think the Pearcy Road boys could believe it. When Navarro, instead of kicking the ball, ran with it and smashed it into their goal, it was like a fairy story. We were actually leading one-nil!

The crowd went mad. Virtually everyone was supporting us as Pearcy Road were so unpopular. The trouble was that once Navarro had scored, he forgot he was a key defender and tried to score another leaving the route to our goal completely open. Zelensky saved about four clear-cut chances; virtually a one-man team in the last few minutes and amazingly, we had won! I'd got my birthday present!

I had an even better present to come. As the Pearcy Road boys miserably entered the changing room, my boys clapped them in and told them how unlucky they'd been. I was so proud of my team; they at least knew how to win.

I'm often reminded of that Pearcy Road coach and his son. If you follow football, you've almost certainly seen the son on television. He's quite a character; at the moment he manages Peterborough United having been the manager at Barnet where he was constantly in the news, Southend and Birmingham. Fancy having to compete with two Frys, both Frank and Barry, when you don't even know the rules properly!

I hadn't seen Noel for some time, not since he gave up the management of the Bedford and District football team, but there he was, larger than life, come to watch the match. He spotted me and made a beeline across the pitch to come and talk to me.

"Hallo Tony, how are you?"

"Well, feeling a bit rough actually. I've ruptured myself and am waiting for an operation for the hernia."

"Good, good and how's the wife?"

Same old Noel, never listened to a word that was said. Good job I knew him otherwise I might have taken offense.

"Have I ever shown you my platform ticket of Llgwyngyllgogerychwyrndrobwllllantysiliogogogoch?" he said, producing a battered platform ticket out of his pocket. "You know it's the longest named place in Great Britain!"

I had in fact realised that, particularly as I'd suffered already three hours of it at his home. I looked at the ticket with interest and handed it back to him.

"You'll need a new one soon," I said cheekily, "this one's almost worn out!"

"Oh, I don't think you can get them any more, boy," he said in his strong northern Welsh accent, "but I must admit if I ever saw one I'd certainly buy one!"

I made a mental note that he ought to buy at least a dozen which would see him out the rest of his life. I wondered if he knew Hong Kong Harry. The two of them could have so much to talk about!

After the match we went round to the Rose and Crown for a glass of Charles Wells, the beer that was reputedly taken straight from the Ouse with no added ingredients! Noel was there looking very agitated.

"What's wrong Noel?" I asked.

"Bloody fools," he muttered.

I wondered which of us he was referring to. It appeared it was none of us.

"Do you know, last night boyo the Chelsea supporters rioted on the train back from Manchester?"

"Oh yes," I said, "I read about it in the paper this morning. Weren't they evicted somewhere?"

"Yes indeed, at Harlington!"

The penny dropped. Noel lived in Harlington.

"I was out taking the dog for a walk. I had to run for my life. I'd never seen so many yobs! What sort of idiot puts hundreds of yobs into Harlington?"

I cruelly thought, someone who had been subjected to three hours of *Llgwyngyllgogerychwyrndrobwllllantysiliogogogoch* at his home, but thought that was a bit mean!

"Was there much damage done?" I asked.

"Oh, broken windows everywhere and they urinated and defecated all over the town. It's a disgrace! By the time the police had got there it was hardly worth them coming, the damage had been done!"

He was quite right of course, it was cretinous. Why they didn't take the train on to a larger town and have the police meet it I just couldn't imagine. Obviously they'd panicked on the train and just simply stopped. It was typical of poor old Noel's luck that it should be his town and he should actually be out amongst it.

"Well, cheer up Noel, it's all over now. Can I buy you a beer?"

"Why, thank you Tony, but it'll have to be a swift one, I got to get back to Harlington. I've got a slide show on this afternoon!"

*Oh dear*, I thought. *Some more suckers subjected to more of Llgwyngyllgogerychwyrndrobwllllantysiliogogogoch in Noel Roberts style.*

\*

At the start of my second year at St Joseph's I felt much more confident. By now, I'd been promoted to Assistant Manager of the Bedford and District Football Team. Noel had been removed and my friend, Roger, had become the boss. My new position involved a tremendous change. I now had responsibility of opening up the school, ensuring the pitch was marked properly, providing refreshments and locking up afterwards. Admittedly, it was the same as last year but I now had a title!

Having won the Cup, I also had some status. I wasn't just another loser.

"This is going to be my year," I confided to Cath, "I'll probably never have another team like this again."

"Careful you're not like Parsee and the Butter pot," replied Cath.

It was one of her favourite stories. Apparently there was once a Parsee who lived with his wife in a little hut near a town. They were very poor, but lived in hope of improving their lot. One day, the Parsee got some cream. His wife churned it into butter and they put it in a pot and hung it on a hook above their bed. The Parsee was very pleased. As they lay in bed and looked at it he said, "Tomorrow I will take that butter into town. I will sell it for two rupees and with the two rupees I will buy a hen. The hen will lay eggs and we will breed the chicks. We will take the chickens to market and sell them for lots of rupees. Then we will buy a pig. We will fatten it and sell it to the pig-eaters for lots of rupees and before you know it we will be very, very rich. He was so delighted with his vision that he kicked his legs in the air, kicked over the pot, spilt the butter and it was all ruined.

"You silly man," said his wife. "With all your wishful thinking you have ruined us entirely. Now we have nothing at all."

"I doubt if there's a team to live with us in Bedford," I went on triumphantly.

The first match was against Roger's team. It was supposedly a friendly. My goalkeeper hadn't come back from Ireland and so I played a very large Italian. Unfortunately, although he was brilliant if the ball was kicked high to him in the goal, he seemed to have trouble bending. I was shattered. We lost very badly at home.

"Did the butter pot break?" asked Cath, sarcastically. "I warned you not to count your chickens!"

We were due to play our first league game the following Thursday. My goalkeeper, Newbury, arrived back from Ireland on the Thursday morning. I borrowed him from Chris and took him up to the pitch to see if he was up to playing. I tried some shots with my right foot and then as the ball came on the left I swung my leg and, to my delight, I found it worked well. I'd never used my left foot but today it was incredible! I must have tried twenty shots with it. I had no doubt that Newbury would be fine so he played that afternoon. With an excellent goalkeeper, we won that and all the other matches that term including the Sydney Black final, giving us the entry in to the London Cup.

I'd been experiencing some dreadful pain in my groin; a nasty burning pain. I thought I must have pulled a muscle, but whatever I did, it didn't go away, in fact it got worse. Eventually I decided to go to the surgery. Apparently, our usual doctor was on holiday so I had to see a new chap just back from Africa, a man called Smiley.

Smiley was a rather small, insignificant-looking chap with thick glasses and long gingery hair.

"You've got blood poisoning," he confidently told me, "take this prescription to the chemist. It will all be gone in a week."

Two weeks later I returned. It was worse.

"Sorry, got it wrong. It's a pulled muscle," he whined. "You need to work it. Do a lot more running and exercise."

I worked it and I pushed myself, despite the pain, but I was back two weeks later.

"I think it's a tropical thing," he suggested. "Have you been to Africa?" he asked.

As I'd never left England, I thought it was unlikely. I was also, by now, getting a little bit worried. Cath and I talked it over and decided that even though it was a bit disloyal, we would see our regular doctor.

I entered the room to see Doctor Jeffrey who was an elderly, round-faced, very competent man who you felt always knew what was wrong with you and could cope perfectly.

"Cough?" he asked. "Yes, well, you've got a hernia."

It was that easy. I felt awful, surely old men got hernias? I was a young, fit games playing teacher. How could I have a hernia?

"Yes, well as you're a games teacher I can probably get you operated on fairly quickly. Meanwhile, take this prescription to the chemist and he'll fit you up."

I felt stunned as we left. I had completely missed the 'fit you up', not realising the implications. When the chemist produced the truss I almost fainted. The thought of wearing that horrible wooden device with a great wooden ball pushing into my body to stop my inner bits coming out; oh, it made me feel sick! I was certainly grateful that I would get a quick snip rather than wait years for the operation.

The rest of the football teaching fraternity were very supportive. They looked up every joke about trusses and never missed a chance to raise a cheap laugh. As I was now all trussed up, I had to change the way I coached. Instead of a track suit and tennis shoes, I wore an overcoat, gumboots and a green hat. I looked an idiot but, as I was a god, it didn't matter!

With school matches I had to get the other teacher

to referee the game while I sat on the touch line. For normal games I sat on the centre circle, turning my chair to face the action. The boys had to play round me. None of them laughed, just took it all for granted.

After Christmas we embarked on our London adventure. We managed to win away in the first two rounds and then found we were away in the quarter finals against the team from Westminster. It had been a particularly wet February. We could hardly find a dry spot to practice and so I was very surprised when the Westminster pitch was playable. I phoned the afternoon before the match and the teacher was adamant the pitch was perfect.

"Oh it's hardly rained here at all," he assured me.

We always travelled early. I'd heard of teachers arriving just in time and the boys being two or three goals down before they'd recovered from the journey or their travel sickness. The pitch was a quagmire; it was a disgrace. It was one of the worst pitches I'd ever seen. I met an old man who appeared to be the grounds man.

"How long has the pitch been like this?" I asked casually.

"Oh, about three weeks," he replied.

"So it wasn't playable yesterday?" I asked.

"Oh no, it rained all day."

Having confirmed my suspicions, I wondered what his game was. The young teacher arrived, who looked to me like a slime ball. He was short with greasy hair, and a particularly nasty little black moustache. Needless to say, I was not biased in any way!

"Sorry about this," he started, "it rained overnight. It was all right yesterday afternoon," he added as an afterthought. "But, don't worry, your boys will get a game. We've got a cinder pitch and I've got permission to use it."

He smiled, a smug self-satisfied sort of smile which said, "I've just stuffed you and there's nothing you can do about it!"

It was obvious that that was his plan. Playing on a cinder pitch would give us absolutely no chance of winning.

"No, sorry. We won't play on the cinders. My boys have never played on that surface before; they wouldn't know what to do, and anyway, we've got the wrong boots. You said this pitch was playable so let's play."

"You must be joking! You can't play on that!" he said jeeringly at me.

"Well, it's your choice. Either it's a swop or I'll report you. I've talked to the groundsman so I know what you're up to. Play on the proper pitch or we'll go straight back!"

He had no choice and he knew it. We would have been awarded the match for his cheating which would be a lot easier than playing.

So, that's how we ended up playing on a mud bath. I took the boys to one side. I had a very good idea.

"Now, if you win the toss, take the kick-off," I told my horrified team. "Here's what you do: kick the ball high up in the air so it drops as near to their penalty box as possible. All of the forwards then run to get as close as you can underneath it. It will plop in the mud and stop. With any luck you can bundle it into the goal and from then onwards every time you get the ball, kick it high in the air so it will drop down in the same way and try the same trick!"

Theory is one thing but practice is another! I couldn't be more pleased when it worked exactly as I'd said. We were one goal up in less than a minute. In five minutes we were three-nil up. After that they worked out what was happening but it was too late. We eventually won four-two and we were in the semi-finals for the first time in Bedford's history! My flat-footed centre-forward had scored a hat-trick, which he would remember all his life. Admittedly, the game was more like rugby but who cares? A win is a win!

*

The school concert was a great success. The only blot on the landscape was that, according to the speech of Sister Mary Benedict, she had done all the work and we'd just turned up. But the, that was par for the course, she even apparently picked my football team!

The evening went very well. All the chosen classes performed well and the audience loved the show. At the end of all of it the Canon came up on stage to draw the winning raffle ticket. The main prize was a very, very large box of chocolates.

"I am sure you're all delighted with the wonderful entertainment we've just seen and would like to show the children and their teachers your appreciation in the usual way."

After the applause died down, his attention turned

to the raffle draw.

"Now, as you know, all the money you've raised through this raffle goes to the orphanage, so we're very grateful for your support." With that, he drew the winning ticket.

"It's a hundred and seventy-nine red," he called out. A little ferret of a man came up to collect his prize.

"Congratulations, Mr. O' Riley," smarmed the Cannon. "I know you're going to donate it to the Saint Ethelburg's draw next week."

The Canon had kept a firm hold on the chocolates. Mr. Oriel obviously had other ideas.

"No, I'll be taking the chocolates home for my wife!" the little Irishman replied.

As he spoke he grabbed at the box. However the Canon was not that easily beaten.

"I'm sure you don't mean that!" he said, pulling the chocolates back towards him.

"I do!" said Mr. Oriel, holding on very tightly to his chocolates.

"Surely, you wouldn't want to let the priest down at Saint Ethelburg's?" repeated the Canon, who by now was very red in the face.

"No, I want my prize," insisted the now fairly angry Mr. Oriel.

For a few minutes they struggled with the box until at last Oriel snatched it and went back to his seat. The audience were trying, in some cases unsuccessfully, not to laugh!

Chris and Joe were laughing about it in the staffroom the next day.

"Do you know the funny thing about those chocolates, Tony?" asked Joe.

"Do you mean other than the hand-to-hand fighting on the stage?" I replied.

"Oh, they've been raffled at least twenty times. The Canon will be furious, he'll need to find a new big prize!"

"Do you mean that's happened twenty times already?" I asked incredulously.

"Previously undefeated in twenty bouts!" remarked Chris.

I had to hand it to the Canon, he very rarely missed a trick!

"By the way," said Joe, "remember you're playing St Joseph's, Luton next week although I shouldn't think you're much bothered by that this year?"

Every year we played St Joseph's, Luton in an annual contest between the two schools. Every team was expected to do their duty, i.e. win! It was a bit like Celtic and Rangers. With the fantastic team I had, I hardly need even consider St Joseph's. Admittedly, I had the problem of the hernia but, even better, I could sit and watch the slaughter.

The game started exactly as I'd expected. From the kick-off we swarmed all over them. Virtually the whole of my team was in their penalty box! This was probably not a good idea as they broke away and we were then one-nil down. To our disbelief, the pattern was repeated three more times. I'd never seen a more one-sided match yet we were losing four-nil! The Luton teacher looked like the cat with the cream, and why not? He must have known it was a smash and grab robbery.

However, with six minutes to go, my lot scrambled in a consolation goal. You could see in his face: four-one. It's a good victory. From the kick-off we grabbed the ball and it was four-two. Still, you could see it in his face: a four-two win isn't bad. At four all, his face showed concern, at five-four, disappointment, six-four disillusionment and finally at seven-four, total disbelief! It would seem my boys suddenly realised they had to get the ball between the two wooden posts! I certainly felt sorry for him, but at the same time very relieved. I hated the dog-house!

"Where's that book I lent you, Christine?" demanded Sister Mary Benedict.

"Ooh, what book?" stuttered Christine in a very surprised tone.

"You know very well, what book! The one on the saints. Where is it? We need it at once."

"I didn't borrow the book about the saints," protested Christine.

"Ach, you young girls, you're all the same! You never remember anything!"

With that she stormed out of the staffroom. Poor Christine, she looked really upset! She got up and slowly left the room. "I've got some marking to do," she said miserably.

A few minutes later, the door burst open again.

"And why was I not informed about the change in

the swimming timetable?" Sister glared at Chris and added, "After all I'm supposed to be the Head of this school!"

"I told you last month, Sister," said Chris in his usual calm and confident manner, "I think you'll find it minuted. Why not ask Mrs. Lincoln?"

"Hmm!" spluttered Sister as she promptly left.

My relationship with Sister deteriorated rapidly over the time I spent at the school. It seemed to me that every time I spoke to her I discovered her further bigotry.

"I'll not recommend that girl to go up to St. Gregory's," she insisted, "her mother's a prostitute!"

"That's not quite fair," argued Chris, "admittedly, she goes out with men but then her husband had left her."

"She's a filthy prostitute and you well know it!" shouted Sister.

"But what about the girl herself? She's a delight, she works hard, keeps herself very smart. I've never heard her swear, surely she deserves her chance? If she doesn't go to St Gregory's its Silver Jubilee Girls and that will finish her."

I was extremely angry. Silver Jubilee was a dreadful school. I knew it well as Cath had started her teaching career there. Marie was a decent girl, I suspected she knew what her mother was and desperately wanted to be different.

"We can't have tarts like that in our schools," continued Sister, "it just won't do!"

"Is this what being a Christian's about?" I asked

sarcastically. "It doesn't seem what it's supposed to be about."

Despite all our best efforts, Maria was rejected and was forced to leave the church system. It was typical of my hypocritical Head.

*

John Brown, my predecessor in the Sports Department, had started his teaching career at Brickhill and obviously, like me, was influenced by the devious old devil himself, John Gunning. Needless to say, with two games teachers coming from one school to another, there was a great inter-school rivalry. It was always sweet, winning against your old school and particularly so as John considered himself a brilliant football coach. Despite this rivalry we always tried to show the boys that it was important to give everything on the field, but the game was over as soon as the final whistle blew. John and I made the point of always standing together as friends to ensure that the game was always played in a tough but fair and friendly manner. It was easy for me because St Joseph's seemed to have the jinx on poor old John's teams. Match after match was played and the result was always the same: St Joseph's always won. John must have hated it but he managed to hide his emotions so we remained good friends.

In my final year at St Joseph's, John had a wonder team, a team to die for! They were brilliant! He had two brothers that were professional footballers' sons and one lad who went on to play for a first division side. In all, it was probably the best team I'd ever seen in the district. The town was divided into two leagues: north and south. At Christmas the two leading teams played each other for the right to represent Bedford in the London Individual Cup. St Joseph's had dominated this competition locally having reached the quarter finals with John Brown and then, with my wonder team, getting to the semi-finals. This year, the difference between Brickhill and St Joseph's was chalk and cheese.

Brickhill had played nine games, won all nine, scoring forty-eight goals and conceding three. We, on the other hand, had played nine, won five, drawn two and lost three. We'd scored twenty-two goals and conceded sixteen. Even the games we'd won were a bit iffy. In the Cup we'd been beaten five-one at home by a very poor team. Still, we were top of the table by one point so we had the right to play in the big game.

It was a game John was really looking forward to. He'd waited a long time for his triumph and was relishing the trip to London to show what he could do.

"Is it worth us turning up?" I asked on the phone the day before the match. John chuckled.

"Have you actually lost a match this year?" I enquired. "Or let's put it another way. Have you not won a match by less than three goals?"

"Come on Tony," said John, "you know anything can happen in a game of football. We're not that good!"

Although he said it, the words didn't hold any conviction. It wouldn't have surprised me if he'd booked a coach for the first match.

"I'll try to be a good loser," I continued, "as long as you promise not to score ten goals!"

"I think I can safely promise that!" he laughed, probably thinking to himself could he actually get ten? That would be something!

John had not won that much silverware and he was obviously looking forward to having the Draper's Shield prominently showing in Brickhill's entrance.

The game was to be played in Goldington Green in the north of Bedford, which meant it was a ground which Brickhill would know and gave them a further advantage.

"Did you know that Brickhill had played two practice matches on the pitch already?" confided Roger. "John's leaving nothing to chance, is he?"

"Well, we can only do our best," I replied. "If it's form and class we need to go by. We'll do well to avoid a fantastic thrashing. I'm not going to be popular tomorrow with Sister Mary Benedict, that's for sure!"

I gathered my team round me before the kick-off.

"All right, we know they're good. I'm not going to try to con you. They've got some very good players indeed. However, they have never beaten us since I've been here and they'll fear us despite all their fantastic results. You'll also be a much stronger and fitter side so try to run them off their feet. Tackle them very hard and give a hundred and fifty per cent effort. As for their stars, I don't think they're very brave. Tackle them hard every time you get a chance, try to shake their confidence. The main thing is: go out there and win!"

The speech was a bit like the Henry V speech on the eve of Agincourt. It certainly was a rabble rouser!

In case any of my readers think I was suggesting cheating or anything underhand when I suggested that they tackled hard, I can assure you that I only meant fair tackles. I'd learnt that some boys didn't like being caught with the ball and even if they had brilliant skills they would get rid of the ball rather quickly rather than risk being tackled. This meant you could always defuse that player.

The pattern of the game was exactly as one would have expected: wonderful skills from Brickhill and enormous effort from St Joseph's. There was only really one team on the field and we were lucky to be only two nil down at half time. The interesting thing I had noticed was that the Brickhill boys were tiring noticeably. They'd had to work much harder than for any other game, and probably expected us to lie down in the second half. I, on the other hand, knew that we were better in the final quarter as we were very fit. Walking to all the matches and daily practices ensured that no team could outlast us.

"You've done very well," I told the lads while they sucked their oranges, "this game can still be won. They don't look a fit side so it's going to get easier for you; step up the pace, run harder, make them work and, who knows, you could still pull off the shock result of the year."

At that point the Canon arrived.

"I think you need my help," he said in that sing-song voice of his. "I'll have to bless the boots. I've had considerable success with boot blessing!" he reassured me seriously.

I had great trouble not laughing.

"Well, if you think it will help," I mumbled, trying not to snigger, "I'll leave you to it!"

It was like something from a comedy film! I really couldn't believe he was serious. However he was a hundred per cent serious and blessed the boots for each member of the team. The other thing that struck me was none of the boys laughed.

The second half started and it was obvious that a change had taken place. Brickhill had expected to cruise and were shocked how hard we hit them. As the minutes went by we became stronger and stronger. Halfway through the half, Munday, one of my favourite lads, scored a beauty of a goal. This really rattled Brickhill. Suddenly they were in a game for the first time that year.

Just when I'd started to hope for a miracle (it couldn't have been the blessing could it?) Munday started to limp very badly. It was obvious I'd have to get him off.

"Munday," I shouted, "come off! Your leg's obviously very painful."

He did a Lord Nelson on me, turning deaf (instead of blind) and disappeared to the side of the field. I walked round and tried again.

"Munday, I want you off now!" I bellowed.

Again, deaf ears and he changed sides yet again. I was walking round to get near to him again, he tackled a Brickhill boy and rushed towards their goal. The Brickhill defense froze. It was like Munday was the only one able to move. It seemed like a lifetime but was probably only a second or so. Everything started to move again and three Brickhill boys desperately tried to stop Munday but it was too late. The ball was sitting at the back of the net. Virtually immediately after the restart the final whistle blew meaning extra time: a further twenty minutes' play.

I gathered the team round me.

"Munday, you've been very stupid. Your leg is more important than a game of football."

Meanwhile, his father, who had been watching, managed to free his leg from the cramp that had caused his problem.

"Next time, do as I say and come off! Now, as for the rest of you, it's your game if you want it. You're the strongest and fittest, you've come back from two-nil down, and you're now the favourites. Get out there and play exactly as you've been going throughout the game. I want that shield; go and get it for me!"

It was again a rabble rousing speech.

"By the way, Munday, well done!"

The team returned to the pitch and I turned to Munday senior.

"You must be very proud of your son," I said.

"Yep!" he replied modestly. "He's not too bad, is he?"

Twenty minutes later we were presented with the Sydney Black Trophy. Munday (who else had scored the s winning goal?) had completed his hat-trick and, cruelly, John Gunning's dreams were shattered.

"I've never seen anything like it," said Roger after the match, "the only reason you won is your boys just didn't know they were beaten. It was just willpower – an amazing result!"

I really did feel sorry for John, he just couldn't believe it. He took it very well but he knew he'd never have a team like that one probably ever again.

"I told you I had great success with my boot blessing," insisted the Canon, "you'll have to tell me when you need me again."

There was a lot of superstition about our team efforts. There were, obviously, the usual jokes going round about us playing with twelve men. Some claimed that we had two goalkeepers and the second goalkeeper, the spirit they saw lurking in the back of the net, was unfair. On one occasion it was alleged that Sister twitched her nose and a ball heading for our goal deviated rapidly and missed. The real old chestnut was when they came out with a broom and swept our goalposts to break any invisible shield we'd put on to stop the ball going in. It was all done with good humour and Sister always used to play up to it which is why, locally, she was thought of as a sweet old nun who drank sherry. Of course, none of those people who thought that had to work with her!

I'd never been very good at athletics. I wasn't the graceful athletic sort so I had to rely on good old-fashioned encouragement when I helped with the teams. Joe, however, was an exceptional high jump coach. I assumed that as he was a long lean-limbed skinny chap that he'd been a high jumper of quality but never actually asked him.

"Have we got any winners, Joe?" I asked one lunchtime as I returned from bashing my head against a brick wall or, as others would describe it, coaching the non-cricketing world to play cricket!

"Oh, yes indeed!" said Joe, in that beautiful Irish accent of his. "We've got a treasure, Anne Devalley, she's only a third year but she's incredible. She won the third year championship last year and I think I think she'll win the fourth year area title this year."

"She's that good? I know that Carol said she was fantastic at netball. So she's going to be a star then, and we'll have her for two more years. That's brilliant!"

"You'll have to come and watch, Tony," said Joe.

"I'll look forward to it, I'll come tomorrow." With that I went back to planning my revolutionary cricket team. It wasn't as bad as I'd made out in the staffroom. I knew we had no chance against Brickhill, although one could always hope.

I hadn't actually started very well with the school sports. As master in charge, I introduced a steeple chase. We had them at Brickhill and they'd worked very well. It did seem a good idea at the time however I never anticipated eight boys arriving to walk the bar at the same time, nor did I expect them to compete quite so hard! Luckily, the boy who was thrown off only broke his wrist and the concussion wasn't too bad!

The next lunchtime, as promised, I went up to see Joe's champion elect. He was right, she was incredible. In fact she was so good she won the event three years running, breaking the records each time. Some years later I noticed in the paper that after getting married she represented England in the high jump.

I worked at the serious running, particularly the relay. It seemed to me that time spent on the changeover would be very worthwhile. One of the girls in my class was very good at running but she always came second. Her dream was to beat the school champion but even in her last year she finished second. This, however, meant she ran for the school in the Borough Sports.

In the first round our champion unexpectedly was eliminated, although Elizabeth managed to scrape through to the second round. When she heard the news that the other girl was eliminated it was almost as if a weight had been taken from her. She ran the race of her life and, for once, came first. The champion of Bedford and District! Even better, it was probably her unexpected points that enabled us to be the top school that year. She must have been the proudest girl in the world!

We were sitting in the staffroom the next day drinking tea, when I said to Joe: "I really can't take it in that Elizabeth won yesterday. She'd never even been close before."

"Ah yes," chuckled Joe, "but do you know the Canon blessed her plimsolls before the race. She probably had divine inspiration!"

"I think I'd better get him to bless the cricket plimsolls of my team each game," I added mischievously, "we could do with some help!"

# CHAPTER 10

## *Goodbye Bedford*

*"The long and winding road*
*That leads to my door."*

Father John looked like he'd come straight from a movie set. He was devilishly handsome; tall with black hair and had that delightful soft Irish accent which, when he spoke very slowly, captivated the whole room. He had a twinkle in his eye and was the sort of priest that could even convert me to Catholicism. He was the Canon's main assistant and, as such, had no church. When asked what his duty was, he always replied: "I am the dogsbody. I do things that nobody else wants to do."

He liked coming to St Joseph's because not only did he get a warm welcome, he also got copious cups of tea, biscuits and any other food that was lying around. If he was lucky he'd get a slice of Mrs Connolly's famous chocolate cake. This cake was remarkable: a really rich chocolate sponge cut in two and filled with a rich fudge chocolate filling and then covered at a great depth with fudge icing. It was the sort of cake that if you ate more than one slice, you were likely to regret it. It was very icky but at the same time very delicious. Father John was particularly fond of this chocolate cake. To be honest, he was fond of anything edible.

"They don't feed you properly," said Mrs Connolly, "a young man like you should be eating more."

"Oh I get my fair share," said Father John, "the trouble is I'm greedy and want more than my fair share."

It was the football pool syndicate time again and Joe was collecting the money. Virtually all of the staff were in the syndicate with the exception of the Sisters however, surprisingly, Father John was also a member.

"What would you do if you won?" I asked Chris.

"Oh that's not hard," said Chris wistfully. "I'd give up teaching, look after my garden, go for more holidays and spoil myself."

"Sounds good to me," I said, "what about you, Joe?"

"Oh, I'd go back to Ireland, buy myself a little place and grow my own food. I'd be self-sufficient. What would you do, Tony?"

"I don't know really, perhaps make my stamp business into a national name, who knows? Become the new Stanley Gibbons!"

"Do you think you could do it?" asked Chris.

"Who knows?" I said. "I've got the confidence, but whether I've got the ability, that's a different matter. The one thing about being young is that you never lack confidence."

Chris laughed. "One thing you'll find as you get more experienced and therefore better, your confidence will go. It's a strange phenomenon."

During all this exchange of ideas, Sister Michael had been sitting quietly thinking. Finally she came out with the question that had been puzzling her.

"I suppose, Father, it would be very difficult for you if you won the pools? Deciding what good cause to give the money to?"

"Oh no," said Father with a chuckle, "it wouldn't be difficult at all. I know exactly what I'd do."

"What would that be?" asked Sister Michael.

"Well, I'd go to the Caribbean and play golf. I've always wanted to play golf in the Caribbean."

"Ah, you're teasing me!" said Sister Michael, and laughed.

"Oh no, I'm deadly serious. I enjoy golf!"

"But don't let the Canon hear you say that," said Sister Michael, "he might not appreciate it!"

With that we all chuckled, the bell went, and off we all went back to lessons.

"Have you gone and lost those eleven plus papers again, Dolly? Where are they? They've got to be returned so I need them at once!" hectored Sister one afternoon break.

"If you remember, Sister," said Dolly sweetly, "Chris had them and, if I remember, he took them back last week!"

"Oh did he?" muttered Sister as she left the Common Room.

It was unusual for me to be in the staffroom, but the main thing I learnt was don't sit near the door. Sister was never wrong so the nearest to the door got the blame. It must have looked very odd to visitors that everybody sat at the far end of the staffroom.

Father John breezed in with an enormous self-satisfied grin on his face.

"Well, we proved the point today," he said triumphantly.

"What's that?" I asked.

"Well, we played the Church of England at golf and we won! That shows we're better. I mean if God had wanted them to win he'd have helped them not us!"

"Oh, you're awful," said Sister Michael, "as if God could care who wins a game of golf!"

"Oh, there you're wrong Sister, golf's important. He'd know that!"

"Do you know, Father John," I said, "you're the sort of priest who might convert me to become a Catholic!"

"Who'd want you?" chuckled Father John, "we're not that desperate!"

"Oh, thank you very much!" I said. "That's the last chance you'll get from me!"

Everyone laughed and they went back to eating the delicious chocolate cake provided, once again, by Mrs Connolly.

After half-term, the main topic of conversation at break-time was whether in fact the school play, being produced by Eileen Moore, was actually being staged. Eileen was producing the play because it was mainly a musical based around her superb choir, but there had been problems.

"There's been another awful row," said Mrs Connolly, "between Eileen and Sister Mary Benedict."

"Oh dear, not another one!" said Sister Michael.

"I think Eileen has walked out and won't do it," said Mrs Connolly, "that's what it sounded like any way!"

"But who'll take over the production?" I asked worriedly, knowing for a fact that it would be me as I'd now acquired the reputation for drama. Drama is one thing, singing is another. I always try to avoid singing as I couldn't actually hit a note if I tried.

"I don't think there's any chance anyone could do it," said Chris, "it's far too musically based and it's really Eileen's work."

"Where does that leave me?" I asked, puzzled.

"And me," said Carol.

We were also producing a work to go on the same night as our remedial classes weren't to be included in the main festivities. I was doing a non-scripted pantomime and Carol was doing a fairy story.

"I don't know," said Chris, "we've sold the tickets and invited the parents. I suppose you'll have to go whatever happens!"

"Well, that should be quite a good entertainment for the school. A full school production based on two remedial classes!"

"Well, let's see what happens anyway," said Chris calmly, "perhaps Eileen will change her mind."

With that, Father John walked in looking white as a sheet.

"Are you all right, Father?" said Sister Michael. "You look really ill."

"Oh, I'm not ill Sister, thank you, just a little bit shocked, I've just had some disturbing news."

"What's the problem?" asked Sister Michael. "Is there anything we can do to help?"

"No, I'm afraid no-one can do anything to help. I've just got news I'm going to be transferred."

"Oh, that's a shame," said Sister Michael.

"Where are you going to?" enquired Mrs Connolly.

"Corby New Town," said Father John sadly.

"Oh dear!" said Joe. "I understand your problem. That's not the best place to go to, is it?"

"No," said Father John, "not the best place. It might even be described as the worst place! I'm not looking forward to it at all."

"But why?" asked Sister Michael. "You're doing so well here!"

"I think the Canon thought I needed more experience, real church work. He thought I ought to learn how to run Bingo and church bazaars and such-like."

He sat down with his cup of tea and biscuit. I had a sneaking suspicion he was just a little bit too popular. He was loved everywhere throughout the Catholic community in Bedford and I suspect that there was an element of jealousy. But then I didn't know anything about the working of the Catholic Church, it may just be the next vacancy came up and he had to take it.

"When are you going?" asked Sister Michael.

"Next week," replied Father John rather sadly.

"Well, you'd better have another slice of my chocolate cake," said Mrs Connolly.

Father John smiled and looked much more cheerful and tucked in to a large slice of the fudge cake.

It was to be a long time before I saw Father John again.

Meanwhile I had offended the Evil Penguin yet again.

"Tony, it's just not good enough! How dare you arrange a football match and not get my permission? You take too much on yourself, what have you got to say?"

Sister was obviously not in a good mood, my answer was not going to help.

"You were not in school last Thursday and Friday, if you remember, Sister," I added with forced politeness. "I-I couldn't wait as it was a Cup match so I cleared it with Chris. I'm sorry I-I should have told you."

I knew Chris would have told her and cleared it, but it really didn't matter. It would serve no useful purpose in telling her that.

"Yes, you should have, it's typical of your cavalier attitude. Don't let it happen again!" She left triumphant as ever. After all, she was never wrong.

"I did tell her," said Chris later that afternoon, "but as you know, it's no good reminding her, it only makes things worse."

I walked in to the staffroom next morning, hot and sweaty, after a particularly strenuous practice, delighted to see, yet again, another chocolate cake from Mrs Connolly.

"Tony, look who's here," said Joe, "it's Father John."

I was horrified. I hardly recognised him. He looked really ill, his face was covered in spots. He was virtually unrecognisable from that handsome young man who had been here a few months ago.

"How are you Father? It's nice to see you."

"Oh, I'm fine," replied Father John, "a little tired, but then the parish is very large and there's lots of problems."

I was shocked. All the swagger and confidence had gone. He spoke almost with an air of defeat. I'd never seen such a transformation in my life. There was one thing, I thought, I'd never take a teaching job in Corby!

Once again it was job-searching time. I'd learnt all I could, I felt, from St Joseph's and wanted to get back into the main stream of teaching and at the same time I thought that I was ready to become a Deputy Headmaster.

Now that we'd got the big powerful Humber Sceptre, we felt more confident about searching for a new place to live and also delivering my first day covers. I say 'we' but, of course, I didn't drive so Cath was my chauffeur. I was a very good passenger and navigator. We vaguely looked at the Times Educational Supplement to look for jobs and spent our weekends driving to distant parts of the country to look at the school where the job was advertised and also the area to see if we wanted to live there.

The one thing we learnt, was never go by names. There was a very attractive job advertised in the romantic sounding town of Gainsborough in Lincolnshire. There was also another one on the Lincolnshire coast so we thought we'd drive up and to see what we thought of the area. Lincolnshire had, at that time, an enormous advantage. Houses were very cheap, and it meant we could have bought a much nicer house and improved our quality of life. However, there's always a downside; if we ever wanted to move back we would find it almost impossible to raise the money for a house elsewhere and so we had to be sure we really wanted to live in the area.

We weren't terribly excited about the Lincolnshire sand dunes where the first school was based. It was very isolated and remote and we couldn't see us fitting in there and so we drove on to Gainsborough. It's amazing how you get a picture of a place in your mind. Certainly in our minds we saw Gainsborough as an unspoilt market town perhaps, possibly a bit like Rye or Stanford; rural and charming. We were not prepared for the industrial town it turned out to be. I noticed with interest the other day in the paper a headline which said "Is this the cheapest house in

England?" Apparently, somebody had just bought a terraced house for fifteen hundred pounds in Gainsborough in 1997.

I started applying in the first instances for rather ambitious jobs. I can remember feeling quite put out that I didn't get an interview for a Group Ten school – not surprising when you consider that St Joseph's was only a Group Five!

I found the going very difficult. Interviews were hard to come by and what was even more disturbing was that on some occasions I had wasted my time going in the first place. I remember being in one staffroom waiting for my interview, talking to one of the other applicants.

"Of course you know it's all a waste of time, don't you?" he said.

"Why's that?" I asked.

"Well old Jones has been appointed already really, all but the shouting. They were told that they have got to have interviews so they are having them. You are the token from away. The rest of us are locals, but it's all a waste of time. Still at least you got your day off and your expenses, didn't you?" he added, as if this would make it all right.

I didn't think that travelling all day trying to get a job that didn't exist was something I was very pleased with. I hadn't realised that many jobs had to be advertised even if the school wanted to appoint somebody from within. It was a hard lesson to learn that even if you got an interview, there was no guarantee that there was a job at the end of it.

Against all the odds, I finally apparently got a job

at a local primary school. After a while I got the idea of how well I was interviewing and on this occasion I felt very pleased with the way things had gone. I was phoned up by F.W.G. and asked to come and see him at the school. When I arrived he offered me a glass of sherry and told me to sit down.

"Well Tony, you're a very, very lucky young man."

"Oh yes," I said, "and how's that?"

"You have got yourself a Deputy Headship and in my opinion you are far too young! However I'm sure that you will make the most of it and do very well. I just wanted to have a few words with you to make sure that you understand how lucky you are and what you've got to do."

I was somewhat staggered. Nothing had been told to me officially, but nevertheless it was inconceivable that F.W.G. would have got it wrong. He was very much a part of the local scene and would have known the Headmaster of the school I was applying to very well.

"Don't be too cocky!" he continued. "You don't know much at the moment, but you are learning fast. Get your head down and listen and learn. It's important that you understand the administration. Make sure that you can fill in the forms and can back up the Head when he is not there. If you do that well, then who knows? You may be one of the youngest Heads in the district! But remember, you are young. You are inexperienced and you will need to learn."

I thanked him for his kindness and went rushing home to tell Cath the good news. To celebrate, we went out and had a meal in a restaurant we had not tried before, where we experienced Calabrese in white sauce for the first time. It probably came out of the deep freeze, but for us it was something exotic. It came with Beef Bourguignon, very continental! We had a nice bottle of wine and happily drifted back home. The next day my new Headmaster phoned St Joseph's. The school secretary, knowing that I had had news, sent someone to inform me, but before I could take the call I was told that it wasn't for me after all. It was for Sister MB. The phone call lasted for over an hour. I don't know what was said during that time but the net result was that I didn't get the job.

A couple of days later Sister MB asked me how I had got on with Mr Smith.

"I haven't seen him for years," she said, "I really must give him a phone call and ask him how he is."

I told her politely that I had failed yet again and I couldn't help noticing the smirk in her face as she offered me her condolences. She hurried back into her room. I couldn't believe it. As I said to Cath that evening, she was on the phone for over an hour and yet still she claimed she hadn't talked to him for over two years.

I felt completely gutted. What on earth had she told him on the phone? I was a Communist, a pervert, a trouble maker, a useless teacher, a bad organiser, a drunkard, and a womaniser? It didn't need much, just a few hints here and there on the phone. Nothing that could be subsequently proved but enough to do the job. I went back to see F.W.G. to see if he could possibly have got it wrong. I entered his study and, for some reason, he seemed smaller than usual. I think he must have been very embarrassed.

"I don't know what to say, Tony," he said, rather slowly. "As far as I was concerned, from what I'd heard, you'd got the job. There was no doubt. There was no misunderstanding. Obviously something happened afterwards that changed his mind."

"I think it may well have been something to do with a phone call to Sister Mary Benedict," I replied bitterly. "They were on the phone for an hour and, obviously, whatever she said made him change his mind."

"Ah, that's very bad," he replied, "because obviously it means that any job you get you're vulnerable to her comments. Can you think why she'd do such a thing?" he enquired.

"Well we don't really get on but I would have thought that would have been even more reason to get rid of me. I'm not a Catholic, I've got no future in her school because no non-Catholic will get promotion. Logically, it would seem better to get a Catholic to do the job. There's no shortage of games teachers. It all seemed very simple to me."

"How many cups have you won for football since you've been there, Tony?"

"Oh, I don't know. We've won the League twice and will probably win it this year. We've won the Cup. We've won the Draper's Shield twice and we've won the Sydney Black Cup twice so I suppose we've won six already and it will probably be seven in a few weeks."

"What about cricket?"

"Well, we haven't won anything. We've been the runner up for the last three years, as you know... Oh,

I see what you're getting at!"

"It doesn't really matter that you don't get on, Tony. You're winning, which is why I say you've got a serious problem."

"What do I do about it? After all, if I can't get out of the school, she's always going to be my Head teacher."

"Well, it's a bit dramatic, but I would drop her from the references. Use me and why not ask Chris if he'll be your referee?"

It all seemed very dramatic but I suppose it was worth considering. I thanked him for his advice and went back to school. A few days later I had my famous talk with Sister Michael.

"She's just not a Christian, Tony!" she said. "Don't worry about promotion, just get yourself a job anywhere. It'll be for the best, I promise you!"

Sister Michael's words, combined with F.W.G's warning, convinced me that I had to drop her as a reference. That night, Cath and I talked it over and decided to apply for three Deputy Headships, two in Kent where we decided we liked the area, and one in the Midlands to be nearer to Cath's parents.

We duly filled in the forms. I have to admit I cheated. Cath wrote them for me. Her writing was absolutely brilliant whereas mine qualified me as a doctor! We posted the applications off and hopefully waited for the results.

The big end of term football showdown was due to be played that evening. We had won the League yet again, the third time in succession, and were due to play John Gunning's Brickhill for the right to be champions of the town. Needless to say, after the shock result with the Sydney Black Cup, John was determined that he would win the Draper's Shield. The year before we'd shared it; neither side able to score a goal. But in all fairness, there should be only one result tonight, Brickhill were a much better team than St Joseph's and it was unlikely we could pull off a shock again – or could we? I was always optimistic. Who knows, I might be able to weave a spell? After all, we'd never lost to Brickhill since I'd been there and it was just possible that something could go for us on the night. It with this sort of spirit that I phoned John to wish him the best of luck as the oncoming game.

I phoned John up to have the usual competitive chat and after trading insults, I wished him the best of luck.

"May the best team win," I said, expecting his to win but hoping for the best. He again wished me the best of luck.

"The main thing is, let's hope it is a super game that all the crowd will enjoy, and show everyone what can be done with junior football!"

As I put the phone down, to my amazement, I found Sister Mary Benedict behind me.

"It's always been the same, Tony. You're disloyal! You've never thought of the school. You've always preferred Brickhill. Disloyal! That's what you are and you always have been!"

I honestly couldn't believe what I was hearing! Firstly, Sister couldn't begin to understand my character. I hated losing, as far as I was concerned, St Joseph's came first, second and third but you had to observe the niceties. She continued with her stream of vitriol. I couldn't really hear it properly, I just was so upset. Almost in tears, I replied to her: "You'll have my letter of resignation in the morning, Sister. I don't want to talk about it any more," and walked out, and somehow managed to get on to the school bus and get home.

When I got home, I found I could hardly stop shaking. I was so angry but so upset at the same time. I don't think I've ever felt quite so low. How could she say such a thing to me? Disloyal? I'd never been disloyal. I also knew my character and I would write the letter of resignation and hand it in the morning. At that point I had no other job to go to but at least I had the stamp business.

"Here's the letter I promised you last night, Sister. I am giving you a terms notice as per my contract." With that, I slapped the letter down on the desk, feeling a bit like the Prisoner, the futuristic TV series starring Patrick McGoohan who slammed in his notice at the beginning of every episode.

"And what do you think you'll do then?" sneered Sister MB. "You won't get promotion in teaching, I'll see to that!"

"I don't need to teach!" I replied arrogantly. "I'm a brilliant businessman. I'll make my business grow into something worthwhile." I replied with much more confidence than I felt at the time. "Now if you'll excuse me, I've got cricket practice." With that I swept out feeling that for once I had won the day.

The cricket practice went well, which was good, because I was determined to win that cricket shield.

"Don't worry," said Cath sympathetically, "we'll sort it all out. I'm still teaching, it's no different from having a baby. You've got a business, it's done very well part-time. Just think what it could do if you were working at it all the time."

I knew what she said made sense but I was so upset that I could hardly drag myself up to even talk about it.

The game itself was played at the Eerie, the Bedford Town Football Club where Bedford, at that time, were playing top southern league football. It was a very big pitch; the larger the pitch, the more it allowed true skill to show its class. I don't know what I said to the boys before the game. I hadn't got much to give and I honestly wasn't in my usual cheerful and hopeful form. The game went very badly. Whatever magic I gave them, obviously, was lacking. The team fell apart. We lost five-nil; the biggest margin of defeat ever recorded in the Sydney Black Cup.

John was over the moon. The first time he'd ever beaten St Joseph's and by a score of five-nil. He tried to be a good winner but his triumphant grin said it all. I didn't know what on earth I was to say to the boys back in the changing room. I slowly walked back trying to pull myself together, trying to think of something reassuring to say to them. I walked to the door with all the cares of the world on my shoulders.

"It's the cricket season, isn't it?" asked Munday in a much more cheerful voice than I could ever have imagined.

"Yes it is," I replied wearily.

"St Joseph's have never won the Cricket Shield, have they sir?" continued Munday in a very positive tone.

"No, we've never won the Cricket Shield, though we've been runner-up three times," I replied a lot more cheerily than previously.

"Brickhill hold the Cricket Shield, don't they?" said Munday indicating the direction his brain was going.

"Yes, they have held it for the last three years."

"Wouldn't it be nice to take it off them, sir?"

"Yes, it would be, very nice."

"Could we have cricket practice tomorrow, sir?"

"Yes, Munday, that would be an excellent idea!"

Although many of the footballers were not necessarily cricket players, for once they were united. "Let's get that Shield this year!" they said. They immediately started talking about bowling, fielding, catching, and the various teams that we would have to beat in order to win the Shield. I would never have believed that one boy could have raised my spirits so easily. I've often wondered what happened to Munday. He ought to have gone far. He was a very clever boy with enormous determination and a very, very pleasant personality. I would always be in his debt for getting me through one of the most difficult situations in my teaching career.

The next day I duly gave in my notice and started the cricket practice as promised, which we hoped would eventually lead to our first ever Cricket Shield.

"Did you never want to be a Head?" I asked Chris one day as we were walking up towards the games field.

"Oh yes, I had ambitions, Tony, but it obviously wasn't to be. I applied to quite a number of schools but whatever they wanted I hadn't got so I accepted my fate and have enjoyed being a Deputy Head here."

Interesting, I thought. I wonder, had his career suffered the same sort of blight that mine had? After all, he was a superb teacher, a brilliant administrator, marvellous with all the staff. In fact, a natural Head Teacher.

I gradually talked my way around the staff and realised that one of the greatest compliments paid to Sister Mary Benedict, the fact that her staff were so loyal and never left, was not all it seemed to be. If you were good, you just didn't get out of the school. The poor ones could get out quickly but in that way she built a superb staff and kept the experience going for many years. It was great for the school but not so good for the various individual teachers. Without realising, I was quite a catalyst at that time. All my colleagues were very religious and for them to even consider that a Sister of their church would actually do something to hinder their future was unthinkable.

After the extraordinary school play of the previous year when the two remedial classes had created the only entertainment. I decided to put on a school play in the F.W.G. style for the end of term. Cath had introduced me to the works of Nicholas Stuart Grey, a teacher who had written plays for his own class which had then been published and even been performed professionally at the Birmingham Hippodrome where

Cath, as a child, had come across them.

My favourite was a play called 'The Tinder Box'. The usual tale of a poor soldier who meets a wicked witch after a magic tinderbox; he gets hold of it by mistake. He becomes the master of three powerful dogs, meets a beautiful princess locked in a tower, rescues her and eventually marries her and lives happily ever after. Of course there's much more to it than that: the chivalrous cats who are the ensnared slaves of the witch, a greedy innkeeper, and a lot of sycophantic courtiers who will friendly with anyone as long as they pay for the bill. Or in other words, it's just like life!

The play was difficult to put on and was not helped by the fact that I insisted on having two complete casts in case one child should be ill. Then at the last minute I felt sorry for the reserve cast, which was brilliant, and decided to put on four performances, two with each cast. Needless to say, Sister kept well away from me, but the rest of the staff were wonderful. Towards the end they rallied round, helped with costumes, scenery, stage management, in fact I couldn't wish a nicer send-off from the school.

# CHAPTER 11

# *I Sit and Watch the Children Play*

*Little Children*
*– Billy J Kramer*

Cath's niece Anne was due to come and stay with us. Cath's brother, another teacher, had got a promotion which took him from the Midlands to distant Essex. He needed some time to go house hunting and a two-year-old is not the best of helpers with such activity. We were quite excited about it all. We'd never had a small child to look after and to be honest we knew very little about them. She was a delight. I proudly carried her on my back around Bedford in a sort of rucksack which was most effective and we enjoyed ourselves looking in the window of the toy shop run by Mrs Clarke, who was now a customer of mine for stamps. Cath had great fun using both English and French names for the toys for as Anne's mother was French, she could understand the basics of both languages. We probably overplayed with her during the brief forty-eight hours that we were in charge and I think that it was during that time that we decided that it was about time to start our own family.

It was a major decision. We would lose one income, but the stamp business was beginning to grow and we both thought, *What the hell?* and decided to give it a try. I had been brought up with precautionary films like 'A Kind of Loving' and 'A Taste of Honey' and 'Room at the Top', and when just one chance encounter led to pregnancy I realised that these things could be very quick. It was obvious then, that a baby would soon come along. I wonder how many couples naïvely believe this until in fact, some time later they find to their horror it isn't that simple.

Cath and I had spent some time looking at baby clothes in the St Neots wool shop which doubled as the St Neots stamp centre and was one of my stamp bases. With such high hopes, it came as quite a shock to us both that it wasn't a matter of us deciding, the Umpire had the final word and he had decided against. The other ironic thing is that when you are not trying for a child you don't notice the insults the jibes, the innuendo concerning your prowess. In the case of me it was snatches of conversation which would go something like, "Of course, I've proved I'm a man. I know I don't fire blanks," or, "It's the ultimate, isn't it really, to prove that you are whole? Having a child is the only way you can do it."

Of course there were many other unpleasant digs about my masculinity or lack of it. Cath experienced similar unpleasantness from married couples with children. It seemed to us at the time, that we posed some form of threat to the established order by not having children. In some ways, I suppose it is a form of jealousy, the act that we could go out any time we liked without the eternal problem of babysitting. Holidays were easy, we could go anywhere at any time. Of course, we had that extra money because not only did we have the extra income from Cath, but also we hadn't the expense of children.

Whatever the reasons, some of the lengths people would go to humiliate us were extraordinary. One New Year's Eve, some years later, we sat next to a couple at the Cricket Club who told Cath that she wasn't a whole woman and was a failure in life and was a waste of space. We left early, very sad but eternally grateful that at least we had each other. Our love was as strong as ever. We decided to go for the tests which is the next step in the humiliation that childless couples have to go through. In my case I was recommended to wear loose baggy pants to keep my vital equipment cool. Of course we should study the timetable – of course by that they didn't mean going on holiday.

In Cath's case it was ten times worse. Her testing was at the same time as the prenatal clinic and she had to deal with the humiliation of all the pregnant ladies being around. There was no privacy for the national health patients and so she was examined behind a curtain while her consultant, who had a bellowing voice, discussed her problems for all and sundry to hear. It was a very painful and humiliating experience for her and even worse that at the end of all the tests, there was apparently no reason why we shouldn't have a family, it was just that we had to be lucky and take it very seriously, working to the calendar. Love is a very spontaneous thing and to try to regulate it according to your body temperature in the morning kills all emotion. All of the love songs speak of being in the mood, and certainly during those dreadful years our relationship was as strained as it had ever been before. In the end, we both come to the conclusion that the whole operation wasn't worth a mess of beans and if we were going to have a child, we would have one, but our relationship was too important to destroy. It was a great relief for both of us to get back to normal and once the decision had been made, we learnt to deal with the jibes. The easiest way was to put them down to jealousy, and point out our advantages.

Cath had talked to Nora when in Malta about children and Nora had said with characteristic vigour, "Who needs children? They need all your attention, time and money. You can have a very nice time without!" So we retaliated with the delights of our next exotic holiday, or the wonderful parties we went to. It may have answered the question to the outside world, but obviously inside we both felt a great emptiness that gnawed away at our insides.

After meeting Betty Brunt at the Civil Defence lecture, where she shocked everyone with her gin story, her daughter Rena had come into my class. Rena's father had disappeared some years before. Rena, aged nine, was very worried that the only family she had was her mother and was constantly enquiring about her mother's health which may have reassured her, but continually reminded Betty that she was considerably older and in Rena's opinion likely to die at any moment. Rena was a very quiet and thoughtful child that caused no problem in class; one of those who get on with their work, so it well and can often be missed by an inexperienced teacher, because of the very fact that they are so quiet.

Betty asked if Cath and I could go and see her one day. We drove out to her house in a local village one Saturday afternoon. It was unusual to be asked so it had to be something serious. Poor Betty. She had to go into hospital and it was going to be a long operation, not potentially life-threatening though of course all operations carry some risk. The trouble was that she had no-one to look after Rena. By now, Cath was teaching at Brickhill and had become friendly with Betty, and I had taught Rena for a year so Rena knew me. We both had a reasonably good relationship with the child and so Betty asked us if we would look after her. I said to Cath after the meeting, "I have a horrible feeling that Betty is concerned if anything happens to her. We only have her word that it is not a very serious operation."

"What? You mean that Rena would stay with us if anything happened?" said Cath incredulously.

"I suppose, probably not. But I wouldn't put it past her. There is nowhere else for her to go and nobody likes adopting children of that age. If the only solution is a children's home or fostering, then it would be far better if she were fostered by us."

Cath thought about it for a while and then as usual came out with the obvious reply, "I think basically we should wait and see. We are crossing our bridges."

Rena came to stay with us, bringing a small case and her piece of blanket which she took with her everywhere. It's funny how so many children have some kind of comforter when parted from their parents.

Rena fitted into our house very quickly. I think she found us a little bit strange. We did have this habit of singing old pop songs in the car and Rena had never come across anyone who sung wherever they went before, nor, I suspect, had she been around a happy relationship ever before. Hopefully it was good for her to see a man and a woman getting on so well and so obviously in love.

As it happened, Stevenage Fair was on during the patch that she stayed with us. I hadn't been to Stevenage Fair since I was a teenager, but as a child, it was one of the landmarks of my life. Stevenage Fair was one of the great medieval fairs. It occupied the centre of the town, right across the A1, The Great North Road from London to Scotland. The Charter was so strong that no lawyer had been able to break it and the net result was that all traffic had to be diverted for around nine days while Stevenage Fair was in progress. Cars piled up by my house, situated in a backwater for those nine days as a constant reminder of the excitement to be found in the High Street.

The Fair had changed since I was a small child. At first it was very much a country fair, with many stalls selling a miscellany of household goods, china, glass, food, all sorts, and amusements around the edges. In those days my mother and father would know almost everyone in the streets. As I grew up, the influence of the New Town became stronger, the Fair changed character, becoming much more of a modern fun fair and less of an old style fair, and the town was full of newcomers who were strangers. But it was not all bad because the fair expanded into an enormous field at the end of town.

We drove over from Bedford to Stevenage, singing as usual. My mother still lived in the town so we parked the car at her house and walked down to the fair. Seeing something attractive through their own eyes is something amazing. Stevenage Fair with Rena was something even more special than I remembered it. I don't think that she had been to a fair before, she was game for everything; her face lit up, eyes sparkling, and she literally bounced from candyfloss to roundabout. I took her on the Whip, one of my own special favourites. Cath reluctantly joined us as she knew my tricks. I was able to spin that car round at speeds you couldn't imagine. Rena loved it and shrieking in delight she begged for another go. Cath begged to be excused! I repeated the operation, spinning harder and faster. We smashed the opposition on the dodgem cars, even though you weren't supposed to, and we faced the horrors of the ghost train. I say horrors but in all fairness it would take more than a few bits of string and the odd mask to frighten a bright eleven-year-old. We ate the toffee apples and cake, and walked until we were almost sick. I won a big fluffy toy on the darts stall; pop music thundered out drowned by the excited squeals of the children as they experienced the various thrills of the fair. The noise was deafening and as we slowly walked back from the big field, Rena asked if she could have just one last go on the Whip. I duly obliged and Cath, despite her misgivings, joined in once again and then all singing together we walked back and had a cup of coffee with my mother before driving back to Bedford, trying desperately to get the harmony for *Silence is Golden* and *Big Girls Don't Cry*. It was one of those nights that you don't forget, but it was bitter sweet in some ways. The fun of having Rena to stay brought the realisation that we may never have our own child to take to Stevenage Fair.

Cath came in chuckling one snowy evening after school.

"All right, I'll buy it," I said, "what's the joke?"

"I've got the ultimate Nancy Barter story," she said. Nancy was always good for a chuckle. Although we were both very fond of her, her theatrical performances were always larger than life.

"You know they are not allowed to slide on the playground?"

I remembered well the rule coming in. Nancy had fallen over because somebody had made a slide right outside her classroom. As the junior and infant teachers crossed the playground regularly to get to the staffroom, it was felt that slides on the main playground were certainly not to be encouraged.

"Well as you know," continued Cath, "the children can't resist a good patch of ice and most of us don't really mind. They got a really good slide going on the playground today, it must have been about thirty or forty feet long. The children were taking runs ups and having a really lovely time gliding effortlessly to the other end of the slide. Just as Alison Purbright, one of my nicest girls hit the ice, Nancy Barter came out at the far end, eyes blazing with annoyance that the rules were being disregarded, important rules which she herself had introduced. She stood at the end of the slide and waited, arms outstretched while the poor girl, helpless to stop herself relentlessly drifted closer and closer, her face a picture of horror and expectation of punishment. She was not disappointed. As she arrived at the end of the slide, Nancy upended her.

"'You-nau-ghty-lit-tle-girl-you-know-it's-wrong-to-make-slides-on-the-playground!'" and she punctuated every syllable with a smack. The whole playground of children dissolved into mass hysteria. The poor girl was bright red with embarrassment. Nancy, also red-faced with exertion, called out to the caretaker.

"Get this broken up and made safe immediately!" and stormed off like a ship in full sail.

The snow and ice had been causing us some problems with our transport. We had finally upgraded our hand-painted minivan to a luxury Vauxhall which had a heater and rear windows! The drawback was that it was unreliable and on cold winter days it had a nasty habit of not starting at all. We resolved to get ourselves something slightly better and drove over to our usual friendly garage to see what he had on offer. What he offered us was to us, unbelievable. He had a Humber Sceptre in silver metallic paint. It gleamed and glistened as if it was new. The seats were red leather and it had overdrive, a sort of extra gear which you could use at high speeds on the motorway. It was the most beautiful car I'd ever seen. It wasn't that expensive. Nobody particularly wanted the old gas-guzzlers. We took it off for a test drive, way out of Bedford, along up to the A1 and then almost up to Peterborough. Cath loved it! The speed, the control, the sheer feel of luxury! They didn't have to do much to convince us, we wanted it! I always thought of it as a big shiny silver bird that glided over the roads.

Cath was in seventh heaven driving it. With such a fantastic car, she became much more inclined to take the first day covers to the various post offices rather than post them. She really enjoyed driving. The big problem about delivering covers was that they had to be there on the day of issue or they did not get a postmark. On one of our adventures, the car actually broke down in a village miles from anywhere. Luckily there was an old-fashioned sort of garage and the kindly mechanic, realising our panic, stopped what he was doing and managed to fix the problem and we were able to get to Slough. We had to wait a couple of hours and I can still feel the fear I felt then as we walked around the village, terrified that we had missed the deadline, our covers would all be ruined, and we'd lost an awful lot of money.

We got back safely and the next day we were phoned up by the Post Office in Slough.

"Can I speak to Mr Benham please?" said the voice on the phone.

"I'm afraid not. That's the name of the company, but you can speak to Mr Buckingham, who runs it."

"Very well then, I have to tell you that Post Office regulations prohibit us from postmarking envelopes that have not been addressed. Your envelopes have not been addressed therefore we will not be able to postmark them."

I was literally stunned. I could not believe that we could have left off the small label we were to put on every envelope.

"Is there nothing we can do?" I asked, terrified.

"Well, you could come and address them here, that would be acceptable. They must be done quickly though."

Getting to Slough was not as easy as it had been in the first place. Cath's half-term was over and I didn't drive. Luckily the great white hope of Bedford football, Roger, my co-manager and also friend had got a day off for an election and he offered to drive me to Slough. I was very up-tight as I honestly couldn't understand how stupid we'd been. When we arrived at the Post Office, the offending envelopes were produced, all four of them! We had taken thousands and thousands of envelopes to Slough and apparently the labels had fallen off four envelopes and they were so b-minded that they wouldn't even cancel them and put them in the boxes with the rest.

"Rules is rules!" said and officious Post Office official. "If we start breaking them, where would we be?"

*Where indeed?* I thought. Possibly human?

On the way down, I'd seen a stamp shop at Rickmansworth, by the station. I'd been too preoccupied with the major problem of unaddressed envelopes that I had not even thought of stopping. I'd mentioned it to Roger and on the way back he suggested we stop and I look to see if I could buy anything to make the trip worthwhile.

"I doubt if it will be worth it," I said. But he insisted, so we stopped and walked over to the dirty, dingy little shop, just by the main station entrance.

As I walked in, I spotted a very rare first day cover on the wall. It had been put together by somebody on the 1$^{st}$ January 1902. Four stamps had been issued on that day – a halfpenny, a penny, a twopenny-halfpenny, and a sixpenny. I don't know how much ten old pence was worth in 1902 – but if you index-linked it to today you would be talking about tens of pounds. Old first day covers are very rare and this envelope was in excellent condition and had been priced at twenty-five pounds. It was in fact a gift! I took it from the wall and handed it to the shopkeeper.

"How long has that been on offer?" I asked. As it was somewhat dusty.

"Oh, probably about two years," he said. "There's no interest for first day covers."

You can imagine my joy when within a few days I had sold it for a hundred pounds profit – more than a month's salary, just by calling in at a shop in Rickmansworth! I took Roger out for a meal to celebrate and vowed to visit more stamp shops!

In between my teaching, drama, cricket, football, and Young Teachers, I managed to fit in my stamp business. It was growing steadily. I used to sit down over the weekend and write in my disgusting handwriting to any stamp shop or dealer I thought might want my services and gradually Benham became THE wholesale dealer of first day covers.

I was also helped by a major historical event. The owner of the Stamp Company from whom I had been buying many of my first day covers was a member of a very strict church. His church told him that the world was due to end very shortly. Apparently the flood was to come and he was to go up to the top of a high hill where he and his brethren would be spared whilst the rest of us sinners would be destroyed. He was a Believer, so he set to work selling off his stamps because obviously they would all be ruined during the flood. During this sell-off, I visited at least every week and sometimes twice a week during the holidays. I could hardly believe what I was buying because it was all so very, very cheap.

The cover that made me laugh the most was the one issued for Sir Francis Chichester when he sailed round the world in the *Gypsy Moth*. Because the dealer lived quite near Chichester, the firm had produced literally tens of thousands of Chichester postmarked covers. They just didn't know what to do with them and so sold them off for sixpence (2½p). As the basic cost would have been around 2/6d (12½p) you can see it was a very good buy.

I sold thousands of those covers at twelve and a half pence and what was even funnier was that most of the stamp dealers commiserated with me for making such a dreadful mistake and having to lose money so badly on them. I said that I had to keep the cash flow going to buy the new first day covers so I was doing the best I could! As fast as I made my money, I reinvested it into more covers, more stamps and then started advertising in a cheap magazine, so I was often selling two or three hundred new issue covers to collectors around the country as well as supplying all my shop customers. I also started advertising in a trade magazine and started to get customers in New Zealand, South Africa, America, Australia, Canada, and other small orders from all over the world. It was certainly heady stuff!

Cath had had many happy holidays in the Scilly

Islands and we had been invited to join her parents for the following summer. It was a very long drive for Cath down to Penzance. I still hadn't passed my test. I rather liked having a chauffeur, but she was in some ways a disappointment – she wouldn't wear the peaked cap I bought for her! I hadn't stopped driving, I just hadn't taken any more lessons.

We retched our way over to Scilly on the *Scillonian*, a ship especially designed to be shallow bottomed to go into St Mary's harbour which made it sway alarmingly with every wave for the full thirty-mile journey. We sympathised with the day-trippers who sat green and weak on the quayside until it was time to make the return trip.

In those days, the Scilly Islands were very unspoiled but at the same time, rather primitive. Our holiday quarters was in a farm house and I must admit that going out to the khazi at the bottom of the garden in the middle of the night with a flash-torch didn't appeal, nor did the fact that it was only flushed once a day because of a shortage of water, especially as it was used by at least ten people. I'd always been a little fastidious and I found this revolting. I couldn't also imagine a harder or more lumpy bed, and as for the pillows, well sleep was not at a premium but cricked backs were. Added to this, the bedrooms were all linked and my parents-in-law were just through a thin wooden door which was a little inhibiting for a young couple! This forced us back into being naughty teenagers disappearing at night into the bracken to get a bit of peace and privacy!

The island we were staying on was St Martins. There was no pub, no hotel, no restaurant, no café, no TV, no transport, just a solitary sub-post office that sold a few provisions. I discovered a very interesting fact about the Post Office. There was no delivery service on St Martins. All mail was collected there, so if you posted anything to yourself, it was duly postmarked and then waited for you to collect it. The British Post Office has never allowed cancelled to order (CTO) – that is you can just have your stamps postmarked and handed back to you. This is strictly against post office regulations, however this was exactly what was on offer at St Martins because of the extraordinary circumstances of the island. I created some wonderful fine used stamps during that holiday and the subsequent one and I am sure that many collectors today wonder how on earth these wonderful blocks of stamps exist with superb St Martins postmarks.

While we were there, I was introduced to the joy of boats and sailing. I must admit that on a hot day with blue skies, there's nothing nicer than bobbing along in a small boat. I was soon to find out though that the waters could turn rough, the skies black and fog could appear from nowhere.

I'd gone out with my brother-in-law through some rather nasty rocks. It was a beautiful day and there was no warning whatsoever of the fog that appeared as if by magic, blocking out all vision and ability to reason where you were. Noises became very muffled and distant, and we knew that between us and the island were vicious rocks. However the other way was the Atlantic Ocean and America next stop! I don't know how many times we actually went in and out through those rocks, I have no idea. Backwards and forwards we went, always convinced we were going the wrong way once we had got there. Eventually though we made it through and back into harbour.

Cath was distraught with worry and had persuaded her father to go out to look for us. The irony was that the lifeboat brought them back in to harbour when we got back by ourselves. I think Cath's father was humiliated as he was a very good sailor who was not in trouble, but the lifeboat crew didn't seem to care. They wanted to tow somebody back in and he would certainly do. I was never really so keen to sail again, being a natural coward, I decided it was safer on dry land.

"You'll be going into hospital soon," said Cath over breakfast one morning.

"Yes," I said, "it's the fifteenth of May."

To be honest, I wasn't looking forward to it. The idea of snipping me open and sewing me up didn't particularly appeal, but at the same time, being trussed up like an old chicken also had its disadvantages. I was more than a little bit fed up of wits saying, "I'll see you in a truss!" or, "I suppose you're a bit tied up at the moment!" I don't suppose anyone looks forward to going into hospital but as the days ticked over, I was frantically trying to get everything in order, particularly the stamp business. I'd written to my main trade customers to warn them that I wouldn't be around for a bit but that hopefully everything would get back to normal very quickly.

The day before the operation was one of those God-given days – very still and sunny when the air is so still that voices carry for miles. Cath and I went to

Olney, one of our favourite weekend visiting spots. I thought that I was being very brave and not showing any sort of emotion, but apparently Cath could see my fear and worry, though she didn't mention it. It was one of those days which you treasure all your life. We strolled round the old village, looked at the antique shops admiring the things we would buy if we could afford them, and walking along the river. I can remember wearing a very outrageous green tie that Cath had made me out of a bit of material left over from one of her dresses, my hair was fashionably long. At the time I thought I looked dashing and handsome, but looking at the photographs today, I am not too sure! It's amazing how fashions change and how dated old photographs make you look.

I took myself off to the hospital the next day, with my little suitcase. I went to the lavatory and there met a very, very old man, bent double, obviously in dreadful agony. I felt very sorry for him as I strolled back to my bed. The next day, I crawled down to the lavatory, bent double in agony to find the little old man, looking much younger and standing bolt upright, shaving!

I was something of a celebrity for the wrong reasons in that hospital. It appears that my hernia was unusual. Most people rip themselves apart picking up heavy weights, not many do it by kicking a football and thus tearing their muscles the wrong way. Because I was somewhat unusual, I was a good attraction for the various medical students. I was twenty-five and I admit to being somewhat prudish! To be examined regularly by bunches of girls younger than myself, with nothing to hide myself behind than my black, blue, yellow, technicolour bruises was somewhat embarrassing. I also wondered what had actually been done during the operation to create such an incredible mass of colour! Surely all they needed to do was sew me up, not beat me at the same time! I worried that my love-life was going to be a long time returning.

I was, though I didn't realise it at the time, very lucky. I'd been given a week to get over the operation. Many of the hernia victims were turfed out after twenty-four hours. During the last few days, I'd been promoted to the convalescent ward, a sun-trap off the main ward with only three or four beds in it. All the patients in this wing were on the mend. We even had a television, a great rarity in hospitals in those days, so we could watch England in the World Cup. We were not encouraged by the reports of Bobby Moore being arrested for apparent shoplifting and taken away from the team for some time and then being allowed to return with no charges at all. But what distressed us the most was Sir Alf taking off some of his key players to rest them when we were beating West Germany two-nil only for the Germans to stage their usual recovery and they beat us three-two. It was bad enough being in hospital, but to be in hospital when England had lost the World Cup in such a stupid way seemed the ultimate punishment.

I eventually got back home in late June and was to be allowed back to school until the following September. It was strange pottering around the house while Cath went off to work. It takes a surprisingly long time for a hernia operation to heal up. I had hoped to be back playing cricket that summer, but realised that I was going to miss a second season and I wondered if I would ever play again.

# CHAPTER 12

## *It's Better to Travel Hopefully Than to Arrive*

*"We're all going on a summer holiday."*
*– Cliff Richard*

My father and holidays did not go together well. I can never remember enjoying them. I think he objected to uncomfortable beds, bad food and a change of routine. On the hottest of days, he could be found in our garden wearing not only a jacket and tie, but possibly a waistcoat as well. He'd read the paper, normally the Financial Pages, whilst enjoying the summer heat in his favourite special garden chair. Trips away were always fraught with problems. When I go back to my boyhood holidays I remember a miscellany of disasters of a minor or major nature.

On one return from our annual holiday on Great Yarmouth we got lost, the suitcases fell off the roof, scattering our dirty linen throughout Norfolk, a bull escaped from a field and, needless to say with our everlasting luck, we were the first car to confront it. We were caught in a flash flood and the water squirted through the bottom our car where there was apparently a hole by the gear stick, and shot straight up my mother's skirt. She took it with remarkable composure. It wasn't the ideal way to return home.

If this catalogue of disasters wasn't enough for one journey, the play still had one act before the final curtain call. The final insult was that the big-end of the car went and the car started making a noise like a heavy hammer striking an anvil. There was nothing we could do but simply push on home. My father, who was never the greatest navigator, missed a diversion sign and drove into a Suffolk market town where a church procession was in full cry. We joined behind, adding some unrehearsed percussion. My mother, sister and I were very embarrassed but my father enjoyed the procession and all the rest of the events apparently oblivious to the annoyance we were causing.

My father, typical of the wartime generation, hated waste. He always seemed to find accommodation through a friend or customer. Why on earth he should have imagined we would want to stay in a small terraced house in Delabole in Cornwall, I can't imagine, particularly as the landlady was a ferocious old rat-bag who served the evening meal at 7pm, not 6.59 nor 7.01. If you were late, you went hungry. To be perfectly honest, it wasn't as if the meal was worth having, but I don't suppose that if ever occurred to my father to skip it – he'd paid for it and he was going to eat it. The rushed journeys back from excursions round Cornwall so that we would be there at 7pm became very strained.

That was the other thing about Dad, he could never stay in one place very long. As soon as we had decamped onto the beach, he was bored and wanted to go on to the next town, beach, church or gravel pit. "Gravel pit?"

I hear you say, "Why on earth would he be interested in gravel pits?" Well, he was very keen on a sand and gravel company called *Inns and Co.* and had invested in it quite heavily. Jerry Inns, one of the main directors was one of his customers. He liked to check on his investments. I was quite an authority on sand and gravel pits as a small boy.

We did once persuade him that it would be a good idea to stay in a decent hotel. Unfortunately though, he hadn't booked and after being turned away from every decent hotel between Beer and Sidmouth, we ended up in the usual dingy Bed and Breakfast. The only time my father did stay in a fairly reasonable hotel was in Bournemouth. This was after he had become crippled with arthritis and he decided that perhaps he needed a little bit more comfort. The hotel was called the Hotel in a Rose Garden. My recollection of the place was that it smelt of the horse manure used on the roses! The hotel itself was run by an old rogue. He used to give me a 'special' drink each night. In reality, it was Andrews Liver Salts in lime juice. I never asked for it and we all assumed that he was being kind. That was until my father found that it cost him £7!

The first time we stayed was at Easter, when it was quiet and fairly pleasant. The food was reasonably good and the hotel was filled with interesting antiques. On the strength of this, my parents booked for the first two weeks in August – which in those days was the Bank Holiday weeks. On arrival we found that the hotel had changed appearance quite considerably. For a start, there were no antiques. Apparently, the owner didn't think that the kind of visitors who came during the first two weeks of August would appreciate his better furniture. He had also allowed the cook to go on holiday at the same time as he didn't think that these people would appreciate decent food. When my mother complained, he explained all this which made her livid. After all these guests were paying the same for a disgusting product. He reassured her that everything would be back to normal the second week when his usual type of guests would return. I suppose that he could have been Basil Fawlty's father! One of the families however, got their own back – possibly not intentionally, but nevertheless it worked very well. The grandmother who was with them was deaf. She had obviously not brought her hearing aid to dinner.

Snippets of the conversation entertained the dining room each evening

"Huh! Warmed up chips! These are disgusting! This cabbage is all watery... Can't the cook do anything in there?"

"*Will you keep your mother quiet?*" hissed the owner.

"I want a glass of water," continued the old lady belligerently. "What sort of meat's this? You can't tell from the taste!"

"*I have asked you please to get your mother to be quiet!*" implored the desperate landlord.

"Where's my water?" demanded the old lady.

"Lumpy custard! We get cream at home!"

"If you don't get your mother to be quiet, I shall have to ask you to leave," continued the now red-faced owner. "She's annoying the other guests."

"THIS IS THE WORST MEAL I'VE EVER HAD IN MY LIFE!"

At this remark the entire dining room clapped in appreciation of an honest critic. The owner was furious and embarrassed but there was little he could do. I think he reinforced my father's bigotry about hotels and holidays.

"We've got to have a holiday!" said Cath firmly as I'd just returned from mowing the couch grass which we called a lawn.

"I don't think we could afford one," I replied dolefully. "They're very expensive."

"Don't have to be. We could go camping."

"Camping!" I exclaimed. "Can you see me in a tent?"

"Well, to be honest, no. But I'm sure you'd enjoy it if you tried. I've had lovely tenting holidays."

That was the thing about Cath, she'd always enjoyed super holidays. Her father, unlike mine, believed in holidays. It was all rather sickening for me to hear about her super experiences when most of mine would feature on Candid Camera. Anyway, despite my desperate attempts to change her mind, she was adamant.

"We're going somewhere and that's that!" said Cath very firmly. Most of the time Cath was very easy going, but it was obvious that on this occasion she really wanted to go away. "Let's look at the map and see where the nearest seaside resort is and just go."

I must add it sounded possible. Then to my horror we found that the nearest resort was Great Yarmouth.

"I don't think you'd like Great Yarmouth, it's very tacky," I said firmly.

"It's not that bad," replied Cath, "I used to go there from the Broads. It's quite a nice town."

Now, if I'd been on the ball, I would have pointed out that Easter or Whitsun wasn't peak August. However I thought of another objection: "We can't go, I'm afraid. There are new stamps out on Tuesday," I said triumphantly.

"All right, we'll stick the stamps in the morning, take them with us and we can post them in Norwich when we change trains." The one thing about Cath, she'd always been an excellent administrator. I had to agree that it was a sensible plan and our collectors would get a different postmark other than Bedford. I had not yet realised that we should be going to Windsor for definitive stamps where the postmark would have had more relevance.

The day of our holiday and the new stamps was perfect. Blue, blue skies and blazing sun, in fact just what you don't want when sticking thousands of stamps on envelopes. We worked steadily and by eleven in the morning, we had finished. As we left for the station, the sun was taking a break popping behind some small clouds. As the train approached Norwich, the small clouds became larger. From Norwich to Yarmouth the sun completely disappeared. Still, we were on our holiday. The sun would come back the next day, wouldn't it?

We had sensibly left our cases in the left luggage office and set out to find a cheap Bed and Breakfast place.

"Nothing too expensive," said Cath, "but hopefully we can find a pretty place."

NO VACANCIES was the sign of Great Yarmouth that August day. I'd never seen so many! We walked and walked and walked, mile after mile. Memories of holiday failures flashed through my mind. Eventually I made a major decision: "All right. We'll go to a decent hotel."

"We can't afford it!" said Cath sensibly.

"Oh, I'll sell some more stamps!" I promised. "Come on!"

With that, I went into an expensive-looking hotel.

"I'm dreadfully sorry," said the clerk. "No vacancies!"

This was the same pattern for all the hotels. Why on earth I thought they should be different, I honestly don't know! It began to get dark at about 8:30. We were by now totally exhausted and desperate. I can't remember whose idea it was to get a taxi, probably Cath's, she's the clever one. We cruised up and down the mean streets of Yarmouth until eventually he found us a room in a council house in the back of nowhere. We'd already picked up our cases to get straight to bed as by now it was approaching 11pm.

"I don't just take in anybody!" confided Mrs Russell. "I'm particular who I have in my house. Why, just last week, an old man came with a young girl.

Well, he was wearing *brown boots*. Brown boots! I knew he was up to no good, so I sent him packing!"

Mrs Russell was a lady of very firm views, and she enjoyed sharing them with us. It wasn't a perfect holiday stay. The washroom was behind her kitchen, virtually in the yard.

"Want a little wash?" she would regularly ask.

The fascinating thing also about Mrs Russell was that she knew so much about other people and she generously shared her information.

"You know that Duke of Edinburgh?" she asked. "Well, *he's* no better than he ought to be. I feel very sorry for the Queen," she confided.

I wondered if she had actually been taken into the Queen's confidence – perhaps over afternoon tea? Or had she gleaned the insight from the Duke of Edinburgh himself?

"Want a little wash?" she added.

Later: "You know that John Wayne?"

*Not personally*, I thought, but waited for the punchline. Was John Wayne having an affair with Princess Anne?

"He's a *real* man! He could beat me up any day," she added wistfully.

I couldn't really see John Wayne coming to the back-end of Yarmouth despite such an attractive offer.

Yarmouth was a very depressing place in early August. Most of the holiday makers seemed to share my father's view of holidays. I had never seen so many miserable people. Most of them seemed hell-bent on spending all their money as quickly as they could by pushing it down the throat of slot machines. As we walked out the second evening, the sea was quite attractive. The moon was shining, virtually nobody wanted to share this beauty with us – they were all hell-bent on losing their money as quickly as possible. I found it very depressing. We had to get away from Yarmouth, and from our digs, so the next day, Cath suggested we took a bus to Southwald. She remembered it as a pretty village by the sea.

The bus journey to Southwald passed by a signpost to Gunton. This had brought back another flash of my distant holidays gone by. We used to go to Gunton for day trips. My father had found the most perfect deserted beach. We parked at the top of a windswept, heather-covered sand dune and walked down a narrow path to a beautiful sandy beach. It was not very well-know and very few people ever went to the beach. My father didn't mind going there because it took so long to get there, and he enjoyed driving. There was also a gravel pit to see on the way there and a gravel pit to see on the way back, and we couldn't stay on the beach too long because obviously we had to get back before it got dark. My mother and sister enjoyed sunbathing and I, heavily covered with scoll and anti-sun remedy, would proceed with my favourite beach occupation of throwing stones at cans, rocks, or anything else I saw of interest. We must have gone to Gunton on many occasions, before one day we went for a walk along the beach and around the headlands. To our horror, we found it was blocked with very large barbed wire barricades. There were notices written on the other side, ominously with a skull and crossbones above them. It appeared we had been enjoying our holidays on a beach that had yet to be cleared from the war and could have landmines, unexploded bombs, shells and anything else which might provide an explosive start to your holiday. Needless to say, we decamped very quickly and very carefully and departed, never to return to Gunton again!

Arriving in Southwald was like visiting another planet. Not only was it very pretty but the people smiled and seemed happy – even though the sun wasn't shining! In fact, the rain wasn't that heavy and as we had raincoats, it didn't really affect our enjoyment that much. We walked round the narrow streets, passed the green and enjoyed, as have thousands of others, the beauty of the church and the lighthouse, built in the town itself. The beach was stony and boasted a run of impressive bathing huts. Despite the unseasonable weather, many families were camped using wind shields, umbrellas and sunshades to make the weather more bearable. In fact, we were witnessing the middle class stoically making the most of their holiday – a sort of Dunkirk spirit. It all seemed perfect to us.

"How about moving down here for the rest of the holiday?" I asked.

"Where would we stay?" replied Cath.

"Oh, I don't know. Let's have a look round!"

It was obvious we couldn't afford the main hotel. It looked fairly posh and there were not many boarding houses. Eventually, we found a pub which took in paying guests.

"Yup, we've got a room from tomorrow night. It will be fifteen shillings a night," said the landlord. "Do you want to see the room?" he added.

"Yes please!" said Cath quickly, knowing that I always got embarrassed about such things and was likely to say 'yes' immediately.

He led us up behind the bar to a flight of well-worn wooden steps.

"Mind your head on the beam!" he warned my before I bashed what few brains I still had left out. "Well, here's the room. What d'you think?"

It was a large, airy room with a double aspect window looking out over the main street. The furniture was old, and the bedspread well darned but nevertheless, very clean. It also had a wash basin, a luxury compared with the ablutions at the back of Mrs Russell's kitchenette.

"Jack!" called the landlord's wife. "Come here quickly! I need you!"

"Excuse me, I'll be back in a few minutes," he called from halfway down the stairs.

We looked again at the room. Cath's eyes went to the basin.

"Want a little wash?" she asked, and we both doubled up giggling like school children. We were still laughing when Jack returned.

"We'll take the room from tomorrow," I said confidently. "We should get here about lunchtime."

We paid a small deposit, made our way out into the street.

"It's a great improvement on Mrs Russell's place!" I said. "And not that much more expensive."

"We better get the bus back and tell Mrs Russell. She won't want us to go because it's easy money for her," replied Cath.

"Oh, I don't know. Perhaps John Wayne will come and take the room, so he can beat her up!" I suggested. "That would make her day! Or maybe one of her intimate royal friends might want to come and stay!"

As it was, Mrs Russell took the news very well.

"I don't blame you! It's not the best place for a holiday and you'll enjoy Southwold. My grandmother came from thereabouts."

We left her after an excellent breakfast, freshly cooked eggs and bacon and hot toast; something that luxury hotels find so difficult to do. Southwold was everything Cath and I wanted for a holiday. It was quiet, there were superb walks all around the area, semi-precious stones to find on the beach and a warmth in the pub which made the holiday very special.

Mind you, we didn't think that the first night. After supper, we had a few drinks in the public bar. It was fairly quiet. Ipswich were playing at home in the League, but we weren't to know that. We amused ourselves playing darts. I had always been good at darts. I had had a dartboard in the garage at home and had practised for hours and hours and at the tender age of fourteen had managed to bluff my way into a pub darts team. I used to play as a guest – they always wanted me to register properly and were disappointed that I didn't. I think they'd have had a bit of a shock to find out that not only was I underage, but by four years! That was one of the big things of being tall.

Cath also had a very good eye and was an excellent partner. I could start and finish and Cath was a canny high-scorer. We enjoyed our lengthy practice and retired for the night.

Our slumbers were shattered with the return of the football supporters, obviously full of high spirits. Judging from the noise of celebrations, it was obvious that Ipswich must have won. It was then we realised that our room was directly above the public bar.

"Not to worry, love," I said to Cath, "it must be very close to closing time. They'll have a few drinks and go. In about half an hour, all will be quiet again."

In theory, that should have been correct. Licensing hours in Britain were very strict and all public houses closed at either ten thirty or eleven o'clock, depending upon what time they opened in the morning. However, the noise continued well on past eleven o'clock. In fact it went on until the early hours of the morning. I wondered if they had got a special licence or was there some special celebration. Whatever it was, we got very little sleep until around two o'clock that morning. Whatever was going on down there, it sounded very interesting and we resolved that the next night we wouldn't go to bed, we would wait and see what happened around closing time.

After Molly, Jack's pleasant but very aggressive wife, had served us our breakfast, we departed out into the town to explore once again. It was very cloudy. There were occasional glimpses of the sun, but not the sort of weather that would encourage you to go on the beach and even the hardy would think twice about swimming. Whilst we were wandering around we found some very interesting shops selling jewellery made out of local precious and semi-precious stones. It also sold stone grinders and books about how to find these rare stones.

"This is one of the best places in the country to find precious stones on the beach," confided the shopkeeper. "You won't find a better place anywhere. You'll find all about it in this book. It's very useful." He was a very good salesman so we bought the book and looked up about the Southwold area. He was quite correct. That part of the coast was famous for all sorts of stones and as we had nothing better to do, we went semi-precious stone hunting. We had a wonderful time, wandering up and down the beach looking for agates and carnelians and hopefully small pieces of amber. We found quite a few and were very excited by our treasure hunt. In all reality, our finds were virtually worthless and we probably knew that at the time. But we were very much in love, we had the beaches to ourselves as the weather was so poor, and it was a very romantic thing to do. I even bought a pair of carnelian cuff-links set in sterling silver from the little shop. I've still got them. They are useless to wear because they are so bulky, but just looking at them brings back memories of that happy holiday on that salt-swept coastline of Suffolk. We must have walked miles and miles in our search for those stones and we returned back to the Red Lion, had a very large evening meal and then joined the locals in the public bar.

Darts had already started. For those who don't know the procedure, what used to happen in pubs and probably still does is that once a pair is on the dartboard, they stay on taking on all comers until they are defeated. Each time the pair wins, the losers buy the drinks. We watched the game with interest and Jack called across from the bar to those playing, "Here, this young couple, they play darts. They were playing darts all last night. They didn't look too bad either! Put them up on the list." So we were added as a pair. Eventually our game came up and we won. Cath used to drink vodka and lime and I drank beer. We won again and again. In fact, we won all evening. Drinks after drinks appeared. How we could see the board, let alone win games I don't know, but we did. To our amazement, we realised that it had gone twelve o'clock and we were still playing and still drinking. We of course, were legal because we were guests in the hotel, but how on earth were all the others?

At around twelve thirty, the police arrived.

*Oh dear!* I thought. *Jack could lose his licence over this!*

How wrong could I be? The policeman took off his helmet and was given a pint of bitter and he joined in the local gossip. It appeared that all was not well in Southwold. The town had been 'occupied'. No, not by the Germans, but by rich Londoners. Most of the village houses had been bought up for holiday homes and the locals could no longer afford to live in Southwold. In fact most of them now lived in a council estate outside the town or in the few cheaper houses that the holiday-makers were not interested in. One of the councillors actually suggested putting a gate on the bridge going into

Southwold to keep out the undesirables. Those undesirables just happened to be the people who lived in Southwold and had to put up with the bad weather in the winter when all the Londoners had gone away. The policeman, being a real local, made sure that the holiday-makers and Londoners stuck to the licensing laws. The fishermen and the few locals who used the Red Lion were given some leeway.

These locals were very friendly to us. We became members of the Southwold Exiles. Each evening, we played on the dartboard and drank with our newfound friends. They were an odd collection of people.

Denzil was very fat. Now fat comes in various ways. You can be fat, very fat or incredibly fat. Now Denzil would come into the incredibly fat brigade. He must have been around thirty stone. One of his favourite tricks was to take his gut and shake it up and down, making a revolting noise as he did it a sort of "Grrrrrrr!" noise. Apparently this didn't go down very well with the posh holiday-makers so he was banned from all pubs bar the Red Lion. It didn't bother Jack however, as Denzil's average consumption of beer was twenty pints a night. He was what was called a very valuable customer. When we first arrived in Southwold, Denzil was out of work, but he had good fortune, he got a job.

"I've got a job!" he yelled in his Suffolk burr when he came into the pub one evening.

"What ye got ter do?" asked Irvin, the local scrap merchant.

"I'm ballast on the council lorry!" he exclaimed. Apparently it was true. They needed extra weight on the lorry and Denzil was employed to sit at the back of the lorry to ensure it stayed on the road – not exactly the most arduous job, but at least it was a job and Denzil was getting paid and no longer on the dole.

George was perhaps the nicest of the Red Lion regulars. He worked in the bedding factory, virtually opposite the pub. He told us about his secret of life and his special diet.

"I get up about seven thirty," he said, "and I have a glass o' water and a piece of bread. Then I go over to the factory and I work till twelve. At twelve, I come over here and I have as many pints as I can drink until one o'clock then I go back to work. I work through till six, I go home to see Mother, have a nap, then I comes down the Red Lion. I drink stout all evening, sometimes I'll have a packet of crisps then I'll go orf 'appy to bed. At weekends, I lay in until the pub opens then I come straight to the Red Lion, I don't have the glass of water nor the bread on those days."

I honestly don't know what a doctor would have made of George's diet, but he thrived on it and Jack had no objections as George must have been consuming up to seventeen pints a day. Between George, Irvine and Denzil, Jack had got a gold mine. In fact every drinker in that part of Suffolk used the Red Lion. Jack confided in me that he had had complaints and suggestions from some of the 'nice' people of Southwold.

"I had one of those councillors in here the other day," he said. "He told me that if I changed a few things and discouraged some of the less desirable people from coming here, I'd get a much better clientele. I told him – yes, a much better clientele, some of them might drink half a pint of bitter of an evening and the wife a gin and tonic. They're welcome to them up at the Swan – personally I prefer the drinkers, there's much more money in it."

As a businessman myself, I took Jack's opinion very much to heart. From what I've seen of the so-called betters, I think that Jack was better off with the so-called undesirables.

One of the other delights I found in Southwold was a small shop selling stamps. I spent many happy hours going through his stock which in the long run probably went part-way to pay for our holiday. That was one of the big delights of being a stamp dealer, there was always a chance of a bargain and as years went by and my knowledge and customer base increased, it was often possible to actually pay for the holiday with bargains bought in local stamp shops.

On one magic holiday in Gran Canaria, we found an upstairs stamp shop in the back of the old town which had some unusual French postal history. By now my stamp business had grown quite considerably. The shopkeeper spoke no English, we spoke no Spanish, but Cath did speak French and he had a little French. Whilst she was talking to him, I was noticing the comments written in English on the envelopes – very rare, only six recorded, very unusual etc. They looked good and my instinct was to go along with the Englishman who had written the comments on the envelopes. I spent about a hundred pounds and on my return, my postal history expert priced the same covers up at over two thousand pounds. Not only did they pay for the holiday, but also made an excellent profit. This was long in the future. Whilst we were in Southwold I had very few customers and very little money and so I had to buy very carefully.

I will never forget the Southwold experience. It taught me never to just put up with what you have to start with. Holidays can be rescued and holidays could even be fun. We returned to Southwold the following year. We rented a caravan from a chap I played cricket with. Whereas the weather had been poor on our first visit, we were to find that it was not always that good in Southwold. It rained virtually continuously, the only consolation being that at least we were in a caravan. We watched in fascinated horror as the poor devils in the tents gradually got flooded out and left one by one. Gradually even the caravan occupiers gave up and at last we were the only people on the whole caravan site. We were on a slightly raised bit but even then we had to wade through the water to get out onto the road. Very little had changed at the Red Lion. Denzil had lost his job. Apparently they didn't need a ballast any more. George was still on his special diet and Irvin's main topic of conversation was still scrap metal. The dartboard was still there and the drinks still flowed, even to the extent that when we arrived late one evening, we found six rounds of drinks waiting for us before we even got on to the dartboard. It was lovely being a part of that community and I often wish we had gone back again. It was a way of life that now is almost extinct.

My father had never actually left Great Britain. He did go to the Isle of Wight, my mother's birthplace and that as far as he was concerned was going abroad.

\*

Cath had had a wonderful experience just before I had met her. She was selected as a British representative to go on a trip with the Commonwealth Youth Movement. They went round England, Scotland and Wales then off to Malta. Malta had made a big impact on her and she had often wanted to go back. For our very first ever overseas holiday it seemed logical that this should be our destination. By this time my stamp business had grown and I had an agent in Malta who supplied me with Maltese stamps and first day covers. Through him we had rented a flat in Sliema, overlooking the sea. It sounded fantastic and not wishing to waste money, I had managed to book ourselves on a very cheap flight. Admittedly it did mean flying night flights both ways, but then we were young. In fact, putting the two together it must only have cost us twice as much as it would have done had we booked a package holiday! Luckily, at the time I didn't know that. We arrived in Malta at around two o'clock in the morning and had an awful job finding a taxi that would take us to Sliema. The thing that amazed me was how many people were still out and about. Mind you it was fairly warm. We arrived at the hotel we had booked for the first night and were shown to a luxurious room with, to our delight, a bathroom ensuite, a luxury we had never come across before. This hotel also had air-conditioning so I had no indication of the real temperature outside. I had arranged to meet our agent, Reg Bonner, the next morning at around ten thirty. I got up and put on my suit and tie. I only had one suit –

it was a dark blue winter heavyweight wool. I thought I looked very smart.

"You can't go out like that!" Cath said. "You'll die!"

"What?" I replied. "It's a business meeting. I've got to look business-like."

"Yes, but the heat! You just won't be able to bear it!"

"Nonsense!" I said. "I'll be all right. Come on!"

I still remember walking out into the street. It was like going into a furnace. I crossed the road and managed to walk about twenty to thirty yards before I said to Cath, "You were right! Come on, I got to get back to the hotel!"

I scuttled back to the hotel, ripped all my clothes off and ran under a cold shower. By God it was hot! I dressed in the smartest casual clothes I could muster and we started out again to walk to Reg Bonner's house. It was a large old terraced house on Isouard Street, not far from the hotel and apparently very close to the flat we had rented. The outside of the house gave no clues as to how lovely it was inside. Once you walked in, it was cool, large, airy and full of many surprises. The biggest surprise was our host, Reg Bonner. He was dressed in an old pair of army shorts held up with a very large safety pin. The well-darned string vest at the top didn't add to the sartorial elegance nor did the rather dirty plimsolls which he had obviously had since the Second World War.

"Come in! Come in!" he invited, beckoning us through to the courtyard. The accent was pure Oxford, very slow and very plummy. Reg introduced us to his hosts Harry and Nora. Reg had been billeted here when he had been Chief Censor during the war and he had never left – leastwise, he did leave. Apparently he had returned to England and wanted to bring his wife back to Malta. She didn't like it, but he did and stayed.

After we had had coffee, Nora took us round and introduced us to the local shopkeeper and told him to look after us as we were friends, then she took us round to our flat. It was in one of the big stone houses facing the sea. From the huge windows of the sitting room we could look out over the bay with the red, yellow and blue boats bobbing about and to our delight, the karrozin horses were brought down each morning and evening to cool their hocks in the water. In spite of the primitive watering can rose of a shower which blasted jets of icy water and a tiny grubby kitchenette, which Cath immediately set about with disinfectant and bleach, we loved the place at first sight. Nora left us to it after having got us to promise to return for the evening.

The three of them were amazing characters. They ushered us through to their little walled garden with a giant fig tree on the wall.

"I think the sun is over the yard arm," said Reg, "time for some mother's milk."

"What?" Cath mouthed at me

I shrugged. Nora laughed.

"It's just Reg," she said, "he calls his whisky mother's milk because he says he can't live without it! What will you have?"

They did not have vodka, so Cath said she would

have a gin and tonic and I went for the whisky.

"Just a small one," I said.

"Of course, we only have small ones ourselves," said Reg with a naughty grin. It was astonishing how much booze these three old people could consume in an evening. The meal was very light, but was followed with tumblers full of whisky for me and gin for Cath. I don't remember much of the conversation of that evening, but I do remember us trying to get home! The flat was only around the corner from Reg's house but it seemed like twenty miles. We hung onto each other and groped our way along the walls. I think drunk would have been an understatement! We eventually reached the flat and passed out until very late the next morning.

Malta, to me, was a fantastic eye-opener. I'd never been anywhere where the sun shone so brightly. It was so delightful to swim in the warm sea. We decided that it would be rather nice to hire a car. Reg phoned around for us but it was high summer and all the Avis and Hertz cars were out. Not to be defeated, we went to Wembley's, the local garage and inquired about the availability of an open-topped car, which we thought would be wonderful.

"You want a Triumpha Sun-roofa?" asked the Maltese clerk in charge of bookings.

"Yes, that would be lovely!" we said.

"We'll have one in tomorrow, not today. You come round about nine o'clock and you will have your car."

With great excitement we went the next morning to collect our Triumph Herald sun-roof. We felt great –

our first open-topped car! We set off to explore Malta for the rest of the holiday. Cath had a vague idea of where we should go and she remembered something called the Blue Lagoon on the far side of the island. We got a map and I navigated her over to it.

There was a small jetty with a lot of brightly coloured fishing boats bobbing in an enclosed bay. It was scorching and we thought the boat-trip out to the caves looked very enticing so we set off across a dazzling blue sea. Although the trip was nothing out of the ordinary if you have been to enough places, to us that day, it was magical.

As we returned to the jetty, we saw a freshly caught swordfish being pulled out of a boat. We went into the café/snack bar at the end of the jetty and ate slices of that swordfish, grilled. It was the most delicious fish I have ever eaten.

We also went to the Buskett Road House, a night club that treated cruise passengers to sophisticated entertainment. It was deep in the orange groves and in the twilight of the Mediterranean night the scent of the trees filled the air. It was an elegant place with small, intimate, white-clothed tables and sparkling glass and silver. All guests had to wear a collar and tie.

We went to Medina, the Silent City, with its medieval sun-warmed stone walls engulfed in total silence – no cars, no TV, no radios, no music; just the sound of the insects chirping in the heat.

Further up the coast we found the aptly named Paradise Bay, one of the most perfect beaches I'd ever seen. We parked the car at the top of the cliff and a man rushed up to us and said he would look after our car for a few pence. We noticed that wherever we went in Malta as soon as you stopped the car someone always rushed up and promised to mind the car for you. We nicknamed them the parasites, but we always paid them. Although you had to walk down hundreds of steps to get there, the result was well worth it. A quiet golden sandy beach, beautiful turquoise water, perfect for swimming. There was a grubby hut at one end, where you could get light meals and drinks. Cath joked that two thousand flies couldn't be wrong therefore it was obviously the place to eat. We spent many happy hours lapping up the brilliant Mediterranean sun. We were constantly warned about the sun by Reg.

"People come here and think it's Blackpool! They lie out in the sun and burn. We've had two people die of burns here this year. I can't understand where they get their brains from!"

Reg was right. When we looked we saw people sun-bathing with horrible festering burns. Some had had medical attention and had flapping bandages, but still they were out in the sun! Where did they keep their brains?

One evening we were invited to go to the Union Club, the last bastion of the British Empire. We were told that we had to dress up. I put my suit on and we went round early to Isouard Street, looking forward to the experience. We were ushered through to the little walled garden for some 'mother's milk' – a giant tumbler full of spirits. Harry was once again in full cry.

"When I was a little boy, we used to keep crickets in cages and feed them on tomatoes." It wasn't a new story. We had heard it many times. It seemed to be the only one that Harry knew. Nora, on the other hand was very upset. She had just been out and had apparently seen something that disgusted her.

"They were wearing bikinis in the street, in Sliema! Just like Hamrun and Gazira!"

We gathered from this that Hamrun and Gazira were not very nice places, possibly something like Sodom and Gomorrah. Nora certainly did not approve of such goings on. By now, I was beginning to get slightly worried. We were on our second glass of mother's milk. Had we got the right evening? Reg was sitting in a pair of dark trousers and a white short-sleeved shirt. Was he not going to change? After all we were going to the famous Union Club! Eventually, he stood up, grabbed an ancient DJ and put it on, quickly clipped on a bow tie and we were ready!

The Union Club had a very stuffy pre-war atmosphere. There was a distance between the British and the Maltese members. It had the distinct air of a club that would not be in existence much longer. Reg told us of his days in the war and how he had felt when he first discovered Malta, with Nora correcting him if his memory slipped and telling us of the glamorous times they had had in the club. Every so often, Harry would wake up and tell us about crickets in cages and feeding them on tomatoes. We ate undistinguished food through an alcoholic haze of wine and brandy, then went back to Isouard Street for "just a little night cap!" All in all it was a very jolly evening, and once again we staggered home giggling and clutching at the wall.

"If we keep this up, we'll be raging alcoholics by the end of the holiday!" I spluttered

"Do you think it will take that long!" said Cath, clutching on to me for dear life.

As we passed our Triumph sun-roof, we grinned at each other. "That's what I really like about Malta," I said happily, "everyone is so honest. Look we can even leave all our stuff in the back of the car and nobody has touched it!"

Two days later, I went down to the car in the morning and realised that we had forgotten to bring our beach towels.

"Bring the towels down with you, love!" I called to Cath.

"We left them in the car!" she shouted back from the upstairs window. "They're not here."

I checked the back of the car and the boot. No towels. I went back upstairs to check again with Cath. No towels.

"Some bugger has stolen them!" I said at last. "You're right, they were in the car last night. So much for Maltese honesty! We'll lock them in the boot in future."

"Better still, take them in with us."

A few nights later we went out to the Hilton Hotel night club. Jess Conrad was there. We remembered him from our early teenage days. He looked very much the same and even sang the same songs we remembered.

"Did I really fancy that?" asked Cath with a giggle. "I must have dodgy taste!" We danced happily to the strains of Gary Glitter's "Come on come on!" belted out by a good local group and it was about one o'clock when we left for home. We went to where we thought we had left the car, but it wasn't there. We went all round the car park in case we had made a mistake about where we had left it. But at last we had to accept that it had been stolen. We went back to the hotel desk to tell them.

"Are you sure you came in a car?" they asked rudely. We were about four miles away from our flat in Sliema and it was rather hot we thought it a rather silly question to ask and it didn't improve our humour. We reported it to the police and got a taxi back to our flat. The next morning we went round to Wembley's Garage.

"I can only think that somebody took the car by mistake," I said

"Oh no. Stolen! Always stolen!" came the reply. "They steal them all the time. They take them up into the cliffs and strip out some of the bits and leave them there."

"What happens then?" I asked.

"We recover the cars then we buy the bits back. The police are useless," they told us very sadly. It did seem ironical that in such a small island that they should be plagued with so much car theft. But then you could start the Triumph sun-roof with a sardine can opener so it wasn't surprising that they had so much theft."

To thank Reg, Nora, and Harry for their kindness and also for our trip to the Union Club, we invited them to the best hotel in Malta, the Dragonara Palace.

It was not just a hotel, but a glittering casino, having once been the home of a rich and exotic princess. It was very snooty and very expensive. We had an excellent meal in the restaurant and went over to the casino for a flutter. Cath tried roulette for the first time in her life. She put some chips on seven. The wheel spun and there, seven had come up! A large number of chips came back to Cath. She then put her money on fourteen. The wheel spun and Yes! Fourteen came up! Another huge pile of chips came across to Cath who was beaming in delight. She put her money on twenty-one. Again it came up! Cath, it seemed had won a small fortune! She would have done better had she managed to put her next bet on twenty-eight, but she couldn't reach and the croupier seemed not to see her. The number came up but she didn't win. It seemed she should have tipped the croupier to ensure his help. She decided to stop and cash up. Not only had we made enough money to pay for the entire evening, we made a hundred and fifty pounds profit – three months' salary as a teacher in those days! It seemed like a fortune.

Years later we took our daughter back to visit Malta to show her all the delights we had found and loved. Cath had booked us in to a flat in the old army barracks which she remembered with great affection from her trip with the Commonwealth Youth Movement. It had been converted into holiday flats when the army pulled out of Malta after their Independence. We arrived late at night, with a sleepy six-year-old. It was filthy. The sheets were dirty, the bathroom black. We made the best of it for one night, then moved next day into the Hilton. It cost a fortune, but at least it salvaged something from the holiday. The Buskett Road House had changed from a luxury night club into a bingo house selling hotdogs and hamburgers. It was a junk filled litter auditorium of no obvious charm. Only the faint scent of orange trees reminded us of what it had been. Medina, the 'Silent city', was filled with blaring pop music and was anything but silent, destroying the magical atmosphere. When we arrived at Paradise Beach, we parked as usual and spoke to the parasite about how we really looked forward to going back down to Paradise Beach as it was one of the nicest places we had ever been to.

"Have you been here since the big storms?" he asked rather incredulously.

"No," I said, "we haven't been here for donkey's years."

"Well, you may find it changed. In fact very changed," he added.

We walked down the hundreds of steps dreading what had happened, but nothing could have prepared us for the picture at the bottom. Why on earth had they allowed it to become a rubbish tip? It couldn't just be the fact that the water was filled with oil and the beach covered with tar. There was also a very unpleasant smell coming from the rubbish. Paradise Lost. The final humiliation for Malta was when we took Elizabeth to the Dragonara Palace for an evening meal. We dressed up, remembering the glamour of a world class hotel, but as we arrived in the foyer, we were somewhat disconcerted to see a blackboard with words written in chalk, "Holiday-makers are requested not to go into dinner wearing their swimming costumes." It was very sad to see a once great hotel fallen so low. The food was appalling, the service disgusting. Harry was dead and Reg and Nora not long for this world.

The holiday to Malta taught us another interesting lesson. Once you have got a business, you can never get away from it. Even though I was a teacher, my stamp business was growing to such a level that I had staff and we were having enormous problems in those days with horrific-looking customs forms. We had only been in Malta for a couple of days when the first of the forms arrived plus other problems and from then onwards daily, we received a wondrous stream of annoying post, just to make sure that we couldn't switch off. I would have liked to have said I enjoyed filling in those customs forms, looking out across the bay at Sliema. I would have liked to have said so, but then I would have been a bloody liar. It was like having to go to the dentist every day, not knowing what was going to come in the post.

# CHAPTER 13

# *To Employ or Not to Employ, That is the Question*

*"All the best things in life are free*
*But you can tell that to the birds and bees*
*Just give me money!"*
*– Bern Elliott and the Fenmen*

The Malthouse at first was a great embarrassment to us. To my horror, on the very first day an international stamp dealer visited us. I tried, unsuccessfully, to hide at the back of our small stand but he spotted me.

"Hallo, Tony, I see you've opened a shop!" Although the words were fine it was the way he said them that indicated he wasn't impressed with my hole in the wall.

"It's the first day, Robin. And, as you can see, we're not very organised! Try us in a month and you'll find something, I promise." I didn't sound terribly confident and he thanked me in his superior voice and moved on.

We'd borrowed some stamps from our namesakes Keith and Kath Buckingham to get us going and, ironically, it was these that caused us the most trouble. Our first customer, or non-customer to be more correct, was an old man dressed in a shabby, brownish raincoat. He was bald with a beaky nose. He seemed just the sort of customer we needed.

"What have we here? Stamps! How interesting! Have you any Great Britain Queen Victoria stamps to show me?" He spoke very slowly with a charming accent.

"Yes, I've got a few books," I replied, passing over the borrowed priced-up approval books.

"Thank you so much," he politely replied. He started flicking through the books and then totally changed character.

"These stamps are priced far too high. Who do you think you are? Stanley Gibbons?"

"Well, to be honest, they aren't mine. I've borrowed them from a top dealer friend." I stuttered my reply.

"They're all rubbish and seconds anyway," he bellowed. "It's almost a crime. Nobody will buy from you, that I can assure you!" With that, he stalked off.

Cath looked at me rather worriedly. "I hope they're not all like that."

"So do I! If they are, we'll give our notice in."

Luckily most of the locals were harmless and were more interested in our cheap stamps and covers. The trouble was we seemed to pick up every sick person in the area. Cath was extremely kind and patient with them so she got lumbered. First day we only took twenty-five pounds, but we gradually built it up so we were averaging a hundred pounds each Saturday.

After about two months, we got the chance to move to a proper shop with a front door. Our takings were now nearly two hundred pounds for the one day. We were also travelling to distant exhibitions on Sundays which meant life was very hard. I was teaching full-time, working on the mail-order in the evenings, running the shop with Cath on Saturday, and then Cath drove us on Sundays to our show and we'd work all day. Seven days a week and twelve to fourteen hours a day was a hard act and I decided to employ a part-time stamp manager for the shop.

My experience with staff had not been a great success so far. As the business expanded I needed a reliable secretary to help me in the evenings. I advertised but I only got one reply. I decided to take her on without any checking. I phoned her up and arranged to meet. Her name was Marguerite and she told me she was blonde, typically Scandinavian and about twenty-four years old. Cath was somewhat dubious but I of course could see no problems. I'd always found beautiful Scandinavian blondes to be very acceptable. In fact, I'd always have voted for the Finnish entrants in the Miss World competition. It would appear that I was the only one, though, as they always got eliminated in the first round.

I waited expectantly for Marguerite to arrive. However, when she did I was in for a great disappointment. Scandinavian yes, but the other sort.

The ones you see in opera wearing pointed helmets. She could have gone five rounds with Thor. This regular Brunnhilde was not the best decision I ever made. To start with, I've never liked long fingernails on girls. I know it's bigoted. I, personally, find them revolting. Marguerite had the longest I'd ever seen and painted them a bright pink-ish red. They looked like talons.

"You know, I work far harder for you than I do at work," she confided one evening in her sickly little girl voice.

*Really,* I thought, *what do you do during the day? Sleep?*

"You know, you're a regular slave driver."

"Oh yes," I replied, wishing I could drive her out of the office.

Cath, of course, could see the funny side. She thought it hilarious. "But you like Swedish blonde bombshells. You know you do, so what's the problem?" she teased.

"The problem is, she's useless and she's irritating! I really must get rid of her," I added.

"Well, tell her!" said Cath. "What's the problem?"

The problem was, I didn't know how. It's easy taking on staff but very difficult to get rid of them. In the end, it took a major problem to lance that particular boil. My business was based on sending my dealer customers the first day covers they required for every British issue as well as a whole range of other covers. All of the information was stored in my standing order book. I had no copy. It was my entire business. In retrospect I was stupid, but you live and learn.

"I can't find my standing order book," I said to Brunnhilda early one evening. "Have you seen it?"

She went a little shifty and coloured slightly. "I took it home so I could make it easier to read," she replied.

"Well, where is it?"

"I think I left it at home."

"What!" I cried.

"At least, I think it's at home. I've sort of misplaced it!" she continued.

"You've what?" I shouted.

"Well, I might have lost it," she added.

"Lost it?" I roared. "That's my business gone if you have!"

"I'm sure it will turn up!" she said confidently. "Eventually!"

"Eventually! I need it now! You should never have taken it away." By now, I was virtually screaming at her.

"Don't shout at me, I was trying to help. You're a nasty man. I don't want to work for you anymore!"

At that point Cath came in, "What on earth's going on?" she asked.

"This idiot's lost my standing order book."

"Haven't you got a copy?" asked Cath hopefully.

"No, everything's in that book." With that I sat down, drained and very worried. It had taken me seven years to get here and I could see it all slipping away. All right, I'd had other problems like the time I sent virtually all my stock to a shop in Scarborough and it got stolen. But this was virtually the end.

"Where do you think you've put it?" Cath asked Marguerite in a more kindly way than I had.

"I don't know. It might be at home or I might have left it on the bus. I can't remember."

"Come on, let's go to your house now," insisted Cath. "I'll drive you home, then you can search for it."

With that, we all piled into the Hillman and rushed over to her house in Folkestone.

"You stay in the car, Tony," ordered Cath, "I'll go in with Marguerite."

I sat in the car for what seemed like hours. Eventually they came out again. Marguerite brandishing the book.

"Here! Here's your silly little book, horrible man. I'm not working for you anymore!"

With that she threw the book into the car and went back into her house, slamming the door after she went.

"Do you know where it was?" asked Cath, as she drove us home. "In the shed with the newspapers and magazines waiting to be taken by the dustbin men tomorrow! She would have gone to work tomorrow and your book would have gone forever."

When we got back, Cath grabbed the standing order book and copied it. "Now, keep both up to date. It's your insurance policy."

I was apprehensive about employing somebody else but, in order to expand and not die of over-work,

I needed some help. This time, I must have got the wording correct as I had about eight applications. One was even from someone who had actually worked for a long time for a proper stamp dealer in the north. He was my favourite on paper but I interviewed three candidates.

"Have you any stamp knowledge?" I enquired of the white-haired old man who came first.

"I should say so," he confidently began, "I've been collecting stamps all my life, and that's a long time."

"What are you like with people? Have you ever worked in a shop?"

"I've run the ticket office in the park last year but I have to admit most of my working life was in an office. You won't regret giving me this job, I'm bored, I don't like retirement. My wife still works and I really want to do something. Wouldn't ever let you down!"

Somehow, on first impressions, I didn't think that he would. I liked him. "Well, Mr Phillips, I've got to see a few more people but I'll let you know very quickly."

The next applicant was a young married woman with a small son. It was obvious that she couldn't do the job but she impressed me and I took a note of her address and phone number in case I wanted secretarial work done. She also volunteered to stick stamps and that was tempting. As we grew bigger, Cath and I were certainly finding the vast numbers of stamps to be stuck on in a short time very difficult.

The final applicant I interviewed was the professional stamp man and didn't he know it! He was a little, round, moon-faced man. Very dapper in dress and very pompous.

He was very condescending towards me and virtually told me I wasn't up to the sort of standard he was used to. According to local gossip, he even told several people after the interview that he didn't give me any chance in the stamp industry.

With virtually no choice, I took Len Phillips, the retiree, who really wanted the job.

As a bonus, we also got Phil, his wife, who besides being a hot saleswoman, enjoyed keeping the shop clean and neat when she wasn't working herself.

Len was a natural salesman. His only fault was he'd sell anything for any price. He would buy and sell quickly and I'm sure many people got some incredible bargains.

But he could be very annoying as well though. He even sold my own stamp collection that I'd left in the shop one day by mistake!

Len and Phil were very popular and we left them to run the Malt house on Fridays and Saturdays while we did more and more exhibitions. One thing that always puzzled me was that we took all the best stock off to the exhibitions and yet Len always managed to take more money back at the Malt house on the Saturday than we did.

Meanwhile, during the week I was still teaching at Lyminge, running clubs and societies during my lunch break, though why I should ever have got involved with swimming is a serious mystery. It's true, I can swim, in the same way as an old age pensioner with a Zimmer-frame could run. I never liked swimming very much as a child. The only good thing about it was the hot Bovril afterwards! We used to go by coach to an open-air bath in Letchworth. The temperature was always at a constant arctic the teacher's job was breaking the ice! It's hard to get enthusiastic about anything when you're worrying about bits dropping off with frostbite. At that centre of excellence for torture, I really learned what brass monkey weather meant. As far as I was concerned, the only time I enjoyed swimming was when the outside temperature was in excess of 80 degrees. On those rare days, plunging in cold water seemed almost a treat.

Things had obviously changed for the better and the trip to the indoor heated pool in Folkestone was poles apart from my previous experiences. Even then I would have not got involved but for the enthusiasm of my class. It was a swimming gala, and four of my girls wanted to enter a team for the individual medley relay. As it was in the evening they needed a teacher and I was the nominated mug. It seemed harmless enough so I agreed to help them, got the forms, sent the money, and duly entered the competition. The girls in the team were all excellent and, possibly even more important, were all very competitive. They practised as much as they could before the event and were really looking forward to doing their best.

The actual gala was normally at the outdoor pool on the sea-shore. This is gone now, but in those days Channel swimmers used to practise before going off to swim across to France and it was a valuable asset to the tourism of Folkestone.

Today, it is a valuable car-park for a massive Boot Fair, but then, that's progress! As it happened, the pool had a problem so the gala had to be switched to the indoor pool which was probably far better for my girls because they'd been used to swimming there.

As we travelled to the event, the excitement of the girls was infectious. They'd never experienced anything like it and the four were on a high. They went off to change and I wandered off round the pool to complete the formalities. When I went into the office the lady in charge seemed flustered.

"Are you Mr Buckingham?" she enquired. "From Lyminge School?"

"Yes! We're entering the medley relay and I've also got a boy going in for the butterfly."

"Oh dear! There seems to be a sort of misunderstanding, I'm afraid," she mumbled.

"What sort of misunderstanding?" I asked.

"Well, I'm afraid your girls can't enter the medley relay. I'm very sorry."

"I don't understand, why on earth not?" I asked as reasonably as I could under the circumstances.

"It's the rules, you see. I'm sorry."

"You keep saying you're sorry but that won't help my girls. What rules? What are you talking about?" By this time I was getting annoyed and I'm afraid my voice was rising.

"It's the school, it's too small. It's just not eligible for the medley relay. It's as simple as that." She said this confidently.

"Too small! What difference does size make? This is just stupid."

"No need to be rude. I didn't make the rules. Your school is just too small and that's that."

She obviously was used to rules being obeyed and thought that would be the end of the matter. I, on the other hand, was not going to tell those girls they couldn't race as the school was too small.

"All right, who makes the rules? I want to see them now!"

"It's Mrs Greenridge and she's busy!"

"I don't care if she is busy. I want to see her now! My girls will race unless somebody can convince me otherwise!"

"Hmm, hmm! Well, very well, I'll see if I can find her but she's very busy."

She gave me a look that should have made me feel like mouldy cheese and then off to find the rule-maker. I waited, getting myself ready for round two. At least I'd not given in at the first hurdle. The two ladies came back quietly talking. I could hear the odd word such as 'rude', 'ill mannered', 'unhelpful' drifting from the conversation.

"Mr Buckingham? I understand you have a problem?" Mrs Greenridge was a plump, country sort of woman, jolly hockey sticks and all that sort of thing.

"No, I don't have a problem. However, four extremely hard-working girls in my school do. I'm told they can't race as the school is too small. As far as I'm concerned that's rubbish. Why can't they race? They've paid the fee and you've accepted them."

"Well, we'll give you your money back, naturally," she said condescendingly.

"It's not the money and you know it! They really want to swim and it'll break their hearts if they can't. Particularly for such a stupid reason."

"Young man, the rules are there to protect them. How do we know they'll be able to swim two lengths? We must think of safety!" she said triumphantly. "We don't want a tragedy, do we?"

So that was it, as we were small we couldn't possibly have four reasonably good swimmers.

"My good woman," I said, knowing it would annoy her, "I'm a Deputy Head. I'm a responsible teacher who takes safety very seriously. Do you think for one minute I would bring children who couldn't swim two lengths and enter them in this competition? That's an insult to my professional standing. If it's just a case of safety, then let them enter." I spoke as reasonably as I could and then glared at both ladies.

"They'll just be humiliated," said Mrs Greenridge, "it would be much better not to."

"I don't care if they finish ten minutes after the other schools. That's not the point. They want to swim, I want them to swim, stop being so stupid and let them swim!" I shouted this point perhaps a little too loud but at least it got the result.

"Very well! But if one drowns, it'll be your responsibility. Anyway, I really can't waste any more time. I've got work to do!" With that, she turned and sailed away like a schooner in full sail.

I returned to my girls who seemed worried.

"Is there anything wrong?" asked Denise, a farmer's daughter who was the keenest of the swimmers.

"Why should there be anything wrong?" I asked.

"Well, we saw you talking to old Greenie," said Alisa, a very fit, athletic-looking, tall Major's daughter.

"Yes, well we had a few points to sort out," I replied, trying not to laugh.

"They were very loud points," giggled Sharon, a delightful fish and chip shop owner's daughter. She was also exceptionally tall and very powerful-looking.

"I like to put my points firmly so perhaps I raised my voice."

"Go on. You were having a row, weren't you?" added Jackie, the local publican's daughter, who liked to be the zany one. "They didn't want us to enter, did they?"

"What makes you think that?" I asked.

"Oh, just what some of the girls said. Are we still in the competition?" she said hopefully.

"Of course you are, but whatever you do, make sure you do don't drown or I will be for the high jump!"

The gala continued and we got nearer and nearer to the medley relay. The event was fairly simple: each girl had to swim one length of her chosen specialist stroke (i.e. backstroke, breaststroke) and the second freestyle. The event started and about nine girls lined up. The whistle went and off they went.

To our amazement, Sharon started pulling away from the rest of the field. The gap got wider and wider and wider. We were about five or six yards ahead at the changeover and Sharon powered back to give Alissa a commanding lead after the first leg.

Alissa's backstroke was very powerful and she not only held the lead but started to increase it.

By the halfway stage we were something like half a length in the lead. Denise's breaststroke was easily the best in the field and the lead just got bigger and bigger and bigger. When Jackie dived in on the final stretch, our lead was a length! She continued to swim as hard and as bravely as she could and held the length so we actually won the medley relay over all the 'big schools' by a fantastic distance. I couldn't believe it. The girls hugged each other and went up to collect the cup. We were then amazed by the announcement over the loud speaker.

"The girls from Lyminge School have not only won the Bryant Cup but they have broken the record that had stood for over thirty years! Congratulations to Lyminge School for a fantastic race!"

There was a great cheer and clapping came from round the pool. The girls were so pleased with themselves. Although I'd done nothing as far as the swimming was concerned, I took pleasure in the fact that, without my belligerence and determination, they would not have been allowed to race. I was also rather pleased with the very large silver trophy that we took back to Lyminge.

I often thought of the way the girls reacted before the race as if they knew something I didn't. I very much got the impression that they thought they wouldn't be allowed to compete, not because they were too small, but for the fact that they were almost certainly going to be amongst the favourites to win the cup and it might have been in someone's interest to pull rules on them to stop them racing. I'm probably being too cynical. Then, I majored in cynicism in the world of hard knocks.

I was getting worried about the legal side of my business and getting my accounts submitted. When I first got down to Hythe, I had consulted an accountant to get some advice. He'd told me that the most sensible course of action was to become a limited company and had promptly charged me an arm and a leg to register me as such and then disappeared. That had been some time ago and I did realise that unless I did something about accounts I would probably be in trouble with the law. Being a very law-abiding sort of person, that was not something to look forward to.

By now I was dragging Cath off to every local exhibition within a fifty-mile radius in order to promote our shop and also our new first issue cover service. We'd gradually built up a collection of local customers who came to us at these exhibitions. It was amazing how far they travelled.

One of these customers had a very strange voice. It was almost Kenneth Williams camp but not quite. It had an incredible quality of its own and it was a sort of natural voice if you wanted a Nancy boy to appear in a stage play. The chap himself was very pleasant; about fifty, roundish red face, blackish hair thinning at the top and obviously a very keen stamp collector. As we got to know him over the weeks and months, we found he was an accountant for Walmer near Deal. I broached the subject of my own particular problem i.e. my accounts.

"And who's doing them at the moment?" he enquired. "I can't take work off another accountant, not without their permission. You've got to understand that!"

"That's not a problem," I said, "in fact, nobody's doing my accounts which is worrying."

"Yes, well you should be worried," he said, "not doing accounts is rather bad. You say you're a limited company, when were you started?"

"Oh, about a year ago."

"Well, that's not too bad. What sort of records have you got?"

"Well, I keep everything I can. I've got it all in boxes and box files and folders."

"Well, I'll have a look. I'm not going to make any promises. I can't give you a decision."

"Well, why don't you come over to my house one evening and we can sort it out?"

"Right, how about next Tuesday? I've got to come over to Saga, then I can come onto you afterwards."

He duly arrived on Tuesday evening at our house. I'd got all my records out and showed him what I'd got.

"This is quite good," he said condescendingly, "I'm surprised, a lot of people don't keep the records properly but these are quite good! I can work from this sort of thing. What do want me to do?"

"Well, I'd like you to get me up to date and then keep me on the straight and narrow."

"Do you want me to go back before the limited company?"

"Just start with that. Yes, I think I'd like you to get it all sorted out and get everything legitimised."

"All right, well I think I can work from most of this. You'll just have to tell me a stock figure at the end of each year. You'll have to make it up obviously because you can't go back and do it now. But I don't think that'll matter, just give us an idea and then we'll get things going."

So I worked out the sort of stock I probably had in hand at the end of each year and Peter got together all my papers and then started to look round.

"Oh yes, that's a nice set of stamps, isn't it? I've always liked those. How much are they?"

"Oh, that's five pounds."

"Oh, that's good. Yes I'll have those. Oh, that's a nice cover as well, isn't it? How much is that?"

"Oh, that's six pounds."

"Oh yes, I'll have that, too and I'll have those too. That's, what, twenty-two isn't it? All right."

He took his stamps and my work off. He was a very efficient accountant and actually very clever. He was back within a few days with my first year's accounts.

"I can't start before 1968, it just won't work. Here's your 1968 accounts."

He presented me his bill and then started to look round. "Oh, I've always liked the George V sets, they're lovely. This set from the Gambia is super. How much is this one?"

"That's nine pounds."

"Oh, I'll have that. Oh, you've got one from the Seychelles. I'll have that too and this set from Bechuanaland."

I gave him a cheque for thirty-five pounds and he gave me a cheque for forty pounds!

He went off and was back again in a few days.

"I've got the 1969 accounts. They're all finished." He gave them back to me and proceeded to buy another lot of stamps. At the end of the evening he gave me a cheque for fifty-five pounds and I gave him a cheque for forty pounds, he disappeared off and was back again within the week.

"That's 1970, we're getting on. I'm very pleased, it's actually amazing how well you kept everything. Mind you, I don't think many other people would find it so easy because, of course, I know the stamp dealers so it makes it easy for me to check the invoices." He again gave me his bill and looked round. At the end of the evening I paid him forty-five pounds and he paid me sixty!

He came back a week later with the 1971 accounts. He gave me the accounts and a bill and again spent an hour or so going through the stamps lying around and this time I gave him a cheque for sixty-five pounds and he gave me a cheque for a hundred and ten! Off he went again and, sure enough, just over a week later he was back again with the 1972 accounts.

"I'm not coming in," he said at the doorway, "here are your accounts and my bill."

I said, "Why aren't you coming in, Peter?"

"I can't afford to. I can't really do your accounts

any more, not unless you promise to put away the stamps. I've worked out it's costing me too much to do your accounts."

"I thought it was rather a good business relationship," I said, "come on Peter, I'll put the stamps away. We'll keep you away from them." He came in and we had a cup of coffee.

"It's all too much temptation," he said worriedly, "I can't resist them. Everywhere I look there's stamps."

He picked up my latest first day cover catalogue. I was in a partnership to produce the bible, as far as first day cover collectors were concerned, and he flipped through it with great interest. "This is good," he said. "Do you send it out to your customers on approval?"

"No I don't!" I said, annoyed at such a suggestion. "I only send it to those that order it."

"Then more fool you then! I get sent the Commonwealth Catalogue from Urch Harris on approval. They always tell me I can send it back if I don't want it. By the time I've looked through it I always keep it. I reckon you ought to send it to all your customers. Give them a nice letter, one of your specials, you're good at that. I bet you'll be surprised how many you sell."

"Oh, I don't know. It seems a bit cheeky," I said.

But after he went, I thought about it. I had about a thousand customers by then and if most of them took it, it would certainly help with the print run. It was a very cheap publication. His idea proved excellent. Not only did most people keep them but I got many letters telling me how interesting the catalogue was and how much they enjoyed receiving it. It also stimulated a lot of orders so, in the end, probably made us a few thousand pounds profit. It was typical of Peter; a sort of wolf in sheep's clothing.

Peter was also extremely nosy. He would wander off round the house.

"And what have we got in here?" he enquired, opening up cupboard doors. "Oh, yes and what's this?"

At the time we thought he was just being nosy. At other times he would taunt us: "What you doing it for?" he'd ask in a sarcastic tone.

"Well, to build a business."

"Yes, but what are you getting out of it?"

"Well, I thought that one day perhaps it would become something large enough to support us."

"Yeah, but what have you got? Why aren't you rich?"

I looked at him sitting on the old settee that we bought when we first got married which had deteriorated so much that he was actually sitting right through it and virtually on to the floor. We'd hung some temporary curtains up when we first moved in, and they were still there. We were working seven days a week. We both were tired out. He had a good point. What were we doing it for? I thought I'd reverse it round and ask him the question.

"Well, what do you think we should be doing?"

"I can't give an opinion," he replied. "That's not my job."

"Well, if it was your job?"

"Oh, that's complicated. It's wheels within wheels."

This was one of his favourite expressions. At the same time he revolved both hands round looking very serious. I think it was meant to represent things were always much more complicated than you think. Changing the subject, I asked him about a friend of ours, a builder who was a very keen stamp collector and was one of his clients.

"How's Dave? Haven't seen him for a while."

"Oh, Dave. Oh dear, what can I say? Boom-boom!" Again, he was very fond of 'boom-boom' and it was a sort of catch thing at the time. "I saw him yesterday actually. I asked him why he didn't like money. He told me he did like money, liked it a lot. I said, 'You can't like money, 'cos soon as you've got it, you throw it away. What's wrong with you? Why don't you keep it yourself?' I'm glad he collects stamps, at least it'll be something to sell at the end of it."

Dave was great fun. He was normally out of the area building in various parts of the country but when he did come over, Cath, myself and Dave had quite a good routine. We all got together and put together the following act:

"What can I say, I can't give an opinion. Wheels within wheels, boom-boom!"

We did it beautifully synchronised, doing the correct Peter mannerisms for each expression. Joking apart though, this eccentric accountant was one of the best things that happened to us in the early days of the business and we were all very fond of him.

Much of my business was done on the phone and I was aware that I was missing quite a lot of sales because I was out most of the day.

"I'm going to rent one of these new-fangled answer phones," I told Cath confidently one morning over breakfast.

Breakfast consisted of milky coffee and toast with either Bovril, Marmite, or marmalade. It was grabbed on the run as we were usually very late for school.

"I suppose it makes some sort of sense," replied Cath doubtfully, "trouble is, I hate them! I honestly think most people do."

"Yeah, I don't like them but it's the future. We're not here all day and many of our customers are full-time. They don't want to phone in the evening."

Everything I said made perfect sense. The trouble was my own customers. We had all sorts. Some were very efficient. "Hallo Tony. John Reid here from Trend Supply Service. Can you please increase my standing order by ten, and can you send me ten of the last three issues? Thanks."

Excellent. Clear, brief and easy. Many of our customers were similar and it was marvellous to come home from school and find an order on the answer phone for a hundred pounds. However, not all was similar. I had one answer phone addict. He spoke in a sort of moronic Goon voice; a cross between Bluebottle and Eccles.

"It's Alan Jones here. Isn't it a lovely day and I thought it might rain but it hasn't and the sun is really warm for this time of the year! I was thinking of going to Brighton for the day. Oh, while I think of it, send me two 1965 Churchill first day covers. I've always liked Brighton, the lanes towns. Oh, increase my Jersey order for commemoratives up to six, please? I've got a new customer, he's not very nice but I suppose beggars can't be choosers. Could you check the invoice you sent me last week with the Salvation Army cover with it? I think it's wrong. Soon be Christmas, won't it? The Salvation Army band will be playing carols. I wonder if it will snow? I'd like the snow at Christmas – wouldn't you? Oh, I'll have three 1966 Christmas first day covers, please. They'd better be phosphor and, oh, they'd better be Bethlehem post-marks. I've never been to Bethlehem. I thought I'd go some time. Oh, with those Churchill first day covers, they needn't be special. Don't want Blaydon or Churchill, just an ordinary post-mark will do."

The conversation would go on, and on, and on which seemed like forever. But you had to listen because every so often an order drifted in as his mind wandered. If he got onto the machine first, he filled up the entire tape. He also phoned regularly!

Perhaps the one I liked the most was a customer in Bury in Lanes. He was very careful to ensure that every word was spoken with great clarity so there could be no possibility that I got it wrong. He spoke very slowly indeed with a very strong Lancashire accent.

"Fra-aa-nk Bar-rnes, 18, Mo-orgate, Bury, Lancs. That's Frank Barnes, 18 Moorgate, Bury, Lancs. Please send a 1948 Olympic Games first day cover. That's an Olympic Games first day cover from 1948

and it's for Frank Barnes, 18 Moorgate, Bury, Lanes."
He phoned virtually every day for one cover.

I was getting rather worried about money. On paper, as my father always used to put it, I had plenty. Trouble is, paper wouldn't pay the Post Office and I was running out of actual cash. I suppose I should say I had a short-term liquidity problem. It was all my own fault as I didn't chase the debts hard enough. I found it embarrassing to ask for money, which I think is a problem that most small-businessmen have.

Our friend and customer, Dave Lewis, told us once about a doctor who owed him thousands and thousands of pounds for building work. However he tried he didn't get paid so he booked an appointment to see the doctor.

"What seems to be the problem?" started the doctor pompously.

"I've got a very bad case of financial blues. There's only one cure. You write me a prescription or let's call it a cheque? After all, I don't want anything of yours, I only want what's mine." It apparently worked and Dave got his money.

"I'm going to have to become tough with the people who owe me money," I confided to Cath one evening. "Stop laughing! It's not that funny."

"You? You hate anything to do with chasing money. How are you going to do it?"

"Well, for a start I'm going to visit some of them." Cath looked at me doubtfully.

"But I'll phone first." My debt collecting was quite an eye-opener.

"There's no need to get shirty," said Colin in a broad Suffolk accent. He was one of my oldest customers. He was always very slow in paying and in fact he owed me money that went back over nine months. "Your money's perfectly safe, I've got it on deposit at the bank."

*Great!* I thought. *I'm worried sick and he's earning interest on my money!* Ironically, the interest he was earning was coming out of the interest I was paying to borrow my own money!

Some turned nasty when I asked for money. "You owe me two hundred and sixty-eight pounds," I would tell them confidently, "and most of its very overdue. Please send me a cheque?"

"Ah, I've been intending to talk to you. Now, I've never received an invoice, obviously not paid the bill. Sort it out, will you?"

When I checked the invoice. It was for one pound fifty and had only been just sent. I phoned back. "I've checked invoice 1621 and it's only for one pound recent. So you may well not have received it. Just send the balance, two hundred and sixty-six pounds fifty, and send the one pound fifty when it turns up. Perhaps that will make you happy?" I said hopefully.

"No, no I like things straight. I'll wait for the missing goods. It'll be better that way," came the clever reply.

"Look, I need the money! You haven't paid for three months," I replied, my voice getting louder. "Send me, say, two hundred pounds on account if you're short of money."

"How dare you? I'm not staying on the phone

listening to rubbish like this!" With that, he slammed the phone down. I was upset and he had again avoided paying me anything.

"Bit late in paying. At least you'll get it in the next day or so."

A week later I was back on the phone. "Er, the cheque hasn't turned up. Are you sure you sent it?" I enquired hopefully.

"Oh dear, it must have got lost in the post. Look, wait until the end of the week and then if it hasn't turned up I'll cancel it and send you a replacement."

It all sounded plausible but I'm now three weeks away and I've still got no money.

Eventually after five weeks I get the cheque. "Old Wiseman's paid at last!" I told Cath on Saturday morning. "Look, I've got a cheque for two hundred and fifty pounds!"

"Aren't they worth more signed?" asked Cath sarcastically.

"Oh no!" I groaned. "He hasn't signed the bloody cheque!" Back goes the cheque and two weeks later I get it back. It's now six weeks since I started and he owes me twice as much as he did when I first started, with new invoices. However, at least it's something.

A week later I get a letter back from the bank saying please represent the cheque, which meant he hadn't got the money at that time but he might have when I represented it. I pay it in again. A week later it's back from the bank with a second 'please represent'. We're now eight weeks from when I started and I'm beginning to get worried. A week later the cheque was back, this time rubber stamped in red 'refer to drawer'. This in broad financial terms means that it's a rubber cheque and if I drop it it'll bounce up and smash me in the face. Now, I'm worried! The miserable so-and-so had actually doubled the money he owed me by being tricky. However, there were further lessons to be learned.

One of my customers ran a small shop in the Midlands. I had met him once and he'd complained about his arthritis. How he could hardly walk or use his hands. He knew about my father and knowing the agony it caused I was very sympathetic to his problems. His problems, I must admit, were mainly non-payment of my bills. This went on for a long, long time when one day I phoned and he was out and I got his wife.

"Oh, how's Bill?" I asked.

"Fine," she said in a sort of country accent, "he's playing table tennis at the moment. Did you know he plays for the town?" She told me this very proudly.

"Hasn't he been ill?" I asked.

"Well, he did have a cold about a month a cold, but you know Bill, he's never ill! Can I take a message?"

"Yes," I said, "tell him Tony Buckingham phoned and my solicitor will write to him."

"The trouble with you Tony is you're just too kind," confided Bill Brown, one of my nicer customers. "I pay the horrible ones first and leave people like you to know it's not fair but that's life." It was all too true. I had to change my act or leave the play altogether.

"I'm going up to Manchester for a couple of days, debt collecting," I told Cath one beautiful sunny morning, "do you want to come?"

"No, I'll go to Birmingham to see Dad. Why don't you go with another dealer?"

"That's a good idea. I'll see if Gerald wants to come." Gerald was one of my customers and he lived in the Midlands. He liked the idea of a buying trip to the north-west so off we went.

My first visit was to the famous Frank Barnes. His shop was shut so I went into the adjoining premises which sold wet fish.

"Excuse me," I asked the aggressive-looking woman who was running the shop, "any idea when the stamp shop will be open?"

"Frank!" she screamed in broad Lancashire, "customers for you!"

At that point I realised the shops were adjoined; a door opened into the stamp shop.

"Hallo!" said Frank, smiling. He was a short, tubby man with dirty grey hair and loud check braces. "Come on through. What do you collect?"

"Money," I said, "I'm Tony Buckingham from Benham." The smile froze and then completely disappeared.

"Well, I'll just shut this door, if you don't mind. It stops the fish smell getting in." He quickly shut the door. His voice became much softer. "I've been meaning to send you a cheque, Tony, but I've been so busy, you can't imagine."

That was certainly true. I couldn't imagine. Frank

busy? The shop was filthy and chaotic.

"I'll write one out straight away," he continued. I got the impression he didn't want his wife to know he owed money. He probably only did the stamps to get away from the wet fish. I had to admit, she did look rather terrifying. I never had any problem with Frank over money after my visit.

My next visit was to the largest and most prestigious stamp shop in the north-west.

They were not my customers at that time but I certainly wished they were. We met the son first, who was very pleasant. Although he was referred to as "Young Mr Lee," he was considerably older than me. Eventually, the great old man came out. He was a legend in the north. We were introduced and I put my hand out. He turned his back on me, muttering: "I don't deal with the trade" and walked out.

"I'm sorry about that," said young Mr Lee, "I'm afraid he makes the decisions." It was a shame. We both wanted to buy some covers but his word was law – in those parts.

We visited many stamp shops, buying and collecting money and eventually I tracked down another of my very bad debts. The man was an Alderman. I'd taken him to court but the summons apparently couldn't be served. They said they couldn't find his house. We thought a visit to the police station might help to locate him. The tired-looking policemen looked up across the counters at us.

"What can I do you for?"

"Do you know where this house is?" I asked, passing the address over the counter.

"There!" he pointed through the window. "Not hard, was it?"

The house was opposite the police station and the authorities couldn't find it to service my warrant! So much for justice!

"Thank you very much, you've helped us enormously."

"Oh, I wish all my jobs were that easy!" he replied, laughing.

We walked across the road and knocked on the door. A large, fat, ruddy-faced man opened the door.

"What is it you want?" he asked.

"My name's Buckingham, Tony Buckingham from Benham. I called because you haven't paid your bills for a while."

"Oh yes? You'd better come in then." He let us through into his living room. "You'd better make yourself a cup of tea because I'm going out. I'll be back." He left.

I looked at Gerald and he looked at me. "You don't think he's going out to get help, do you?" asked Gerald, worriedly. "He looks the sort who might have some rough friends.

"I shouldn't think so."

"Well, I'm going to make some tea anyway," said Gerald, so he went into the kitchen and set about finding the tea, teapot, kettle etc. while I looked round the room.

It was absolutely amazing. It was full of my covers. None of them had been taken out of the envelopes.

They must go back five, six, seven years. The whole wall was covered. There was a fortune sitting there. "Gerald, look at this lot! He hasn't done anything with any of the covers I've sent him and lots of them aren't even opened. No wonder he doesn't know he owes me money!"

So we sat in that cosy sitting room, drinking tea and waiting. Eventually the alderman came back.

"Sorry about that. I had to go out. Here, how much do I owe you?"

With that, we left. I couldn't believe my luck. I thought I'd lost the money. Not only had I not lost the debt but I'd also regained a customer and had some more business.

The only problem is I had to fill in the cheque. Would you believe it, I actually got it wrong and had to botch it up, knowing I wouldn't get another one from him. The other extraordinary thing was, it didn't come back 'please represent', it didn't come back 'refer to drawer', it went straight through with absolutely no problem at all. I don't know what he bought the covers for and I often wondered what happened to them.

*

I had a particularly bad day at school. Nothing had gone right. It was wet, it was cold.

I'd walked home and got caught in a heavy shower. I had to change my clothes. I went into my office. I flicked the answer machine on.

"Hallo Tony, it's Alan Jones here. Oh, it's raining cats and dogs 'ere."

That's all I need! Half an hour of Alan Jones – that's just perfect. I couldn't face it at that moment and so I opened the post. There was a very smart-looking letter from the Ohio Stamp and Coin Company from America. I opened it carefully. It was an amazingly large order. One of the biggest I'd ever seen. I looked and thought, *Well, this changes the day. It's not such a bad one after all!*

At the bottom of the order was a large red sticker which said, "Please see conditions attached to this order. If conditions are not met no payment will be made." Very strange, I thought, so I looked at the conditions. They were very elaborate. They stated the way I had to send the covers, the way they had to be packed, the wording that had to be on the outside of the packing, that they had to be broken into four separate parcels, they had to be sent to different addresses, they had to be insured at my expense. The list went on forever.

*You petty little sod*, I thought. *At least, if he's that fussy, he's hardly likely to be dishonest!* I organised all the covers together, put them into four separate packets, packed them exactly as he instructed, wrapped them carefully, addressed them in the way he'd asked and posted them the next day off to America.

The next night I boasted to Peter Mabey about my major export drive. "Do you know, I've got customers now in Australia, New Zealand, Canada, Japan, Hong Kong, Cyprus, Malta, most of Europe and a large number of customers in the States. I really am becoming an international stamp dealer!"

"Well, that's good," said Peter, "I don't know if you'll like what I've got for you, though. It's your accounts for 1972."

"Oh yes? Why shouldn't I like them?"

"Well, you better look."

I opened it up and we made a profit of nearly two thousand pounds which meant I had to pay a lot of tax. "What? How on earth have I got all this tax to pay? I gave you the stock figure, Peter."

"Yeah, you gave me the stock figure. Yes, no problem but you didn't tell me about the cash, did you?"

"What cash?"

"You had a lot of money at the bank. Well, you can't do anything with that. Money's money, if you've got it, you've got it. You've got to pay the tax."

"But it's nearly a thousand pounds!"

"Well, I can't help it. If you made it, you got to pay it. That's the trouble with all my clients. If they have a bad year they blame me. If they have a good year they blame me for the tax. I can't win!"

"Why is it so high?" I asked.

"Well, if I remember rightly, you found those missing Queen's heads on those Church stamps. You have to pay the tax on your evil gains." Peter continued in that extraordinary camp, South London voice of his. "I've brought your bill and I'm not going to buy anything today."

"Oh, that's a shame," I said, as I paid him his cheque, "that means you've actually got some money out of me at last!"

"It won't last long. You'll soon have it back.

Anyway I must go, I'm going dancing with Gloria."
The way he said dancing, making every letter very
long and the emphasis on Gloria, was extraordinary. I
had visions of him with a rose in his mouth dancing
with a Spanish flamenco dancer. But then, perhaps
not!

Peter made his excuses and headed off for his
dancing date and I got back to doing my orders. *I'd
better check the answer phone*, I thought.

"It's Alan Jones here, God it's windy, don't know
if it's blowing your way. Really is blowing here. I
thought of having a curry tonight. You can get good
curries from a take-away. Have you got a take-away
curry place?" *Here we go again!* I thought. *Half an hour of
rubbish and I do wish he'd just give me the orders.*

# CHAPTER 14

## *Taking the Plunge*

I had a letter from the bank. It was curt and to the point.

"Dear Mr Buckingham, I would be glad if you would call to see me at your earliest convenience. Signed P. Pelham Plunket, Manager."

"Oh my God!" I said to Cath. "If he's going to take my overdraft away I've got real problems!"

I'd never actually met a bank manager in my life. When I was at Bedford I dealt with the chief clerk's assistant's assistant – if he was available that was. If not, I saw the assistant. The only time I actually got a letter from the bank was to point out I was six pounds overdrawn. Like most people I was terrified of bank managers. I duly made my appointment and with great apprehension and worry and concern, I turned up at the bank.

"Can I help you?" said a bright young thing behind the counter.

"Ah, yes, I I've got an, er, an appointment to see the bank, the bank manager um, er, er a Mr Plunket?"

"He is expecting you, is he?" she asked firmly.

"Ah, yes, yes I did say I'd come."

"Well, you'd better sit down over there then."

I sat down and glanced at the magazines. You know the sort of thing:

"Bankruptcy – is it really necessary?"

"Why take that risk?"

"Are you never too late to get a pension, who knows what's going to happen to you next up when you're worried anyway."

I sat for about half an hour getting myself more and more into a state. *I know he's going to stop my overdraft. How am I going to buy the stamps? I should have chased the debtors harder*, I thought. *It's my own fault, I'm so soft.* Eventually, the girl came across.

"Mr Buckingham? Mr Plunket will see you now."

As I got up a very worried-looking man came out of the bank manager's office, white in the face and looking terrified. He walked slowly out of the bank and I thought, *Oh dear, my turn next!*

I went into the room and a short, fat-ish, middle-aged man with an impressive moustache greeted me. He was wearing a brown tweed suit with waistcoat and when he spoke his voice seemed totally wrong for the body.

"Good afternoon Mr Buckingham," he said; the most beautiful, deep and, I'm told by my wife, sexy voice you could imagine. It was very impressive. "Won't you sit down?"

I sat down, hands slightly shaking and sweating.

"I'm very grateful that you've come in. I've been

looking at your account and I'm very worried about it."

I thought, *Oh no, it confirms my worst suspicion – he's going to take my overdraft away.*

"I honestly don't understand how you can work on the overdraft facility we are allowing you," he continued. "It really is giving you no scope whatsoever to run your business. I thought, the best thing I can do is multiply it by three for a start."

*Am I hearing what he's saying?* I thought in astonishment. *He's not going to take away my overdraft, he's going to treble it!*

"Your account is most impressive," he continued, "I've actually used it recently at a talk at the Banker's Institute. You have a classic swing."

With that he wasn't actually referring to my bowling technique or even my golf swing, but apparently I borrowed money, paid it back, borrowed it again, paid it back. It worked on a monthly cycle.

"You are the classic bank account. Exactly what an overdraft's about. I'd also like you to know that if you need any extra money for something that comes up, please do not hesitate to come and see me. I'm sure it can be arranged. By the way, I'm having a little party for my better customers next Tuesday evening at seven thirty. I'd be delighted if you and your wife would attend. I live at Oak Walk at the end of the High Street. Thank you for coming in to see me, Mr Buckingham."

I left in a sort of daze. With that extra money I could certainly do more with the business. I'd often had to turn away good collections simply because I hadn't got the money. In most cases, I could have bought and sold within a few days but I just couldn't take the risk, knowing I needed the money for the next.

"I've been thinking about these EEC stamps," I said to Cath one cold day just after Christmas. "Wouldn't it be fabulous to get a French post-mark on them? Our customers would be very pleased with it. It would be quite a nice day out."

"How do you get a French post-mark on English stamps?" asked Cath.

"Well, they've got to be on ship and they've got to go into a French port. It's called a paquebot. In other words, posted at sea. I thought we'd just go across on the boat to Calais and see if we can talk the French post-office into doing them for us."

"Well, it would be a nice day out and I've never been to Calais," replied Cath.

"Calais? France? I've never been out of the country," I said, "it will be the very first time I've ever left Great Britain."

We caught the ferry in the early morning, explained what we wanted to do, and were sent down to an office where we found a very hairy old man who apparently was doing the same thing. At the time, we didn't realise that it was his project, he'd got all the official permissions. We were literally muscling in on his idea.

However, he was a very nice man. Not only did he allow us to join in but he even let us use his own ship's cachet which he'd had specially designed and made. The old fellow was Eric Ivens who we'd get to know much better when we became full-time stamp dealers. His company was known as 'Historic Relics' and we always thought of him as the old relic. He had wonderful Victorian sideburns and would be ideal for any Victorian melodrama.

I spent the whole of the journey over putting ship's cachets on all of our covers. Mr Ivens was only putting one on but as there were two different ones I put two on all of our covers. Mr Ivens kindly organised our covers into the French post office and also arranged for some of ours to go back to Folkestone to get a Folkestone paquebot. It was really nice of him as without our covers, his would have been worth a lot more.

The value of collectables is all about scarcity.

We left the ship and went ashore to have a few hours in Calais. I don't know what I expected but certainly not grey sky, sparrows and the same cold weather. Why should it be any different? After all, we could see Calais from Folkestone, but I just imagined foreign parts would be different. We found a small café and went in.

We looked at the menu and I started to laugh.

"Look!" I giggled to Cath. "They've got raped carrot and crudities. What are we coming to, a whore house?"

Cath laughed. "I don't know what they are. Perhaps it's worth ordering to find out."

I did order the crudités. They were really crude and revolting, oily nasty things. Cath had the raped carrot which simply was grated carrot with some form of salad. In all, the meal was not memorable.

"I thought the French were supposed to be good at food. That was disgusting," I said as we left.

"We must have picked badly," said Cath, "I'm sure they're not all like that.

We returned home on the ferry and the next day our covers arrived from the post office.

They were superb. It was just after we'd managed to get hold of the business of John Read of Trend Supply Services and we sent out all the covers with the paquebot post-mark to them and all our other customers.

At the time we charged thirty pence which was the same as we always charged. We made no allowance for the cost of our trip to France. We never thought of charging any extra. We were just pleased that we'd managed to do it. The collectors that received those covers from us must have been very pleased particularly as today the covers sell for about thirty-five pounds. Although we didn't make any profit those covers we certainly did make a lot of friends and that goodwill obviously helped us greatly in the future.

Now that John Read had gone from Trend Supply Services, my best customer had become Martin Stead. He ran a very successful business from home and his orders were getting bigger and bigger. I was very surprised one day to get a phone call from him:

"Tony, I've got new curtains!" he said.

"Oh yes?"

"And a new desk, it's much bigger than before. I've also got carpet for the first time and a car-parking space."

"Oh, well done!" I said. "You'll be telling me next you've got a picture to go on the wall." I thought this was very strange phone call, normally he was asking me for covers or putting up his standing order. It seemed very odd to tell me he's got a new desk, curtains, carpet, car-parking space. *What's he on about?*

"Oh I see, Tony, you don't know much about business, do you? What I'm telling you is, I've got a very big promotion. So big that I'm having to give up stamps. Do want to buy the business?"

"Well, yes, of course, if the price is right," I said. "How much are we talking about?"

"Well, I don't know. I suppose if we work on the value of the stock which obviously is the main cost, about eight thousand pounds. And then there's some mint stamps I want to sell at the same time but I'll sell those at face."

"Well, it sounds all right. Perhaps I can come and see you?"

Cath and I went that weekend to somewhere near Reading.

His house was what would be described today as a four bedroomed detached executive-style home. A little bit like Brookside but obviously in a much more expensive area; the 'Silicon Valley' of Britain.

Looking at Martin's stock it was obvious that the price was a fair one. The only problem is, I had to take about three thousand pounds worth of Jersey and Guernsey mint stamps that I didn't really want. But as they were costing just face value it wasn't really much risk. I could always sell them to somebody for postage if I couldn't find another dealer to buy them.

He allowed me to buy it in four sections: two thousand pounds a month for four months and this would work very well as it would enable me to chase many of my debts and get them back in and also use this new overdraft facility that I'd been given by Percival Plunket. I also thought I'd better pop in and see the bank manager and just tell him what I was doing.

As we drove back to Hythe, I told Cath the best bit of the deal. "The amazing thing is that no-one values the customers. Every time I buy a business I only buy stock. I buy the stock at a price that I think is fair and would buy anyway, possibly slightly paying a little bit more, but it means if I can sell the stock I get the customers for nothing."

Although Martin Stead was one of the most impressive purchases with so many new customers, this had been happening in a small way for a long time. Many people started up as stamp dealers, got a few customers, then lost interest and would pass on their customers to me with what stock they had accumulated. As I had so many trade customers, I could normally sell the stock I didn't want to them and sell the rest of it to the collectors that I was gradually building up.

I also was full of all sorts of silly gimmicks. For example, I used to have a 'Pay the Taxman' sale. This is the one that I told the customers that, according to my accountant, we'd had a very good year but the trouble is, the good profit was simply in covers and as I can't pay the tax with covers, I've got to sell the covers to pay the tax.

I'd then follow that up with a 'Pay the VAT man'

sale. We'd been so successful in selling the covers to pay the tax, we now owe so much money to the VAT authorities that we've got to sell covers to raise that money.

So we'd follow all that up with a summer sale. The collectors loved it. We always put in silly things like:

"Offer 327: if you've read this far you can knock 50p off your order."

"Offer 471: congratulations, you've read 471 offers therefore you can claim 10% discount."

It had a jolly good effect of making people look right through my offers and spot all sorts of things that they might not have noticed. It also helped to make us much more successful.

After we'd taken over Martin Stead, our largest customer was an RAF officer called Graham Lewis. He was as mad as I was and the two of us got on very well on the phone for many years. He was a super chap; a natural salesman and dealer. He told me that he once went to his local shop and they had a very cheap offer of shampoo. In fact amazingly cheap. He bought the lot and sold it all at a fifty per cent profit round the RAF station. He couldn't resist a bargain and I don't think it mattered to him what business he was in as long as he was enjoying himself. He helped me once at an exhibition in Bath and he was absolutely outrageous. The two of us put on a vaudeville act for the collectors and our stand was packed for the entire two-day exhibition.

Just after, I'd been very lucky with an auction purchase in Hythe, where I'd managed to buy a large and valuable collection for way under its true value simply because it was put into the wrong auction. I'd become a bit blasé with this collection because I'd done so well. I priced each page very cheaply so it was very popular with the collectors. At the same time I was making an incredible profit. While we were in Bath, one of the more pompous and serious dealers came up to my stand. He looked through the collection and finally picked up a page that had a number of penny blacks on it. It was priced at two hundred and twenty pounds. He looked at it carefully, took out a magnifying glass and looked at one of the stamps, smirked and then said: "I'll take this," and threw two hundred and twenty pounds down on the table. He then removed the one stamp he'd looked at it and said, "I only want this one, you can keep the rest. This is a double re-entry plate six and it's very rare. Thank you for making my exhibition!"

He walked off triumphantly confiding to all his friend what a stupid idiot I was for selling the stamp so cheaply. I looked at the page, rubbed out two hundred and twenty pounds and re-priced it at two hundred pounds. About ten minutes later I sold the page for two hundred pounds. I was quite pleased, an extra two hundred pounds pure profit and I'd got no idea what he was talking about anyway! Ironically, the dealer denies the event ever happened there, or has absolutely no recollection of it!

I could never understand the stupidity of most of the stamp dealers. When they bought a bargain, they didn't buy it quietly and go away hoping to find another one, which is what I did. They liked to rub it in and tell you how stupid you were. I learnt a lot from their lectures and in the long run all of them paid dear for their triumph because it made me look more carefully in the future.

Some of the established dealers were really unpleasant and never missed a chance to put down newcomers. One day, a collector who was a world class expert came into the Malt house. He wanted me to sell a proof stamp for him. A proof is a printer's trial of a particular stamp. He gave me a ten minute lecture on it, told me it was worth two hundred pounds but he thought I could probably make more than that. As far as he was concerned, if I gave him two hundred pounds for it, he didn't care what I made. So I took it to Bath and showed it to one or two people and they said I ought to take it to the Bournemouth exhibition where a particular dealer would be keen to buy it.

When we'd finished at Bath, we drove down to Bournemouth and stayed overnight.

The exhibition was interesting and I was able to buy many covers at very cheap prices which made the trip very profitable. I finally saw the important dealer who wanted to buy the proof. He was very interested and so was another dealer with him. They suggested we had a mini auction and four people sat down with me and bid for the proof, eventually getting up to four hundred and fifty pounds.

I accepted the final offer and was very pleased to do so as it had made me two hundred and fifty pounds, and handed over the stamp. Then, they started to laugh.

There had been no auction. All four of them worked for his firm and they just did it for a bit of a joke. The main dealer sneered at me and told me that it was worth far more. I shouldn't even be allowed to be in business as I was so stupid.

"You even buy badly at auction," he continued, "you bought a cover in the Western Auctions at Cardiff last month for two hundred pounds. I put it in, it was only worth fifty pounds!" And with that, they all laughed at me again.

I let them finish their laughter, got up slowly and replied: "Well, thank you very much for the very interesting lesson in ethics in the stamp trade.

"I thought you'd like to know just two things. Firstly, the proof bought for two hundred pounds and so I made two hundred and fifty pounds, what you make is up to you. I'm delighted and so was the owner of the proof. Secondly, the cover that I bought for two hundred pounds. You think I overpaid for it. Well, the collector that bought from me for nine hundred and fifty pounds thought I'd under-priced it. It's all in the eye of the purchaser, isn't it? As you say, probably I'm too innocent to actually survive in the stamp world. Thanks for your advice." As I walked off I noticed they weren't laughing anymore!

Business was growing and doing very well and I ought to really have quit my job and run it full time, but we were very scared. We had a mortgage and didn't want to end up with financial problems like so many of the other stamp dealers. In the end, Cath came up with a compromise.

"Look, why don't I give up teaching?" she said. "I could keep the business going for you. In that way, if it works you can join me as soon as possible. If it doesn't, you haven't damaged your career."

"Yeah, but you don't even like stamps," I replied. "It'd be pretty ghastly for you. I know it makes sense but is that really the best idea?"

"I think so," she said, "it would be silly for you to give up and then have to go back into teaching. It wouldn't look good on your record."

We argued and discussed about it for some time and eventually we both agreed it did make sense, and so Cath resigned from her teaching post and became a full time dealer. It was a very lonely year for her. In the first instance, she had to wander round with a catalogue trying to learn what covers were what. Her other major problem was my organisation, or should I say, lack of organisation? I knew where everything was, but I was the only one and her first job was to reorganise our complete stock so she could find a cover when she looked for it.

It was obvious as the year went on that our business was growing faster and faster.

Peter Maybe, our loveable accountant, had refused to get involved with VAT as he put it, "The only VAT I want to get to know is VAT 69!" We had to deal with the complexities of this horrible new tax ourselves.

Cath was still very new in the business when there was a firm knocking at the door.

She opened it, and to her horror, it appeared that a Nazi Stormtrooper had got misplaced in 1943 and had appeared in Martins Way!

"Gut Morning!" The visitor spoke with a Germanic accent, had small gold-rimmed glasses, a

Tyrolian hat and wore jack-boots. "I am the VAT inspector. I vish to inspect your books."

"My husband's not here!" stammered Cath, for whom books were not a strong point (yet).

"Ven will he be here?" demanded the visitor suspiciously, by now appearing to have a small, black moustache growing on his lip.

"Tonight. He is Deputy Head at Lyminge School and will probably be running an after-school club, but he should be home by six."

"Very vell, I shall return at six!" and with that, he left.

Cath picked me up that evening and broke the bad news.

"He's terrifying!" she told me. "And he'll be back at six o'clock!"

"Don't worry! We've done nothing wrong. It'll probably only be routine, I think!"

Although I tried to sound confident, I too was very worried. I'd heard dreadful stories about these new inspectors, many of whom had come from Customs and Excise and were more used to dealing with drug dealers. They had horrifying powers and you did not have to intentionally do wrong to be in real trouble with them.

On the dot of six, the VAT-man once again knocked on our door.

"Gut evening!" the man started. "I am Mr Fassbender and I must inspect your books!"

"Come in, I've got them all ready for you. I'm

sorry I was out when you called, but it's only really my hobby business. I'm really a teacher."

"It makes no difference. If you are VAT registered, you must obey the rules," he said coldly.

*Oh my God!* I thought with a sinking heart. *The man's got no sense of humour.*

We gave him a cup of tea and he sat concentrating on our books. After about an hour he spoke again.

"Please, you come here! This is wrong and must be corrected! This is not allowable and must be removed and here are some minor mistakes. You will put these right, I think. I will call again in one month, then check it. Thank you for the cup of tea." With that, he left.

"Oh goody," said Cath after he'd gone, "we'll look forward to that!"

"I don't think he's too bad, but he certainly has vays of making you get your books right! The German accent must be a great asset to a VAT inspector! Anyway, I'd like to ask you a favour."

"Oh yes?" said Cath suspiciously. "What's that?"

"Well. You know I have to teach netball," I started, as Cath started to laugh. Cath knew only too well. My team had played hers the year before and she described my rules as a form of net-football. "Well, will you come and help me up at Lyminge? I reckon we could have a superb team this year. I got a great bunch of girls and none of the other teachers will do it."

"Of course I will. I'd love it. I really miss teaching sometimes. It would keep my hand in."

The netball did go well and it gave us immense

pleasure whopping up the larger Folkestone schools who had been condescending to my girls because they came from a village school.

*

My trade society sent out a monthly list of possible problem customers, you know the sort of thing, those who didn't pay their bills or who claimed they did not receive the goods in the first place. It was all done on a coding system. For example, Code 1 probably meant that they didn't say thank you after they got their order; Code 35 told you that they were a mass murderer. In reality it only went up to thirty and this meant that something was seriously wrong and you should phone the trade society immediately.

I was looking through the new copy over breakfast, when to my horror, I spotted the Ohio Stamp Company marked thirty! I phoned immediately.

"'Allo Tony," came the Czechoslovakian voice of our Trade Secretary, "how can I help you this morning?"

"It's about the Ohio Stamp Company, Otto. What's going on?"

"Twelve British dealers are taking him to court in America. Whatever you do, don't send them anything on credit." As he went on, I felt more and more sick.

"Too late, Otto. I'm afraid he's already got £1,800 worth of my covers."

"I'm so sorry, Tony. You should have checked with us first!" He was right of course, but it did not make me feel any better. So much for my export drive.

That evening, Cath was back to one of her favourite subjects.

"We've got to get out more. How about Bridge? We used to enjoy playing."

"Well, it's easy to say, but how do we go about it? We don't know anyone who plays bridge down here."

"I've seen an ad from the adult education service offering bridge. We haven't played for a long time so how about a refresher course? It very cheap and in fact it's on tonight."

"All right, let's go then!"

We had a quick scrambled egg, toast and bacon then rushed to the school where the bridge course was taking place. As we arrived, we heard a familiar Germanic voice.

"There are heavy penalties if you don't make these tricks!" Sure enough, it was the dreaded VAT man.

"I don't think I'm that keen!" said Cath.

"Nah, let's have a drink instead."

As promised, exactly two weeks later, Mr Fassbender was back at our door. This time without the jack-boots – had they been our imagination? He seemed far more human this time, perhaps we were just getting used to him.

"Gut! Your books are fine now. I will be back in a year to check again."

After he went, we had a very large schooner of Harvey's Bristol Cream and waited for Peter Maybe, who was coming over for one of his regular visits.

"How's your export drive going?" he teased. "Is it

Ohio or Goodbye-oh!"

"Ha-bloody-ha!" I replied. "It's not funny!"

"No it isn't. Business isn't funny. It's like a game of snakes and ladders. The important thing is not to tread on too many snakes! Anyway, it's not all bad news, you have doubled your turnover again. I've just finished your 1973-74 accounts. Do you realise you've doubled your turnover every year since I started doing your accounts?\You really must think about where you're going. What are you doing it for? Do you want to be the richest man in the graveyard?"

"I think he should give up teaching," said Cath. "What do you think, Peter?"

"Oh, I couldn't give an opinion. There's wheels within wheels. You'll have to make the decision, Boom-boom."

"What would you say if you could give an opinion?" I asked hopefully.

"I couldn't say! But if you double again, you'll have to give it very serious thought."

There was no doubt that we were growing very quickly. Stamps were in fashion, prices were going up every day, and I had a very large stock. Two or three things influenced my final decision. Jersey and Guernsey had independent postal administrations since 1969. When I had bought the business of Martin Stead, I'd had to buy £3,000 of mint Channel Islands stamps at face value. I had put them away and had been so busy that I hadn't got round to selling them.

Suddenly, to quote an Americanism, they were HOT. Everybody wanted these new stamps. I worked out that I could sell the entire package for £9,000 or more, which would mean that I had got the entire business and the rest of the stock free. I'd never been greedy to get the very top price, so despite the fact that prices were still rising, I sent them off immediately. I was told by many stamp dealers how stupid I was because I could have made thousands more profit. As it turned out, I was one of the lucky ones. I actually got paid. The greedy ones who held on for a better price lost everything. It was nice to have a business decision proved right.

The second major change was my friend Graeme Lewis decided to sell his business and offered it to me first. I bought it with the £9,000 from the Channel Islands stamps.

With Graeme's RAF business combined with our own, Benham became the King of the RAF covers.

It was over Christmas that I finally made the decision. I looked at myself in the mirror and, quite honestly didn't like what I saw. Tired did not do justice to my looks. My captain at Hythe Cricket Club, who was an undertaker, probably worked with more healthy-looking people. I was working seven days a week, fifteen hours a day and it was showing.

"Peter's right," I said to Cath and my mother on Boxing Day. "I don't want to be the richest man in the cemetery. I'm going to give my notice in and that will give Lyminge two terms to replace me. I'm going to be a full-time stamp dealer."

"Oh Anthony," said my mother anxiously, "think of your pension!"

13172221R00232

Printed in Great Britain
by Amazon.co.uk, Ltd.,
Marston Gate.